PSYCHOTHERAPY WITH THE ELDERLY

PSYCHOTHERAPY WITH THE ELDERLY

BECOMING METHUSELAH'S ECHO

George Bouklas, Ph.D.

JASON ARONSON INC.
Northvale, New Jersey
London

The author gratefully acknowledges permission to quote from the poetry of Edward Bjorkman and David Levinsky.

Production Editor: Elaine Lindenblatt

This book was set in 11 pt. New Baskerville by Alabama Book Composition of Deatsville, Alabama and printed and bound by Book-mart Press, Inc. of North Bergen, New Jersey.

Library of Congress Cataloging-in-Publication Data

Bouklas, George.
    Psychotherapy with the elderly : becoming Methuselah's echo /
George Bouklas.
      p. cm.
    Includes bibliographical references and index.
    ISBN 0-7657-0051-4 (alk. paper)
    1. Psychotherapy for the aged. 2. Psychotherapist and patient.
3. Aged—Mental health. 4. Maturation (Psychology) 5. Nursing home
patients—Mental health. I. Title.
RC480.54.B68 1997
618.97'68914—dc21   96-46668

Printed in the United States of America on acid-free paper. For information and catalog write to Jason Aronson Inc., 230 Livingston Street, Northvale, New Jersey 07647-1731. Or visit our website: http://www.aronson.com

I dedicate this book to my wife Naomi,

who is my loving Echo,

and to our beloved Bella Chaim

Our culture protests against servitude to death. It attempts to blot out death's presence and so erase any sense of obligation. The only relationship it seems to tolerate is a rugged alienation. But there is another way to be with that which gives life its boundaries, its purpose, its joys. Come and let us echo Methuselah, and we shall see the way.

Contents

Preface

This book is addressed to my colleagues, friends, and contemporaries. It is about the forms of therapy I use with my elderly clients and contains vignettes about people 70 to 106 years of age. Because of my interest in gaining an overview of the role of therapy in our society, the book is also about the treatment relationship as a model for understanding how we are and how we grow. Finally, it is about middle age, and the developmental challenges we face as we round the ages of 40 and 50 and see less in front of us than behind us.

Methuselah and Echo refer to the elderly patient and the therapist. Echo has been borrowed from the larger world of psychoanalysis, and so there is a discussion of the treatment approaches that this field has generated. Our prime players are also an inseparable duality. Each of us is Methuselah and Echo, too. The therapeutic attitude we take with our own selves now will set the groundwork for actualizing in our seventies and beyond.

We are at once the helper and the helped. We are the hurt and vulnerable self given to fragmentation and on the verge of losing everything. At the same time we are the healing power that lies beyond the prosaic and dwells in the realm of pure being. To merge these two aspects of ourselves is an act of self-blessing. To establish relations where we echo others, and where we teach others to echo us, is to transmute the self and invite integration.

Methuselah is our final self. This self can be the epitome of grace. It can be an extension of our early, character-forming pleasures and travails. And it can be a grand reiteration of the hurts of a lifetime with little hint of redemption. As we lived our life earlier, so shall we finish it, that strong is the urge to repeat. We encourage our children to take advantage of opportunities for self-expression and development so that their adult lives can be rich and fulfilling. In our middle adulthood we need similar encouragements to prepare for a transpersonal status as elders. We need to examine life in the middle, to alter and influence the way in which deterministic forces will exert themselves upon our future.

Methuselah's Echo within our own hearts is the harbinger of our old age, wrought of the insistent silence between each beat, of the exhaustion that surrounds life, of the will to decompose. As life preponderates over death in infancy, it accedes to death in old age. All that has been breaking down, every moment, no longer finds fruitful challenge in the powers of building up. But this death is not nothing. It is not merely the absence of life. It has will, it has contours, it has a voice. The voice is an echo that manages to bounce off the encrustations of denial, to let us know it is part of us. To allow the forces of entropy to gain access to the conscious and reflecting mind is to gain wisdom.

In the course of maturing, we learn that death and life have created the harmonic of being. Death, which has paraded before us in all its guises, is able to be grasped. It is the desire to wall off the experience of others. It is hatred for the Other. It is the wish to destroy oneself. It is the demons that populate our imagination, projected outward and given body. It is the wall against the dangerous outside, and since that wall is conjured up in the psyche, death is us.

It is rejection for those who are not like us. It is sadism and masochism. It is destructive behavior, limitations on the expansive-

ness of the self, meanness of spirit, selfishness. It is the bile we bring
to relationships, the control we exert over others, the hurt that
satisfies. If we stopped there, we would be blessed with a special
maturity, but wisdom takes one more leap.

When properly perceived, death is the force that gives life
meaning. Love finds further definition in the presence of hate.
Altruism is more powerful for having as its frolicking bedmate
naked self-interest. Amor is swept forward on the sharp arrow shaft
of murder and would not find its mark were it not for the terrible
need to reduce unbearable tensions. Anguish, bittersweet romance,
unrequited love are more real because they give equal access to the
life and the death force. What is felt as the commonplace is merely
the muting of the two forces in a standoff. The malaise of daily living
is evidence of how each neutralizes the other. The harmonics are
given no access to a wider range and clearer notes, and we dully
move through life.

This egalitarian notion of being opens the way for accepting
our faults, missteps, urges, and mistakes. The other person loses his
unique outline. He becomes us. The most marvelous and most
horrible person have a match in our own souls. Within the culture,
those who end up at the extremes are dramatizing our own wish to
be purely one or the other. They enact the collective force of the
group's will and serve as external guideposts for our hunger to
experience the basic drives more clearly. And when we are sated,
new hungers emerge, maturational ones that suggest all the ways we
wish to know ourselves through the mirror of society's monsters and
angels. The aged are at present one of the canvases on which we
work our magic, and they suffer for our projections. They also suffer
for the projections they have maintained over the course of their
long lives.

I have treated many elderly people and have found myself
negotiating a vast plain of bitterness. Neither money nor degree of
physical health nor contacts from a loving family functioned as an
effective talisman against the disfigurement of their momentary
experience. The acting out of dying robs them of living. Maintaining
an aggressive view of a neglectful and hateful world has become its

own odd reward, and the supposed fear that everything is awful is revealed over the course of life to have been the person's superordinate wish. He is a god and has created the universe that will cage him and eventually engulf him. I have watched such people die in a state of muted horror, having animated death as a malevolent force.

The difficulties described in the literature concerning the therapeutic care of the elderly become a difficulty in the self of the therapist. What he cannot face in his own life he must now face in the person of the octogenarian. Either he can use the experience of the treatment relationship to work out the issues that at present foretell of his troubles in his later years, or he can reject the opportunity. Elderly patients are notorious for their regressive resistances and the sense of incurability they communicate. This is another way of saying that we who treat cannot fully apprehend our elderly status. Our cosmologies prevent the formation of redeeming conceptions about late-life emotions, attitudes, and behavior patterns.

The challenge for therapists, physicians, health care professionals, and family members is to locate the precursors of great-grandparently wisdom in ourselves. This is an act of precocity within the confines of our present society, and therefore an extraordinary event in the life of the typical person. It is my hope that this book will urge the reader on in his quest for the great-grandparently vision, by sharing a more intimate view of what ails the elderly and what returns them to the path of maturation.

Acknowledgments

I am a wealthy man. I have learned with many people who were willing to share what they knew, and who personified their work. Drs. Buck, Balasny, and Gilman were my professors at Adelphi Suffolk College, now Dowling College. They gave me a formative experience of psychology that has stood the test of time, couching knowledge within the craft of the field. Professor David Levinsky took this to its logical extreme by embodying every therapeutic technique he presented. He stood as a peer among peers at Adelphi University, committed to educating students through relationships as well as ideas. Dave became my close friend and together we went on to teach many graduate classes where we worked to integrate therapeutic approaches.

"Ace" Watkins showed me what was possible in education with his unceasing quest to create environments for schoolchildren that were safe and comfortable at the same time that they were challenging. "Pop" Robinson engaged me in moving freely between the cognitive and affective domains, in reaching out to undergraduates. Drs. Roz and Lenny Schwartz gave lovingly to those of us who worked for the State University, sparing nothing to help the professors become whole people. Frank Falanga and Harriet Greenspan left me with everlasting gifts in the field of special education. Phyllis Meadow, Benjamin Margolis, Mark Clevans, Yonata Feldman, Gerald Fishbein, Hyman Spotnitz, and their colleagues brought the intriguing world of psychoanalysis into focus as they worked with us to understand literally a thousand treatments, until we, too, lived, ate, breathed, and became psychoanalysis. I especially thank Dr. Margolis for his unwavering therapeutic stance. He is surely a role model for all analysts.

Harold Stern, Don Shapiro, and the people of the Union Institute underwrote interdisciplinary study bravely and without ever blinking. Their trust in us produced a very different kind of attitude—expansive, inclusive, hungering for the novel. They believed in our quests to find commonalities, to reach for underlying grand concepts, and to be hunters of integration. Ari Blumenfeld helped me resonate with the East. His astute comments gave me the transpersonal context for telling Methuselah's story. Ed Wallach freely shared his knowledge about modern psychoanalysis, with a grace and compassion that were special. Dr. Wallach is one of our great contemporary educators and therapists.

My spiritual life has also received the most direct of feedings. Hazel Moy's duty was to teach us Latin, but she connected with our family and became our guardian angel, too. Father Theodore performed the sacraments of our church with a vulnerability that allowed him to shiver, quake, and weep. I will never forget the holiness of this man. Rabbi Rafael Loeb prayed in a simple way, opening himself to such bliss that I could truly feel the presence of God in the room. Dr. Bentzion Sorotzkin reached out across cultures to make an everlasting friendship, as did Rabbi Zev Shostak, and it was with these men that I discovered my spiritual voice in middle age.

Naomi, my beloved wife, has been at the center of my evolution. Before she came into my life, the mundane was more than equal to the transcendent. She helped the transcendent win out. She is proof that angels do exist, that one can live in this world but also sidestep its corrosive influence. What I learned in forty years of schooling Naomi happens to know naturally. She absorbed much of it from Bella and Harold Chaim, her parents, who took the full impact of the Holocaust. I would be hard-pressed to find more loving and accepting people. They saw death and decided on life.

A final thanks to the patients, who taught me how to work with them, and who left behind a legacy that I now share with you.

Introduction

To work, to love, to play, and to contemplate. That is the formula for the second round of our lives, as we pass the age of 40 and look beyond short-lived goals, to the achievement of longevity. The contemplative life affords us the sweetest later years, as we savor every memory and use the past to inform the present and to structure the future that remains to us.

The reintegration of all happenings into the present and the adoption of guiding cosmologies to understand everything about ourselves become our life's work in the second half. This work has its painful moments, because we progressively remember everything that we had worked to forget in our search for an uneasy equipoise. The therapist's role is to carefully shape the reflecting efforts of the patient, to leave a good taste in the person's mouth about this endeavor, to encourage the will to continue self-study. For this is a life worth living.

Along with the pleasures of therapy there is also pain, but what can be excruciating can also bear the most beautiful fruit. As a new child is created from labor, so is a new person created out of the old organizations of character. Every pain hides a pleasure of its own, and here is the secret of therapy. The pain of finding out what you lost when you were 3 is offset by the resurrection of that whole important year, with all its happiness and polymorphous gratifications. The verbalizing of unbearable emptiness felt in one's adolescence itself creates a satisfying wholeness. To validate that emptiness in words turns it into a fullness. In this we see that the healing powers have always been present, but inaccessible. Each of us has the magic to turn nothing into something. The therapy creates access, releases magic.

Hates are discovered, but as they are illuminated, so are the loves they sought to repress. There is delight in the love, until that, too, gives way to the illumination of a more primitive hatred underneath. So goes the story of a life; love and behind it hate, behind that love, and yet more hate, until the interstices in this mosaic melt away, and fragmentation yields to integration. But this yielding will not come without a proper invitation. The therapist has formally dedicated himself to addressing the patient in a special way. He has accepted a role as the translator moving among the hidden aspects of the individual, helping each aspect find a voice. This is "inside" work with a view to mastering the "outside" life.

In our present world, the mind is called only to certain, select endeavors, and the body only to others. The soul is all but forgotten. We live in an evermore compartmentalizing culture. "I only want this part of you," hollers society's bursar. "I will not pay for the rest." The drive to become whole gets no special help from our present society. The equally prevailing drive to mosaic, to fragment, to repress is thus rewarded in the most literal fashion. We also see in this the group dynamics of culture, the primitive force of hate seeking an institutional presence. For the compartmentalizations of work in business and industry are nothing more than the fragmentation of the individual, projected onto all and used as a device to train the indiscreet lest they pretend to a greater wholeness and incite the resentments of the enslaved selves who are watching carefully.

This may be the way the world is, but it is not the world as it has to be, and our patients learn that they can create new realities, make a good life for themselves, and leave a rich legacy to their children and their culture. From the forties on, our work, whether in or outside therapy, is to extend life by re-merging what was once one. The mind, body, and soul easily follow the call to fragment, but they equally respond to a hunger that has them cascading toward the same dimensionless point, where time stands still and the past, present, and future have been captured. The power of healthy narcissism wants release from the negating influence of destructive narcissism. Under the right conditions, the ego is willing to give up its terrible polarizations. There is inestimable value to a cosmology that will take the sting out of failure, the rapture out of success, the pain out of loss, and the obsessiveness out of incorporation.

Therapy is one way to hone a personal cosmology that will create solutions for present problems and will leave the person with a way of being more of himself in the world. This is the promise of middle age in general, and people find all kinds of ways to fulfill it. The confining circle is broken, and the person learns how to leave society as he continues to function within it, how to give something up and in the process create something more powerful. The semantic pull on perception, behavior, attitudes, and philosophy can exhaust, leaving the person to the whatness of the moment, and a style of life that will keep this quiddity forever accessible.

This book is about elderly people who lost the path of self-development at some point in their lives, or who seemed never to have found it. If there is one common feature capturing the essence of the group I have treated, it is that very few have lived a life of contemplation. These people are fragmented, even shattered, in their old age. The history of their fragmentation reaches deep into their twenties, teens, preadolescence, and infancy. Dementia complicates rather than alters the original picture. My experience has been that cognitive and memory deficits are not the source of most patients' fragmentation, but an amplifier. There are ways to work dynamically with people who have different degrees of dementia, and the methods described here sustain at least some impact as we work with progressively impaired elderly.

When a patient comes to us after seven or eight decades of neglecting his integration needs, the task of therapy seems daunting. In the countertransference, the therapist is dismayed by the vestigial nature of the patient's reflective powers. He does not think that he can develop therapeutic leverage in time and is infused with a feeling of helplessness. My position is that the therapist's helplessness is also his power, that his dismay is more akin to optimism than any other feeling, that the challenge of the elderly patient reveals to him just how he has been using Western thought to fool himself, that the ideal opposites of our language melt away to reveal the whatness of the treatment relationship, as the therapist becomes Echo.

Echo is neither happy nor sad, here nor there, powerful nor helpless. She is a reflection of Methuselah, and her capacity for reflection restores access to the old person's healing and magical powers. In Greek myth she played a powerful role in the story of Narcissus. She was the life-giving alternative to the inorganic mirror created within the pool's surface. When Echo sang back Narcissus to Narcissus, he was able to stay alive without damaging himself or his shy admirer. It was when he chanced to see his reflection in the pool that his transfixed stare incapacitated him. His feet branched out into roots and he languished from self-love at the pool's edge.

Psychoanalysis has taken this story for its own, to exemplify how aggression stunts the developmental flowering of the child and leads him dangerously close to a destructive lifestyle. The pool as dead matter reflected Narcissus's deadness of feeling, so he rooted himself right there, to absorb the waves of understanding he experienced for this insistent inorganic propensity within himself. Aggression is the content of this rush to return to a previous, undisturbed state, and if it is not educated in the example of others who have learned to make peace with their own aggressive drives, this entropy acts out its destiny in destructiveness.

Echo has moved on. Her Narcissus has been left to his cold and deadening rapprochement with his static image. But she still has work to do. Methuselah awaits her.

The Garden

Methuselah rested in the corner by the cemented walls, his eyes closed, his weathered hands clasping a bony knee, softly rocking, humming nothing that was recognizable, oblivious of the ebb and flow of sensory activity around him, he in a long-sought suspension between life and death. This was earlier a cloaked and disguised goal that progressively clarified over the long span of his years until he was here in the garden, wholly identified by this suspension, in all its exquisite equilibrium.

He struggled long and hard for this clarity, with years of depression, numbness, insomnia, self-limitation, dissatisfying petits morts, years of indirect but unmistakable expressions of a life that was dead, and of a death that was living. He was at this point one with his goal.

He rocked and let his expiring breaths create random hums, an aural rendering of his inner parts, the earliest chords of the organic in him exciting the inorganic with scenes of song flight, and the inorganic beckoning back with the possibility of utter peace. He hummed without hearing, when behind him a hum like his own arose, one that shadowed him and followed him and suggested him. He listened to this hum, heard himself captured in it, and drew from it a mental picture of a figure rocking as he was rocking, in matched equivalence.

It was then that Methuselah turned and opened his eyes to behold his Echo, his companion in the corner. He stared transfixed at his Echo, at the mirror of him in her face, at the clarity and beauty she bestowed on him with her mirror. Methuselah fell in love with his Echo, his own image, who used that love to draw the old man into the garden.

1

The Therapeutic Action of Echoing

The air lay still in the room, without a noise to disturb it, without a breath to move it, neither hot nor cold, neither there nor palpably gone. The 99-year-old woman in a cloth cap and flannel nightgown rested her arm against the bed rail. Her mouth remained agape and her unseeing eyes open. She fiddled carefully with the rough edge of her woolen afghan and whispered to herself.

"This is not my afghan. I don't know whose it is." She repeated this in speech deliberate enough to offset the slight amplitude of her voice. "Why do I have someone else's afghan?" she inquired softly. "Where is my afghan?" This went on for quite some time. I had caught the woman in a refractory period, where she was relatively calm and regaining her strength.

"Why don't I know whose it is?" she finally shrieked. Now she could be heard throughout the wing, as she roiled the air with tidal waves of terror. In the midst of this, I loudly asked back, "Why don't I know whose it is?" The terror, which seemed so unswayable, washed away in a moment. She turned to my voice. "Would you say that for me once more, sir?" In some fashion her dread feelings had been transmuted to an orientation reaction. "I said, why don't I know whose it is?"

How many themes played themselves across her face: bemusement, playfulness, the recognition that she had discovered a potential soul mate. She picked her words carefully: "Sir, I do not understand why you should worry about an afghan." Addressing the feeling, I answered, "Why shouldn't I worry?" She fell into cogitative silence.

After a long while of considering my mirroring response, she answered: "It does not get you anywhere. My mother, may she rest in peace, who I loved with all my heart, tried to teach me how to accept." We sat in a comfortable silence, and I got the experience that she was feeling my contours, as blind people do, but with her mind. In the countertransference I felt enlivened in her presence. The atmosphere of the room had altered completely. She smiled, "Can it be that you, too, are blind?" It was easy to answer, "Am I not blind, too?" She agreed. "Of course it is true; you are blind."

IT IS THE CONTINUITY BETWEEN US THAT BEGINS THE HEALING PROCESS.

The close intimacies of human services can rigidify us against knowing what it is essential to know. Our challenge is to create for ourselves a loving atmosphere that defuses the urge to defend and rigidify. We need to pick friends, trainers, and associates who soften us without reminding us of our disquieting vulnerability. If this happens, then we can relearn how to cry for a lost blanket, and we can locate within ourselves the part of us that is blind.

"Where is the blasted aide? He told me he'd be back! But he's gone! Gone! Lost! Doing hanky panky in some back room! I need my arm stretched now! These kids are the worst. I need him now, not when he's done playing around! I swear they should roast these people alive! Damn it, I'm for capital punishment! Nobody believes me but I'm serious. Pull the switch!" The patient was overcome with consternation, rolling back and forth in his wheelchair, gripping the handbrake until his knuckles lost all color.

"Fry them!" I added. "Give them a good roasting!" The patient's fretting subsided, and he sat musing. This was a reaction he had not gotten before, and he was not ready for it. He chortled, "If you only meant that." I replied, "What makes you think I don't mean it?" He stared at me in incipient recognition, a gauze lifted from his eyes. "I believe you mean business, you know that? I sincerely believe you'd roast them kids." Nodding in agreement, I said, "Look, our only problem is that we're not inventive. If we thought about it, we could really come up with something better than roasting!"

The patient drew up his wheelchair and did his best to cooperate with my call to his inventiveness. His physiognomy declared a shift from muscular action to verbal expression, as he got the opportunity to put his feelings into words in a way that finally gratified him. In the ensuing weeks we went on a killing spree, remembering each and every person who ever crossed him. It was an unremitting orgy of fantastic murders, conceived and perpetrated in the mind's eye. Then he was exhausted, sated. Self-understanding came as a mirror of my understanding. "I believe I have always been this angry. As far back as I can remember. In my infancy. I could have killed my parents." We spent the rest of our sessions incorporating this truth into his daily affairs and getting him to hold back this aspect of his emotionality in his dealings with others.

His ability to face such ideas was heroic in scope. He had made the most perilous journey of all for the human being in modern culture. He placed himself on a course where his projections would become known to him as elements of his shadow side. He did it with so little fear because he knew he was not going to have to go there alone. He had me as his traveling companion.

BEFRIEND THE INSTINCTS. SAY IN QUIET SELF-ACCEPTANCE, "I AM AN ARSONIST, A MURDERER, A RAPIST; I HAVE THE WORST OF HUMANITY WITHIN ME."

It is the forbidden impulse we need to befriend in ourselves and in others. Consider our reaction against the person who indulges himself in some impulse we renounced under harsh terms. "Not I!" we yell. Thus all society's engines turn on the dynamic of projection and the conjuring up of the hateful Other to blind us to our shadow side. Religion suggests a sympathetic reaction to the indulger, "There but for the grace of God go I," for religion allows vulnerability. Psychotherapy observes the same person and nods, "There am I." It is our growing comfort with the instincts that becomes the seat of our healing capacity and our wisdom.

The patient loved to smoke his cigarettes. He had smoked five packs a day for as long as he could remember. He thought of himself as a connoisseur of tobaccos, having tried every kind from various parts of the world. American brands were his favorite. His teeth were yellowed and those right behind the dangling cigarette were nearly black, as were two fingers of his left hand.

He was very ill. His lung capacity had dwindled to nothing, and he breathed in short gasps. The social worker tried to block his smoking due to its serious effects on his health, but he invoked resident's rights and neutralized her efforts. He and his psychotherapist stopped meeting after he disagreed with proposed health-related goals, and they could negotiate neither a treatment target nor therapeutic modality. The man held to the opinion that he was not particularly ill, was not suffering emotionally, and was certainly not dying.

His wife visited him daily, and he had her doing errands of a sort that filled up her time and also left her as breathless as he. "Move the cup. Closer. No. Put it there. There! Now. Get my footrest. Don't forget. Empty the ashtray." She cried that he had gotten worse in every way. She was sure he was destroying himself and felt an intimation that he was going to take her with him. She invited me to visit them, and he agreed to couples therapy.

He accepted the restriction that he not smoke during the sessions, and then refused to say anything more about cigarettes. The first theme was his wife's breathlessness. He ordered her here, ordered her there, sent her outside the room, beckoned her back. She was utterly distraught, for she sensed that his tempo was picking up as he became more ill. She sensed his death was imminent. Somehow she felt he was using her feelings to communicate his own.

Once she could say this hated and fearful thing, both of them seemed to come under control in the treatment. This subject did not come up again for a while. Neither of them wanted to tackle anything unpleasant. He helped her reminisce in an amiable sort of way, describing their married life, their love, issues surrounding their childlessness, and the husband's frequent traveling, which had whetted her need for him. She spoke, and he encouraged. She did her best to highlight positive experiences and capture the former optimism of their healthy youth. However, this talk did little to alleviate the problems between them outside the sessions. She found him becoming more demanding and controlling with each week that passed.

My understanding was that he was trying to work her to death, to push up the timetable so that they could die together. At the start of his medical crisis, they both preferred to act the drama out without the vitiating of their passion by interfering reflections. And they would have persisted were it not for the accompanying pain caused the wife. It was she who had called for the therapy. For as entranced as she was by the siren of death, the urge to live was still strong within her. Her efforts increasingly focused on all the things she had to live for, and her reaction to this talk was to find the peace she was looking for. She was not going to let her husband kill her after all. The husband listened intently and accepted all that was said without much comment. During one session he told us he was terrified at the prospect of dying alone, but he would not permit any further exploration. However, in an act of compromise, he gave his wife wide berth and stopped his demands.

Death came a few months later than the doctors had expected. The patient became immobile and needed oxygen continuously. In a panic he gave up his cigarettes and promised never to touch them again. He reverted to his earlier behavior of attempting to exhaust his wife to death. But this time she openly resisted him. The new problem was that a vacuum had been created by her relinquishing of lifelong enabling patterns. She asked me how she should be with her husband, who was getting quite frenetic and doubly regressed in the face of her independence.

During a session where both were in a state of complete misery,

I told the wife what she must say. She stood over her husband, clasped his gray hand between hers, and told him, "I will see you on the other side." She repeated this until they both gained the full sense of it: No, I will not give up my life now; it is not my time. But I will join you in no time, in a mutual eternity. "I will see you on the other side."

They both relaxed. Properly joined with his wife, the husband felt strengthened. He reached out his hand to me. I took it and told him that I would also see him again on the other side. The nurses and aides said the same. He died in a state of peace and reconciliation. For over a year I had watched this man from afar and had noticed how he held a cigarette in his mouth, sucked on it, made love to it, drew sustenance from it. I saw what a rush he was in to light another. All he ever wanted was that one perfect cigarette that would accompany him into eternity.

WE ARE SEPARATED FROM THE OCEANIC, AND SPEND THE REST OF OUR LIVES TRYING TO RETURN TO IT. TO KNOW THIS IS TO UNDERSTAND PEOPLE'S ADDICTIONS AND OBSESSIONS.

Control over one's life is always thought to be the result of ego differentiation and further ego complexity. Psychoanalytic theory does not consider regression a maturational solution to one's struggles. It lionizes the differentiated ego as the sole agent of progression, but as we near the end of our lives, we seek a healing with the universe. Regression-in-the-service-of-transcendence identifies the power of our early, polymorphous pre-selves to effect a spiritual connection to everything around us.

THE NATURE OF THERAPEUTIC PROGRESS

We should be warned to beware therapeutic ambition. As soon as we *want* for the patient more than he wants for himself, we are setting the stage for patient resistances created by our own needs. We come by these feelings honestly, reacting to a society that is on the fast track. Learning and change are expected to happen quickly, and we are partly responsible for this prevailing attitude. As developmental psychologists, we have failed to effectively communicate to our society how human beings first assimilate and then accommodate to new circumstances that require an adaptive response. Somehow we allowed the behavioral model to swamp and neuter the developmental model of learning. It is up to us to explain how people progress, so that we may take the steps necessary to treat each patient properly.

If we feel pressured to conjure up some quick results and do not take the time to share with our colleagues how we understand clinical phenomena to unfold, we are in for trouble. We are referred nursing home residents whose suffering and functional maladjustments are sufficient to merit our expertise, but who do not enter therapy with the baseline skills, knowledge, and understanding that would augur a quick and short-term therapy. As we treat our new patients, we have to keep the attending physician and his designees informed as to progress and educated as to the research dimension of our work. Because therapy and research psychology use the same approach, we should employ an empirical method to better understand the patient and to design the right holding environment and interventions.

I had been treating an 89-year-old woman for major depression. She reluctantly agreed to see me but let me know during the first session that she had no interest in talking. If I was going to talk, she was going to leave. We sat quietly. Content that I was not going to force her to talk, she agreed to meet again. She leaned forward the next session, huffed and puffed, examined her fingernails, and looked at me. After the passage of some time, I asked if the silence was okay. She thought it was fine. She offered that, for a change, she was in the room with someone who was not trying to get something out of her. We went on like this for months. Her record indicated that she experienced her first major depression at 25, following the loss of her only child during delivery. After that she had numerous psychiatric placements and was seen for some time as an outpatient for medication. Another major depression followed the death of her husband, a few years before. Ill and unable to care for herself, estranged from her family, she came to live in the nursing home.

After a dozen sessions, she asked me about her progress. I told her she was doing fine. She shook her head in disbelief and continued to sit stoically through the next month. Her request became more insistent. "I want your real opinion. How do you think I am doing in this therapy?" I repeated that she was doing fine. "How can I be doing fine, when I sit here and don't say a word, meeting after meeting?" I asked her what I might be doing wrong, that she did not feel she was doing enough in the therapy?

This added to her general movement toward relaxing. She was anxious in the first session; in the countertransference, I experienced that she could barely tolerate my presence in the room. This ameliorated over time. At first, she seemed to react with a hidden horror of my presence, not even daring to look in my direction. This also changed, as she became more daring and was lately spending a lot of time looking me up and down. In the beginning, much of her consciousness was tied up with her alienative regard of me as a looming Other. She did not want a dialogue; she just wanted to see where I was at all times, out of a sense of self-protection. This changed as I achieved more human proportions. As she allowed herself to take her eyes off me and look away, I got the distinct impression that she was allowing more thoughts and memories to come into consciousness.

The staff reported she was less abrupt and alienative with them and had taken care to learn some names. She laughed for the first time. This was not accomplished by the treatment alone. While I was treating the patient, I was also alerting staff to different ways to alleviate depression. People were urged to offer simple choices: "Would you like your green sweater or your blue sweater?" Autonomy through choice and decision-making had been found to be a major curative in dealing with depression in nursing homes, and we all worked to adopt a different style with the residents. Thus the staff became more real and human to her.

Toward the eighth month, the patient and I enjoyed a free and easy feeling in the room. The groundwork for a working relationship had been carefully laid for months, and she was letting it be known she was ready to change. Unless I made a major error, I could play a facilitative role in her growth. She was already telling me that she was willing to be angry with me. In psychodynamics, we understand depression as anger turned against the self, or introjected. The patient graduates when she is able to use the treatment relationship profitably and project the anger onto the therapist. She created the opportunity by starting the session with, "I am only giving you two more months to cure me, and then I'm out." I asked her where she got the idea I wanted to cure her.

Her jaw dropped. "What do you mean? You're not interested in curing me?" I asked her if that was what she wanted. "Of course I want to be cured! Why do you think I have sat here with you week after week? Because you are a fine conversationalist?" Now that it was safe, now that she was infinitely sure of my dedication to protecting her defenses, she spoke the whole session. We explored the idea of cure, why she wanted it, whether I should go along, how she saw me effecting this cure, how I was doing so far. "How are you doing so far? I'd say pretty lousy." I encouraged her to be more specific, and when we were finishing up, I thanked her for her frankness and directness.

She returned to her quiet stance, but now the feeling in the room was different. She was angry with me. She was burning. Yet it was safe. Soon she offered, "We are going on eight months with this nowhere-therapy. Can you tell me what to expect?" Sure, I could tell her. She could expect to get exactly what she wanted. "Are you telling me that I can be cured? After all the psychologists and psychiatrists and shots and pills and hospitals?" I told her all was going according to plan. "Whose plan?" she muttered, shaking her head and falling into silence. She withdrew this half-invitation for information as quickly as she had proffered it.

The next week she demonstrated clear motivation, the kind of motivation other patients will show early in treatment. She had not been ready the first month. She was ready now. "So I want to know exactly what you plan for this therapy." I told her all we had to do was continue to meet weekly and be with each other. Her progress would follow. Her anger deepening, she articulated, "And how long is this going to take?" I amiably and disinterestedly responded that "the research suggests about thirty years." Arthritis, weak knees, hip fracture, and all, she bounded up out of the wheelchair and yelled at me, "Well, I don't have thirty years, doctor. Are you blind? I am an old woman!"

I replied that this "research" also showed that if the patient talks freely every session, things could speed up appreciably. This offer that she cooperate only if she wanted to, timed in response to her motivation, engendered a treatment alliance. Central to this therapy was the maturational need for her to take ownership of it. After that she spoke with dedication and animation. She told me about her life, her self-hate, her fear of trying, and her hopeless feeling of getting any gratification in the nursing home. As she told me the worst thing that would happen if she left her room or spoke to a peer or attended a singalong, her attitudes changed. Reflection on her beliefs led her to conclude she may have been mistaken. Telling the therapist all the reasons why something will not work many times paves the way for things to start working again. Echoing the resistances helped reduce their strangulating hold on her adaptive repertoire. She conquered her paralysis slowly, but by the next year had two close friends in the building, attended recreation daily, and experienced more sustained happiness and peace.

She developed tender feelings for me, and I for her. Her yearning for intimate contact had been reawakened, and she generalized this to her peer relations. The staff followed the case, learning how to echo her feelings while still encouraging her to do the right thing for herself. By echoing her, they found it easier to press her to shower, to do her hair, to leave her room, and to spend time in day areas with fellow residents. As we all worked together on behalf of this patient, the staff learned about the level and quality of the resident's contacts, and how to effectively mirror them.

ONE OF THE THERAPIST'S RESPONSIBILITIES IS TO EDUCATE OTHERS ABOUT THE THERAPEUTIC PROCESS, TO HELP PEOPLE UNDERSTAND ITS COURSE AND BECOME HELPERS.

People insulate themselves against suffering with varying degrees of success. Some locate suffering in a phobia that is highly differentiable from the self and can give up their symptom with the application of conditioning principles. Others experience it in interpersonal affairs and can learn new ways to behave in order to get what they want. This learning can also follow conditioning principles. Still others were exposed to suffering during a formative period, and they took the suffering into the self. They are their pain. They could no sooner give up their depression, for example, than dislocate an arm and hand it to the therapist. The suffering is implicit in the schematic organizations of the self.

Here the learning paradigm becomes the internalization of the therapeutic relationship as a new schema. This is complex human learning, where highly reinforced maladaptive organizations must soften and disorganize. Then they can give themselves up to the reorganizing influence of the stable and predictable activities of the treatment, in a process of accommodation. This type of complex learning is to operant conditioning, as calculus is to the learning of the multiplication tables. The difference between the challenges is vast. A simple phobia, interpersonal dilemmas, and depression within the character: it is no wonder that some therapies take fifteen sessions, some take fifty sessions, and some take 200 or more sessions.

Upon entering a new nursing home, I was greeted by the facility gauntlet. A number of facilities have a gauntlet, in the form of a confrontational resident who knows how to embarrass and shame anyone who might come through the door. Because all the people in the building have run the gauntlet, and faced terrible embarrassment, they do not warn the newcomer. This way, with each subsequent dramatic incident, they get to reenact the trauma and perhaps work off some of the anxiety attendant upon it. They tend to linger within earshot or watch expectantly.

This woman gave me a big grin and looked me up and down. As I approached the nurse's station, she announced, "Hey fella! You sure got a big one! Know what I mean? A big dick!" She eyed me closely for a reaction, laughing with glee. I kept walking toward her, got down to eye level, and answered, "You noticed. I must find more modest clothing. I am sorry to have aroused you to this degree." She stopped and blushed. Flustered and angered by a novel response to her game, she experienced a superego reaction: "You shouldn't talk that way to a woman." I agreed. "I have a lot to learn. Perhaps you can teach me." Now the superego reaction shifted to the self. She laughed harshly, attacking herself: "Teach you? I have a filthy mouth!" I offered that we might learn together. Now tears came to her eyes.

Afterward others asked me how they might also disarm her. I brought their attention to their immediate reaction of freezing, blushing, confoundment, stuttering, backing off, and getting flustered. These acted as reinforcers topically accentuating the operant nature of the behavior. She had to be approached with a plan. We must know her and know what she needed. She was angry because she still saw herself as vibrant, whole, and youthful. She froze, blushed, stuttered, backed off, and got flustered when she was forced by outside circumstance to regard her broken, frail self in the wheelchair. We were the culprits, showing up in our wholeness and reminding her of her self-ideal. The discrepancy created shame. She was getting us to act out her warded off feelings. If we acted properly, she could regain ownership of her shame and we could help her.

After this, the staff approached her knowledgeably, understanding the self-hate that was conjured up every time she had to take stock of her condition. This was enough to break the pattern.

CONSIDER THE DIFFERENT PERSON AS A VEHICLE TO INTRODUCING YOU TO AN UNEXPLORED SIDE OF YOUR SELF.

Our capacity to blush diminishes with our self-understanding. What is a blush? We have been found out, denuded, and revealed, and we react. Being found out by another person is secondary. It is that the other has acted as a mirror, so that we have been found out by ourselves. The more we learn about our impulses, desires, and wishes, the less surprise there is.

Blushes are also informed by shame. Shame is the experience of recognizing our fragmentary nature. It is a precocious introduction to the facts of entropy, that something ungenerative and seeking a lower form of order is working within us. We integrate by accepting our basic nature. As we become whole, that source of the blush also relents. As a young teacher, I complained to the principal, "Johnny keeps calling me a son of a bitch." It was driving me to distraction, until the beleaguered principal informed me, "Maybe it's because you *are* a son of a bitch." His acceptance of me as a rascal helped heal a split and helped me deal with the rascal in my class.

THE COMMANDING PRESENCE OF EROS

The patient was sickly and morose. Her last heart attack had reduced her capacity to swallow, and she had to go on a puree diet. She felt weak and ineffectual. She struggled to achieve some redeeming understanding of her present situation, but this understanding would not come. She talked freely enough, with little interest in the treatment relationship, recounting the week's difficulties. It took her a few months to appreciate that she was in the room alone with someone who was giving attention, listening, and attempting to understand.

The resistance to transference did not resolve as much as it shattered, like an overtired dike that lost its capacity to hold back the floods. She looked at me one day and protested her love and desire for me. She had been widowed in her early twenties, had donned black, and had not paid any interest to a man for the next seventy years. She told me that I did not physically resemble her young husband, but that I could be his emotional twin.

The sessions became an ongoing paean to my lovable and desirable dimensions. She woke up with a picture of me in her mind, she thought about me all day, and I was the last vision she had as she fell asleep. She frequently dreamt about me. She brought a calendar into her room in order to know when I would visit next. She wrote me notes, ate her puree for me, and even tolerated being handled by the aides. She accepted showers, shampoos, and manicures, in order to be prepared for my visits. This was not a transitory phase. She kept to this theme throughout the therapy, working to become more evocative about the whole way in which she wished to know me.

She addressed arete, agape, and eros. And how she did address the eros! She told me what she would like to do with me, to what heights of pleasure she wanted to return both of us, how she would go far beyond anything she had tried before, in an effort to fuse us in everlasting love.

The next phase of the treatment concerned her efforts at getting me into bed. She made all kinds of offers, expanded her assertive repertoire, tried various seductions. She begged for a kiss, for a touch, for a hug. My role was to fully investigate her wishes and requests and not to go into action. Because a touch of any kind might carry an unforeseen wallop, I was careful to keep the therapy at the level of talk. Was I the cool clinician? Absolutely not. Did I feel erotically for the patient? Yes I did. It was the maintenance, validation, and expression of the feelings, with control over the impulses, that were the curative action of the therapy. In this accepting atmosphere, she allowed herself to think and to feel and to say things that had remained repressed for all her life, except for that three-year window of experience during her marriage.

As long as she could develop this persona in the therapy and promote an erotic relationship with me, her behavior in the facility normalized and she met her treatment goals. We continued into our second and third year together, in order to maintain her functional adaptation to nursing home living, taking into account her declining physical and mental status and need for ongoing supports.

IN OUR CULTURE, THE EROTIC SERVES AS THE METAPHOR FOR FUSION AND MERGER. WE TALK ABOUT THE BEDROOM, BUT IT IS THE NURSERY WE WISH TO RETURN TO, AND BEYOND THAT TO THE DIMENSIONLESS POINT THAT REPRESENTS ALL THAT IS THE UNIVERSE.

Erotic love invades the other with hot urgency. It is unquenchable, for it is in the head. It does not wax and wane, come and go. What comes and goes is the other, who is allured by it and burnt by it. It knows no refractory period and it is excruciating. When it is brought into the treatment relationship, it is given venue to burn brightly. This is a component to every treatment relationship and the central theme to some. The challenge to us is clear. Can we learn to handle the unremitting heat? For there is real heat, of an angry kind. Love is thrust forward by the ballistic force of aggression. The erotic transference is a negative transference and a way to bring to a higher level of consciousness the anger that is connected to the love. It is camouflaged as burning. That is why the therapist prefers to interpret the love transference and get off stage, even when it is obvious that the continued expression of the erotic state is best for the patient. This is also why the partners go into action and consummate the desires aroused in the therapy. At times it is a sacrifice at the altar of Pluto, and not Venus. The love affairs and marriages created of these dynamics are no less sweet, and for many are the only way to bring into focus and to manage the destructive urges that might otherwise spin out of control.

A DAY WITH THE ELDERLY

There are few epiphanies in a typical treatment day. A rugged homeostasis seems to mark the lives of most people referred for psychotherapy. Insights come after much work, and movement would appear to be incremental, although what is going on is a shuffling and reshuffling of possibilities just below the surface. This reincarnation of possibility finds an equal counterforce in resistance to change; thus there is the resulting sense of slow progress. The elderly are no different as a treatment population.

The first patient of the morning refuses her heart medications and does not believe she needs showers. She throws papers and spits all over the floor and blames the confused roommate. She finds her behavior syntonic and experiences no regret or shame. When others receive visits from family, she loses control and becomes argumentative and verbally abusive with fellow residents and the nursing aides. She misses her own family members, who have given up on her and no longer want to visit. Her loss feelings justify to her the need for psychotherapy, but she vigorously maintains her right to continue acting out and refuses to acknowledge the behaviors of concern identified by the facility. She has tended to talk nonstop and to give the therapist little opportunity to question or interact. But as she has recognized that I have not come to enforce the reality of the nursing home upon her, she has recently taken the chance to become more revelatory. EVEN THOUGH THE NURSING HOME MADE THE REFERRAL, THE THERAPY IS THE PATIENT'S ALONE. The therapy has become more effective as she has trusted the idea that I work for her and not for the nursing home. She is vigilant lest I think poorly of her, as her behavior becomes more dystonic to her. Now she takes the time to check with me. We explore her concerns, but I also gratify her requests and answer her. She is usually quite close to acting out, and we are working to heighten her threshhold.

The fourth patient had experienced a lapse in her cognitive and emotional cohesiveness months before. Her intellectual faculties, memory, and emotional stability were significantly jarred for a number of hours, secondary to some oxygen-depriving event, we suppose. Her first reaction was depression and self-doubt, until her confabulations took over and she found relief in blaming staff for attempting to alter her mind. Now it is clear to her that there was a plot among the staff to destroy her. She fulminates at carefully chosen staff members—ones who are attackable and can be moved off her floor. She uses me as her "intelligence check," to meter her mental status. She is expecting that I will join her in her positive self-view. I explore this with her, and this is sufficient for her to conclude that I concur heartily. Each session ends with, "The doctor himself knows that I have kept all my marbles!"

Her paranoia extends to other areas of her life. She checks her food, observes residents and staff to see if they are talking about her, and thinks now that any escape from the nursing home would be blocked by nefarious forces. She thinks this way even though she is aware of the finality of the placement. She cannot bring herself to attack her family over the placement. She is desperate and avoids cutting off lines of communication, but she does wish the children would react to her as I do. So we study how to get them to cooperate and to talk to her the way she wants. She finds their version of reality offensive, as when they retort, "Ma, you're no spring chicken." She wants to feel as smart and whole as she did when she was 26. In fact, the inner age of just about every elderly person I have treated can be placed thereabouts. There are no self-proclaimed octogenarians that I have ever met. FORGET THE WRINKLES AND STOOPED SHOULDERS. EVERY ONE OF OUR PATIENTS IS 26 YEARS OLD.

The seventh patient, who has been referred for hostile and aggressive acts against the nurses, has little use for therapy. He only attends because of his wife. She went to great lengths to get him involved, promising certain gratifications and then making good on them. He frequently tells me he does not want me as a therapist and seems able to talk freely only when I retort that I do not want him as a patient. WE CAN BE TOO "GOOD" TO GIVE SOME PATIENTS THE OPPORTUNITY TO GAIN FROM THE THERAPY. In fact, the more I attempt to dissuade his contact and his revelations, the more driven he seems to try to foil me and talk. This was accomplished in an angry way during the first few sessions, but after that a playful dimension evolved. He spends a lot of time (rather accurately) analyzing my character. He says if I can sit there and "take" *him* "apart"— something that I have never done—then I can certainly tolerate some of my own medicine. We explore my failings, gaps, and peccadilloes each week. My understanding is that we have learned how to share the badness in the room, and now he is able to work on his social interactions with staff.

The ninth patient is slowly losing her eyesight to glaucoma. She is particularly disturbed because her style of commerce with the world is highly visual. She painted, loved to observe, and loved to read. Her metaphors are visual. This loss is the worst yet in a recent life of accelerating losses. She gains stability one week, but loses it the next to the ongoing stressors she cannot yet master. Buffeted by relentless pressure, she asks for more sessions per week. The therapy reliably comforts her, and she needs someone to talk to who won't drown her in pity. She hates pity, she says, but it is the direct and unadorned feeling of others that sickens and regresses her. As her style is visual, it is also intellectual. IT IS OUR CONSCIOUS SACRIFICE TO REFLECT THE PATIENT'S DEFENSE THAT HELPS, AS MUCH AS ANY SANGUINE AND PROPRIETARY FEELINGS. She needs the carefully offered mirror of intellectual response. If I revealed the feelings generated in me, she warns, she would kick me out of her room. She needs to use her preferred defense of intellectualization to grapple with her challenge and avoid the feeling of fragmenting.

The tenth patient is 100, frail, and enjoying a respite from her severe depression. When I was out for a two-week vacation, her status deteriorated markedly. She is maintained by the therapy, where I provide especially fashioned supports that create for her a continuing sense of mental and emotional integration. The sessions continue in much the same manner each week, she recounting the events as she remembers them and benefitting from questions and comments designed to help her function well. She claims that there are large areas of her life that she will never be able to remember, yet each week she brings in new information. She is driven to integrate a larger picture describing her life and its meaning. THE URGE TO MASTER LIES BEHIND OUR DREAD REPETITIONS AND ALSO OUR SELF-PIONEERING IN EXPANDING THE EGO.

It may be true that some or all of these patients will rebound after thirteen weeks of a behavioral therapy. It is my responsibility to see that the most effective interventions are employed, and I do use my training in behavioral and brief therapies where I can. It may also be that behaviorally trained professionals need to consider less direct, more subtle approaches to take into account the patient's style of relating, patterns of resistance, belief systems, and cooperation in role-playing, in taking instructions, and in doing homework (Lazarus et al. 1992).

Some behavioral approaches can be too demanding for certain types of patients, and the entry-level requirements have to be made easier to accommodate the person's repertoire. That has been happening in all the therapies. We have had to resensitize at the lower end to make it easier for people who would otherwise be considered untreatable. Orthodoxies give way to realities, and at this level the various schools of therapy seem to have more in common.

There is a role for behaviorism in the nursing home setting. Where I can, I share my assessment with the patient and join in a mutual exploration. As a result, the assessment articulates into understandable, succinct, observable behaviors. The principles of learning are employed to traverse the distance between the patient's entry-level behavior and target goals. Practice, role-playing, and homework are used. The operant nature of behavior is highlighted, and I use a multimodal, eclectic approach to set the stage for change.

But more often, my assessment and goal-setting are silent, because the patient demonstrates an inability to participate with the requisite entry-level skills. Addressing the patient's ego mobilizes resistance. The psychologist is seen as someone likely to pathologize the patient's experience, and so the person will not allow a dialectic to discover whether that is in fact true. Even gently guiding the patient through a Socratic process to uncover his beliefs and their effect on his behavior can produce a resistance.

The developmental nature of the person's coping strategies are more prominent. Powers of assimilation have been stunted by immediate precipitators, and by a lifelong pattern of distorting the incoming world so that only the thinnest slivers of it survive intact for the perceptual system to have to decode. The behavioral movement has increasingly adopted its own version of such guiding *schemata*, but perhaps the word *schema* does not impart the constricting nature of this process. Freud (1912) used the analogy of a colander in a more powerful way. He saw character functioning like a spaghetti strainer. The less pliant the character, the more brittle and fixed it was, then the more steel there was to the colander, and the smaller the holes were. What gets through from the outside is only that which is highly polarized and distorted. The form and the content of these distortions are preverbal communications about what happened in the person's early life to block maturation.

Psychodynamic therapy has the goal of relaxing the steel, dilating the holes, turning armor back into fluid stuff. Directness, pressure, and challenge constrict the holes further. That is the reason behind the nondirectiveness of some of our therapies: Do not press for authentic encounter. Shift the attention away from the ego. Have it arranged when to meet, how long to meet, how and when you will be paid. Instruct the patient to say anything he wants to say. Then watch how the patient resists along these dimensions. Let him surprise you. If he has more ego strength than he has let on, he will reveal this through his contacts, but more often he will become more fully realized as Methuselah in the garden.

The patient who enters therapy fully open to a working alliance may exist in the community, but he is rarely seen in a nursing home setting. Our patient is most likely to be frightened about the potential for narcissistic insult that a therapy session represents. He needs us to move carefully and deliberately. He is on the verge of ending the therapy from the very start and requires us to be a certain way so that early termination is not provoked.

Thus we silently analyze the situation of the treatment and intervene in ways that reduce our iatrogenic dimensions. This is the image of Echo. She controls her toxicity. The steel of Freud's conceived *character* is nothing more than patterned self-protection from overpowering and potentially destructive forces. As with the first prokaryote that established itself as durable life in our primordial seas three billion years ago, the ego "had to render its outside inorganic in order to preserve the core" (Freud 1920). This biological metaphor suggested that life had to partly die in order for the soft stuff of it to gain protection from the heat, the cold, the jagged rocks, and the lightning of primeval Earth. It is in our earliest inheritance that life and death are one within us. In its biological dimensions, our ego is that first prokaryote. As we can generate protoplasm and weave more complex reticula and signaling systems, so can we turn the living, breathing part of ourselves into dead stuff.

But when this deadened colander of character resonates only to the mirror of itself in the sweet voice of Echo, what need is there for steel? As the holes open to admit more light and find there is no extreme temperature or jagged edges or lightning, then why reinforce the rind? The *modus thanatos* is rendered unimportant. If everything out there is like me in here, then why expend inordinate amounts of energy to establish a boundary of defense? It is this boundarying reflex that has prevented the person from more freely following his unique, maturational path. Echo stands for a schema, a therapeutic organization of ourselves that eschews psychotoxicity in favor of analysis, patience, timing, and an enduring concern for the protection of the patient's defenses, all as a way of promoting movement.

CREATIVE OPPORTUNITIES

Part of our therapeutic acumen consists of knowing when to press, and when to let things be. I am more given to employing the healing aspects of the milieu, because of my background as an educator. My experience with groups ranging from ten to seven hundred people has given me a sense of how to accent a milieu's therapeutic properties. The one caveat is that I must keep an eye on the aggressive potential of the people involved. What I have retained of my long years in psychoanalysis is a strong regard for its toxipsychological warnings. Be aware of where the murder is, in the patient and in you. Know it and acknowledge it, so that no one is going to have to go into action in order to express it. If you know where it is, more treatment options are available.

The four-story facility was home to 250 residents, most of them ambulatory, but allowed to remain in the home under a grand-fathering provision. As nursing home costs steadily climbed, requirements for placement were becoming more stringent and from this point on most people reviewed and accepted for long-term care would be wheelchair- or bed-bound. The physical mobility of this group was therefore unique.

Staff and consultants waited on line in the resident dining room to get their own lunch trays. As I stood with fellow workers I could observe my forty patients walking in with their peers and taking their places at the tables. There were over fifty tables in the dining room and four settings per table. Despite the large numbers of people in this area, it was only those in the lunch line who talked.

It was surprising that I had not noticed this earlier. None of the residents spoke. They managed to look through each other, around each other, at the floor, and out the windows. Though their trays abutted to create squares enclosing flower vases and metal stands with their names, these people assiduously avoided touching one another. Occasionally a squabble would erupt over transgressions of personal space. "Move that walker out of my way so I don't knock your teeth down your throat!" and "Hey, you're in my #@! seat! Get out of my seat!" and "Don't rush me or I'm not moving at all!"

However there were many more pleasant than unpleasant people in the room and an ordered calmness was maintained. There was an impression that everyone was getting along, in spite of the episodic outbreaks from known curmudgeons. I got the sense of sociability, until I observed more closely. It was then clear how pervasive was the encapsulation of each person in his own world. Many of my patients had been referred for their poor adaptation. The physicians and staff usually wanted me to work with the patients' withdrawal, isolation, poor reality testing, poor social anticipation, and reduced relatedness.

As a principal and a teacher before that, I always volunteered for lunch duty. I enjoyed the busyness of that large room and the vivacity of the youngsters and did my part to keep behavior within reasonable bounds so everyone could have a good time socializing. I also loved Horn and Hardart, the bustle of the crowds, the deep sound created by the clatter of plates, and the ringing of silverware punctuating the constant and satisfying din.

There was something very wrong in this environment. So I looked for an invitation to eat with the residents. Soon after, one of my patients asked me to join her, and we discussed the issue in treatment. At the appointed day, I pulled up a chair next to her and immediately disturbed the equanimity at the table. Where would I place my tray, was there going to be room for me, how would we position the chairs, did I mind such cramped arrangements? Pleasantness and delight prevailed. I chatted a bit and then eased back. Three of the people talked with animation. My patient was very gratified with my honoring her wishes and she energized the table. The fourth person remained quiet. I told this woman we'd all had something to say. Was there anything she'd like to add? That was all it took. She joined right in.

The cook passed by and I called him to the table. I told him the salad was excellent, the green beans were succulent, and the lasagna made just right, with the top a little crusty, just as I liked it. Flustered, he smiled and backed out of the room. The elderly people laughed in appreciation of his inability to take a compliment. Before he left, others added their compliments. I had nodded to the table as I had made each assertion about the meal, promoting such comments among the residents. This occurred on a Monday, and I was due back Wednesday and Friday. The diners at table six instructed me that I must return on those days.

A gentleman from table five called over, "I loved the conversation. Make sure you come back." Table four joined in and the forty or fifty people surrounding us broke into laughter as new tables voiced their invitations. I returned on Wednesday and passed among the people in this west corner of the room. I saw that with rare exception, no one knew anyone else's name. To avoid narcissistic mortifications, I spoke as if everyone did know everyone else, and I liberally used people's names in an effort to teach them to others. "Libby, Dan here tells me that the Turkey Surprise was really a surprise. Right, Dan?" Dan chuckled, "Oh, she knows all right. We were all looking for the turkey in this patty. Only, surprise! There wasn't any!" Libby blushed brightly, because Dan not only addressed her but looked into her eyes for the first time. "Dan, is this the first time you showed Libby your sense of humor?" He quickly rejoined, "It's the first time I've shown anyone my sense of humor."

Everyone laughed. Later, Dan and Libby would get a lot more serious and became lovers. Their relationship humanified the environment for their peers. The home was even a place where two people could find love. We kept meeting in our large group, week after week. My group of four grew to forty. In three months it was more like six groups, loosely knit, with the facilitator up and around. I made sure to contact each and every person during the lunch hour. I used everyone's names, got people to talk, and taught them how to get their peers to talk. This became a ritual that lasted a year.

The lunch room was now loud. People had to talk over one

another to be heard. Plates clattered, people gesticulated with their forks, spirited controversies broke out. The noise was balming. First names sounded out with regularity. There were greetings, interplay, humor. People acted more kindly to the staff, thanking them for serving, appreciating the cleanup, giving the cook feedback. Humanity undeclared and hidden behind masks of impassivity sometimes needs to receive permission, and a path for expression. I modeled each of these behaviors from the first day I began this practice.

A group has a corporate identity that mirrors the dimensions of an individual. Constructive and destructive trends harmonize to create character. This collection of people had a character of aloofness, fear, carefulness, encapsulation. The angrier and more regressed people among the crowd set the tone and accentuated these values in the people around them. But the mildest intervention, asking help in deciding where to sit at that first table, revealed the pervasive interest to relate. This was the acid test. If I had driven the residents into regression, I would have tactfully withdrawn, but my observations suggested that this was not going to happen at all. A great healing power was released. This can occur with groups of various sizes.

I was asked to represent my university years ago at a teachers' convention. I decided to demonstrate how potent a force free operant conditioning was. If the teacher did nothing more during a lesson than reinforce successive approximations of desirable behaviors, a whole different kind of learning emerged. I expected twenty people would show up for this presentation. So the night before I filled my pockets with all manner of candies and little doodads. Since I could not do a reinforcer search beforehand, I made some logical choices in pretzels, candies, pieces of Turkish Taffy, and toys that cost a penny.

To my dismay, the lecture hall was packed to the rafters. There were hundreds and hundreds of people in this room. They waited expectantly as I stared back at them. I thought to myself, "I am not going through with this." My stage fright was strong and building, but then I took a good look at the people. They seemed positive toward me, and they were expecting something good. I considered that I had a few hundred tangible reinforcers on my person. There was really no way out. So I made some opening comments. As a lady in the first row looked up at me adoringly, I walked over and handed her a pretzel. "That's excellent. I love your attentiveness and your willingness to learn. I am so pleased to have you with us." Adoring was an attitude I wanted to see a lot of that day.

A man way in the back was caught by surprise and laughed heartily. I sprinted up to him and offered him a piece of Turkish taffy: "You have good humor and an open mind. We are going to have a splendid afternoon together." I did this for an hour, praising people for focus, attention, eye contact, bodily orientation. I would lecture for three minutes about a technical aspect of behaviorism, and then ask back what I had just taught. Handing someone a Captains Courageous ring, for example, I might say, "You definitely caught the sense of reinforcement. It has to be immediate, it has to come in small packages so the student does not satiate before you are done, and it is best associated with natural activities such as evaluative feedback, so you can slim the schedule later on."

The group seemed to act as one. Its constructive powers had been tapped. I have been lucky in the field of education to have had many such experiences, which have enriched my opportunities to act as a change agent in the field of psychotherapy. For if I had depended wholly on my psychotherapy group training, it might not have occurred to me to take this approach with my audience. I probably would have psychologized the experience of the assembly by easing back more. This might well have led to discomforts, regressions, or disequilibrations. Our models can blind us to the obvious. Sometimes people just need a good feeding.

THE INITIAL VALUE OF TRAINING IS THAT IT STRUCTURES OUR WORK. AS WE CONTINUE, HOWEVER, WE LEARN TO MOVE OUTSIDE THE STRUCTURE AND USE OUR SELVES AS A THERAPEUTIC TOOL.

The therapeutic task has two elements. We go with the patient, allowing our own character outlines to diminish in order to resonate with him. At the same time, we preserve a part of our ego that suggests where the patient is going to be when he has resolved his resistance to progress and growth. In the beginning of our career, we feel like we are a bit unlike ourselves. As we go along, we realize everything about us can be used to help others, and we feel more like ourselves than we ever did.

2

The Therapist and the Elderly Patient

ECHO

Echo was a beautiful and graceful naif. She was a wood nymph slipping in and out of the warm glades of central Greece, at one with nature, a concentration and exposition of the life around her. She admired Narcissus, a young man who shared the wood with her. To admire someone is to bring the mirror to him. His beauty animated her to seek the beauty within herself, and all admiration is the search for an external form to one's ego ideal.

She admired him from afar, showing a carefulness innate to so vulnerable a creature. And what a resonation she made with him. Her vulnerability was a match for his own. She called back to him exactly as he called out, her voice neither louder nor softer, her answers neither longer nor shorter, her insights neither greater nor less. If he had ever chanced to mutter, "What ails me?" she would not tell him, "You are a depressed young man riven by powerful forces you cannot understand." She would reply, "What ails me?" Of all the contacts Narcissus was said to have had, those with Echo were unique. They were not deleterious to either party.

In the persona of the therapist, Echo addresses her naivete in two ways. She moves beyond youth and middle age and precociously adopts the worldview of the great-grandparent. At the same time she grows by reaching below herself, giving conscious experience to her preverbal and most primitive roots. Echoing starts out as a collection of techniques that have us resonating with Methuselah, but if we are in the proper learning environment, we can thankfully expand on this phase of our professional growth. Within the caressing hammock of supportive teachers, peers, and our own therapy, we learn to take the very risks we ask of our patients.

We change in the most drastic way a human being can change. This is largely unnoticeable to those around us, because our behavior shows no great discontinuity. We seem to be the same in our thirties, forties, and fifties. Discrete evidence of this change is in our attractiveness to a greater range of people. We are learning to admire all sorts of things that we would have reflexively rejected when we were younger. We work out our fears and prejudices and along the way conclude that all of them—all that have gone before and will appear in the future—are aspects of our shadow side. As the shadow comes into the light, we integrate and so we can accept, and then admire. At this point, we have left society, in such a way that we can be more in it.

There is further evidence of deep change in the sincerity with which we join seemingly opposite sentiments, in quick order, throughout the day. With the first patient, we steep ourselves in feelings of misery; with the second, we agree that things are looking up; with the third, we follow the struggle to embrace life as poetry; with the fourth, we go with his confusion and do not even know what day it is. The sincerity comes from our recognition that it is all true. We are depressed and hopeful, brilliant and slow, resourceful and powerless; we are all the extremes and everything in the middle. And the greatest part of us lies outside these semantic opposites. We not only can be, but actually are, all things at once.

Somehow it does not seem safe to study such ideas as a young person. What can be freeing and transcendent in the second half of life can be a provocation to toxic regression in the first half. The ego has its own plan and its own rhythm. It has a necessity to grow and recover what ground it can from the id, and threats to the *ego project* release destructive powers that can hamper further growth. When the denial of death has been met and destructiveness is brought into consciousness, the ego's main work is done. Its thicker contours can relent.

"Only once have I been made mute," wrote Kahlil Gibran (1989). "It was when a man asked me, 'Who are you?'" (p. 2). What is the great impasse of modern man, upon enough exploration, turns into the source of our healing. I am everyman, I am no man; I have the universe imprinted in me and held within me. What we cannot deal with the first half of our lives, we can answer in an all-inclusive way when we are older.

The schema of Echo has cognitive, affective, and transcendent dimensions. And it is nothing less than a schema, the grandest and broadest one that erases the distance between the most primitive and the most advanced within us, the one schema that is hardest to construct but paradoxically has all its elements within tantalizing reach. For we all have the pretensions to be the best we can be with those around us. There are moments of crystal clarity, where it seems so obvious how it is done and where to reach within us to schematize transcendence. Yet look at the extreme difficulty most people find joining, mirroring, or quietly accepting the other person's point of view. It is not possible to maintain an I–thou relationship with the world for long periods without a great degree of training and focus.

Part of the pattern of growth is accepting and understanding failure, recognizing that we are going to be making mistakes of all kinds all the time, and providing less than a best fit for those we work with. The near disaster in my professional work occurred when I attempted to enlist the families of my elderly patients as co-therapists. Efforts at directly educating the grown children in increasing their agreeability have rarely met with success. The family members are certainly motivated when they contact the therapist and ask for help with the regressed elderly parent, but this is quickly confounded by the boundarying needs of the family members.

People find it hard to join parents who have been hurtful to them all their lives. To ask them to be agreeable is to take away the defenses that kept them intact when they were being raised.

My experience with families has been more successful when I take their needs into account equally and invite everyone in for family therapy. Bring everyone to the table and invite them to partake. Let the family members benefit from the same resonating that is afforded the parents. Allow the family to resist with the same ardor as the elderly patient resists. Understand the resistance. Embrace it. Love it. Aspects of subsequent progress may fall under the description of behavior modification, but so much is happening in so many areas that the quantities of conditioning amass to yield something qualitatively different, a developmental learning pattern.

So it is that failure improves us. Our only care is to avoid iatrogenic insult and be relaxed enough about our work to learn from the minor empathic failures. They are enough. The patient's comments about such errors keeps us from getting off the track. At the same time, our failures help them critique us in a way that is reparative to them. Our dedication to this point of view is therapeutic in its own right. We are accepting, believe in continual learning, and know we must continue to reorient ourselves to be the way people need us to be. In so doing we model a special resilience the average patient does not get to see in his life.

The therapist is one among a few in modern culture who has taken it into his heart to reflect on his own life. He finds that people have a hard enough time focusing on love and work—forget about play—in getting through the week. The culture is not at present congenial to self-reflection. Indeed, its tempo is exaggerated, pre-orgasmic. Through subtle and not-so-subtle agents, we are beckoned to go through the day in a semitumescent state. When one is in a partial lather, it makes more sense to go up before going down. This atmosphere legislates against contemplation.

And this is as it should be. The culture is making its pendulum swings, seeking the right spot and also seeking the right amount of stimulation. It is not our role to retreat to the mountain in isolation. We are village monks, moving among the people, sharing in the culture, appreciating the semitumescent urges, valuing the environment as the start-off point for people who come to us and wish to be understood. We have to be in the culture to afford it our contributions. It is the part of us that accepts but also contemplates that leads the way for our patients. It teaches them that they have options in reschematizing and that a protean multitude awaits behind the mirage of the fixity of character.

If it is the relationship that creates progress in all therapies, then Echo's agreeability has the distinctive characteristics of a wise elder. She is wary of the human need to discharge her aggression into relationships. She keeps an eye on the murderous feelings and will eventually conclude that they are an old friend to be embraced, not an enemy to be feared and squelched. She has maximized her capacity to see herself in the foibles of others. She has looked upon her life, upon all the things she should not have done that she did, upon all the things she did that she should not have done, and she has held the whole sorry mess to her heart, as the one life given to her by God, as Erik Erikson describes the challenge of late life.

Echo has maintained her ability to civilize the power of the murderous introjects within her, as she has moved out of her teens and into middle adulthood. She used to hide behind a rock to protect herself. Now she does it by relenting under the prodding desire of entropy in its search for more direct expression. It has been pressing for equal say, to move beyond an alienative to a dialogic relationship with the rest of the self in its multiple forms. She accepts these introjects and works on loving them. If the truth be told, Echo is a dual-drive theorist. She knows how tension builds and wanes, peaks and discharges within her. She senses the tension stories and tension songs that are created deep at the interface of her biology and her psychology. She accepts that she was a vibrant fetus creating consciousness anew, and a parasite eating up her mother, and a Methuselah in the amnion seeking splendid equipoise. She accepts the joy and excitement of her budding infancy lodged throughout every cell of her being and recognizes if there was any witch in her childhood nursery to frighten her with death, it was an artifact of her own tension-reducing instinct.

Echo has determined it is her work to come into balance with the negative introjects that form the reflexive and primitive base of the intrapunitive superego. Let these forces wash over her; they need to. And when they are done, there is more to her, and more beyond that. Echo has found a way to let as much of her elemental being directly into the world as is humanly possible, within the constraints of social interdiction. Her cosmology guides her to seek unalloyed love and hate, to feel them both deeply, so she can be of help in showing Methuselah the way. For Narcissus never really vanished. He grew old. Now he is Methuselah.

Patient	*Therapist*
"I am terribly ill and can think of nothing but dying."	"How could you possibly think of anything else?"
"My bed is an uncomfortable contraption and noisy, too. The plastic crinkles when I move around at night. I hate it!"	"It sounds like a horrible bed."
"The nurse is abrupt with me. She treats me like a child. Before I retired, I had fifty men working under me! Who does she think she is!"	"Who can blame you for feeling frustrated?"
"This is my last session with you. We're getting nowhere fast."	"It sounds to me like this is a good time to end."
"You are the smartest doctor I ever met. I am a blessed person. I am the luckiest person alive, to have you."	"You are probably the luckiest person alive."
"I know if I started a fight with the aide, you'd take her side right away."	"How can you say I'd take the aide's side, just because you started the fight?"

"My son made sure he liqui-
dated all my assets and made
himself a rich man before he
locked me up in this home.
The kids are animals."

"They're awful. They deserve
to be put in cages and shown
in the zoo."

"You seem like a very sexual
person. You no doubt have
many lovers. And you please
them all."

"I have a large harem that I
am able to keep quite busy."

"Since I lost my teeth, I can't
eat steak. I miss steak so much.
My life is horrible."

"My teeth are shaky and loose.
It's only a matter of time until
I lose them. You're helping me
see what I'm up against."

"Are you a big shot around
here? Can't you get them to
cook some decent food? Or do
you save all of the good stuff
for yourself?"

"I like selecting the good stuff
for myself before I let the rest
of the groceries go to the
kitchen."

Each patient benefits in his own way from the particular truth
we have chosen to illuminate and send back. Not everyone receives
the same interventions; they are tailored to the aspect that needs to
be echoed. Thus each of these examples, where sentiments about
oneself, the children, the facility, and the therapist have been
mirrored or joined, is specific to the individual situation. In some
work settings the pressures are of a sort that no criticisms of anyone
or anything can be tolerated. In such situations Echo teaches by
taking the attack on herself. Other settings that are more psychologically accepting and astute invite the therapist to the latitudes
that will be best for the patient.

At times the patient's requests can center around very early
needs that will require at least partial gratification for the therapy to
have any impact. The therapist decides the best timing and form for
honoring the patient's request. In fact, all therapy is the research

investigation of parameters. We go along until the patient needs something special, which usually resides outside the classical confines of the therapy. As my trainers told me, any book on therapy is best understood as a treatise on one particular patient that stuck out in the scholar's mind. With each patient we see, it is up to us to "write his book." The concept of *parameter* loses its critical sting when it is understood as the new book that has to be written to capture this particular patient.

Patient	*Therapist*
"You're only listening to me because you get paid. Otherwise, I am an old, boring lady."	"On the contrary, I enjoy visiting, and listening to you."
"All through my miserable life, the only thing that gave me pleasure was an occasional evening at a restaurant. Why can't we ever bring some food in and celebrate?"	"The idea has merit. Let's discuss the details."
"Could you bring in a picture of yourself? I have asked you, and would like it."	"This is surely possible. I will bring one in for you."
"I have asked you all year to escort me to an activity. Now the fashion show is coming up. I want you to take me to it, or at least keep me company."	"Let's get it into our schedules, and work out all the arrangements now."
"I want you to discuss my therapy in your upcoming lecture. This would please me immensely. I want to feel as if my contribution could be equal to yours."	"How would we alter some of the facts in order to preserve your confidentiality, but still get this wonderful story told? Let's get that taken care of."

"There is nothing left in this world precious to me. And now they've taken my watch. It was a keepsake. Something from you—I would regard that as precious."	"I have a watch at home that might fit. Shall I bring it in?"
"As an editor, I commanded respect. Now everyone just sees me as a wasted old man. And I miss the job itself. Why don't you show me what you are writing?"	"I am working on a book. Would you be so kind as to read it and comment?"
"I made a terrible error not marrying. I have no husband, no children. No grandchildren. How I would love a visit from babies. So I could think of them as my own."	"My family is coming to the staff barbecue. Do I have your permission to bring my sons up to your room for a visit?"

Despite the welter of therapy books describing motivated patients zipping through therapy at speeds to warm the heart of managed care executives, the reality is that many patients proceed at a fair pace until they hit the "stone wall of resistance." It is at this emotional spot that further revelations, cooperation, or progress will threaten to foil the disciplined efforts of the defenses. At the same time, the resistance is a communication of the way the person needs to be approached in order to relent in his rigidity and return to healthful assimilation and accommodation processes. During this status quo phase, the person continues to need echoing.

Patient	*Therapist*
"I have nothing more to say."	"Then why talk? We can sit quietly."

"I have told you the same thing for months and you have no solution."

"You have been cooperative in talking freely. I seem stuck."

"All I want to do is sleep on this couch."

"What stops you?"

"Don't change this meeting time. It is just right for me."

"I have a conflict in the schedule. I don't plan to be here at our regular time next week, but then we'll resume at this time."

"You know how much I love you. I have told you a thousand times."

"Why stop at one thousand times? I can hear lots more."

"I only planned on seeing you this one time."

"I only planned on giving you this one session."

"There is no need to return. I feel you have done all you could."

"My work here seems finished. You have done all you could."

"You're a very stupid doctor. What do you say to that?"

"A stupid doctor for a stupid patient."

"I hear that there is a new form of therapy in California. My son is bringing me literature. I want to go."

"Bring in the brochures. I'll help you plan a memorable visit."

"You're not right for me. How did I get you?"

"Who referred you? It doesn't seem I'm right for you."

"My family wanted me to talk to you. But I'm not saying a damn thing."

"I'd prefer it if you remained quiet during this session."

"I refuse to tell you anything personal."

"I am instructing you to avoid discussing anything personal. Everything else is all right."

"Can't you see I'm not worth your attention? Worthless. A worthless human being."

"My first wife dumped me for the tennis instructor. My second wife dumped me for her doctor. Give me a good reason to get married again."

"The big secret is this, as I have told you again and again. If anyone knew me well, they'd hate me."

"My arthritis is bad, like it was in June. Not so bad as July. Worse than May. Here, look at my daily records. It shows how my knees and elbows are doing."

"The nurse came in at 11:37, stayed two minutes, and she calls that a visit? The aide fixed my bed at 9:23 and the housekeeper cleaned the floor at 12:16. I pay thousands to live in this nursing home and I got 27 minutes of attention today. I'm doing an exposé."

"Oh, look at the dandy walking down the hall. He calls himself a professional! He's a fake, like all of them. A fake!"

"What's kept me blinded from the truth this whole time? What do you suppose is the matter with me?"

"With some luck, your third wife will also try to dump you, and so we can finally find out what this is all about. We have a shot at the repetition."

"I know that once people get to know me and are comfortable, they hate me."

"A good start. But do you find you are tracking enough information? How about your hands, neck, back, and ankles?"

"This will become a best seller. It's the most interesting thing I've seen in the last 20 years. You have a mind like a steel trap."

"This world is full of fakes." (Once there is a working relationship): "Why do you always leave me out when it gets interesting?"

(In a barely audible voice):
"Doctor. A pleasure. Your work
fascinates me. Tell me about
it."

(Barely audible): "A pleasure
to be with you. What would
you like to know?"

"You know I hate visitors! Yet
you come! Well, fine! But keep
your mouth shut!"

(Silence)

We echo to create the opportunity for therapeutic movement. These interventions generally relax the patients to the point that they can talk progressively. The goal of this type of supportive therapy is to reduce resistance so that the patient can say everything. Every now and then, the effect of an intervention is stark. The person is surprised. He has never heard anything like this before. Small transformations are made then and there. How could this be?

The steel of the colander, which is character armor, is permanent enough. But this restricting hemisphere, this iron mask, this boon, and this curse upon one's relations with the larger world is also removable. In one deft act, we can shed the mask and confront different possibilities—the greater boon and the greater curse of seeing more of the world as it is. Freud's (1917) other metaphor was the stone wall of resistance. Because resistance is a defense as it is brought into the treatment relationship, and defense is nothing more than the childhood character, he was referring to the steel of the colander, or template, as he called it.

Freud saw his challenge as a martial one: he must smash that stone wall. We know now that the stone wall is created out of the dynamics of our ego, and that it can replenish and thicken itself against all kinds of incursions. The wall just emphasizes more of its wallness, when the person is under attack. And attack is not defined by the intent of the therapist, but by how his stimulation or even lack of stimulation is perceived. It is effect, not intent, that counts.

Spotnitz added to Freud's metaphor. If we stop the fusillade and instead help the patient add stones to the wall, to make it as safe for the patient as he needs, he will eventually step out from behind it and make himself seen (Spotnitz 1976). When we echo, haven't we lost our contours as "something out there to be defended against"? Aren't we behind the wall with the person? If he did not have the energy to step out from behind the wall, or the strength to lift off the restrictive faceplate, haven't we joined with him, shared our energy, and helped him accomplish the undoable?

Colleagues generally consider a number of the interventions above to have arisen from the "paradoxical" approach. Somehow, in order to get forward movement, we seem to go in the opposite direction. But there is nothing paradoxical about Echo. "Technique" itself usually bears a protean value, suggesting endless movability to be with the patient in the right way, but what seems paradoxical and protean in Echo is more precisely her increasing ability to match within herself anything and everything of Methuselah.

It could be said that Echo possesses a litheness to slip in and out of personas. Or, this could be the Machiavellianism that is supposed to typify the personality of a clinical psychologist. But it is neither. It is that she has identified the biological substratum to everything. At one with nature, she is aware of the bubbling smokepot over whose surface congeals the iron mask of character. The smokepot is real, and to look into it is to lose the self. The self organizes above it and uses the stories of culture to secure relatively stable patterns that will render social likenesses and allow the uneasy peace and sharing of space with other smokepots.

The protean side of us is a concatenation of texts, and we are Gilgamesh, Beowulf, Parcival, Moses, Christ, an admixing of story lines that have cultural value; that is, story lines that reliably allow enough of our raw being to come into exposure to make life worth living. We are who Cervantes, Hugo, Hemingway, Cheever, and Updike have been able to form out of their own smokepots. For each artist reaches deeper into himself to expose this easier continuity between smokepot and society. Smokepot is ceaseless and borderless and, without guiding texts, a rather noxious infant who must in the end be destroyed by offended but more powerful infants.

These vicissitudes are met with like destructive power. The amount of destructiveness that the smokepot is exposed to equals the amount of steel in the protective colander. The child turns such powers upon the developing self: "Destructive power come upon this place? It must be me. It is the I and so let the thickening steel of my colander show this." Introjection is the first defense, the most primitive, the one with the most far-reaching consequences for reducing the versatility to deal with a spectrum of demands from the society later on.

This is why Echo retains an all-thereness with murder. She works to know where it is all the time and lives at the site of congealing and remelting of steel, right there at the miasma where smokepot and character touch in a state of flux.

METHUSELAH

Methuselah lived to be 969 years of age. This age was thought to have been picked by the architects of the Bible as an answer to the cultures of the Tigris-Euphrates, where kings were given ages in excess of one thousand years. The Babylonians were placing their kings in the godlike realm. To the Hebrews, God stood alone, one thousand years marking one of His days. Thus Methuselah, grandfather of Noah, was one lifetime less than a day in God's life. He was still a man, and *metu*, the beginning of his name, meant *man* (Kolatch 1984, p. 160).

Our Methuselah is human, not God, but close to having a taste of the millenial day. He falls tantalizingly but firmly short. Entering my thousandth treatment relationship with an elderly person, I see a symmetry taking form. I have treated as many people as Methuselah was old. His persona is filling out. If the aspects of the individual aggregate and combine to offer a larger reality, then who is he turning out to be?

He is the old man in the garden. His preverbal experience is rich, and yet without the words to say it, he cannot perceive it as distinct from himself. He is focused on cupping in his hands the thinnest of gruel, only a momentary equanimity, and because he errs largely on either side of that just-right point in his effort to achieve there-ness, his experience is a collection of hurts and frustrations. To get what he wants is only to fear losing it again.

If he had a ruling mental ego, it lost its hold and he recentered on a body ego. He worships each muscular and glandular gratification and grits his teeth against spasm, pain, imbalance, tension, and hungers. Frustrated and hurt in his infancy, he became the institutionalization of his insults. There were fewer resources left over to tackle the prime and only issue of human existence—to bring as much of his being directly into the world, in order to get enough gratification to want to grow further and to do this without ruining others in the society: the human as the vibrant animal who stays within the guidelines of the social contract.

He introjected more aggression than was good for subsequent efforts at assimilation and accommodation. Thereafter, he was more given to solidify a self in repetitive mimicking of the dead wall that crushed against him. Emotional scar tissue is composed of introjects—our effort to master the death-dealing blows we encounter by resonating with them and constructing in our psyches walls in honor of them. We then forever pray at the base of these structures, using the love force to forestall further wallings. This rind saps us of the strength to live in and of the world. A great malaise settles upon us. The more ideal capacity to feel love and hate singly and purely has been confounded at its inception. Our love is aimed at "fetishizing" the walls, praying to them in the hopes they will relent and release the vast potential energies stored within them.

Methuselah, the-man-who-was-sent, the messenger, is our own superannuated self, a man a footstep away from a moment with God, not yet there, painfully mortal. He serves to highlight the present search for nearness with the spiritual. Years ago I listened to a philosopher-scientist making a case for the ascent of man. He argued that evolution had created the potential for us to refine our powers to ever greater degrees. Monumental advances were within reach. A rabbi stood in the audience and humbly suggested the opposite. The first people were created in God's image. Each succeeding generation finds us farther away from that original equivalence, and the powers of transcendence continue to weaken among humankind. This was not a confrontation between evolution and creationism. I understood it as a call to reflect on the fracturing nature of our present existence. The call to compartmentalize cognitions and skills pushes us farther away from integration. Homo sapiens have to worry about refining one special talent or another in order to figure in the competition. The time is yet to come for us as a species to integrate mind, body, and spirit.

In today's world, it is difficult to configure the spiritual self. The larger arena we find ourselves in abounds with highly conflicting attitudes. It seems the only choices are to exit into secular humanism or submit to religion's tug and turn to fundamentalism. Balancing spiritual belief in the face of modern pressures is an art form in itself, and we have little accumulated wisdom about how this is done. Culture shock is complete. A new and not necessarily better human consciousness is emerging that expects one to handle the buffetings and pressures of technological life without uttering a peep.

Methuselah's symbolism is in his late, late old age. He has at least been granted the time to try to figure things out. Ideally, he has seized on this golden opportunity to find solutions. On a more practical level, he is somewhere along the path, or close by but lost. Our ministrations as therapists return him to the one destiny that has never changed. For his destiny is to learn to more fully and directly translate his being into daily living and consciousness. Our acceptance of the role of guides means that we get to experience it all, and in the process find our own path.

The full form of humankind, and humankind's destiny, has become known to us in our work of resonating with the old man. We see ourselves in him, until we can clearly see ourselves. He comes within conceptual grasp in all his various forms. On the one hand, he is the person who has known only work all his life. Now that he is retired, and the work is gone, he feels dead. Or he is the person who loved and worked, but never had time to play. Now that his job is over and his spouse dead, he feels dead. Or he is the person who learned how to play, and he approaches his second childhood never having given up his first. His is the most ecstatic side of old age.

Less often, he is the person who did everything in balance, and thought to reflect, too. He has discovered things about himself that the average young adult or middle-aged adult could never know. His job is gone, but he animates all that is around him with energy. His spouse is gone, but he has grown to find her loving face in everyone around him and especially in the prolific family branches he has spawned. He aches too much to play physically, but he engages the world at its primary process level anyway and laughs as the Buddha laughs, as Don Gennaro laughs. Above all, he has relinquished the neuroticisms of youth and has chanced to venture back to the miasma, which he can dip into in order to find his pure being. He knows how to be, so that his living and dying are equal and knowable.

In his most regressed state, the old man rests in the garden. When he is of the world, he is in the village. When he has reflected on his life cycle, he is at the celestial gate.

3

Methuselah at the Celestial Gate: Elderly Who Are Ready to Transcend

John was 82 years old when we began therapy. A leather manufacturer, he developed his trade as an offshoot of his work with livestock on the family farm. Devoutly religious, he married in his twenties and took part in the activities of his church, raising his four sons in it. One became a reverend, one a lawyer, one a carpenter, and one a doctor. He moved his family to New York to take advantage of international trade and contacts. His thoughts strayed to his early youth. He recounted how his mother would give him a few pennies every day, and how he husbanded the money rather than spend it on himself. He was able to comment on many different stages of his life in most sessions. Even early in the therapy he demonstrated a grasp of the many faces of personality.

John's talk about himself makes us wonder about the reality of cohesive self. He was gifted in his powers of self-exploration and -description, and so we get an altogether novel idea from his commentary of what it means to be in the world. Everything he said seemed so right, and I wonder why writers in the field of personality study have not captured such sentiments in describing the lives of people. He said he was 82, but he was equally 67, 35, 26, and 15 years old. He remembered those periods in his life with undiminished clarity, and so he was an elder, a retiree, a man in the prime of his physical life, a young man with burgeoning powers, and an adolescent.

The knowledge of these different sides and, indeed, a plethora of sides, seemed to him evoked by different stimuli. He described his youth on the farm, his apprenticeships, his marital relationship, his fatherly duties, and all manner of competing and equally moving concepts. They were not memories so much as they were concepts, for it did not matter to him if he had the data to substantiate a picture he wished to develop of his life. These were strivings. These were attempts to explain the press of being, on a conscious level.

What emerged was profundity over scheme. He seemed literally able to react with the universe of thoughts, feelings, and behaviors given the evocative nature of the demand characteristics in the environment. Further, he could function as a character polymath without any outside invitation. He could be strong and weak, masculine and feminine, worshipping of the spiritual and of lucre, powerful and without power, a learner and a teacher, a leader and a follower, intellectual and emotional, impulsive and reflective, overly energetic and calmly sober, and every shade that fell in every direction over these artificially created opposites. Words cannot adequately capture this, because of our semantically supported elision of most of experience. Ideal opposites reign in the formation and use of our language, submerging the broader experience so that it never gains a voice. The extremes superimpose themselves on everything, so that the words fail us when we try to explain ordinary experience.

In our therapy sessions, John learned to better articulate the protean nature of his self, to capture the spontaneity of its changeability. He was confronted in a therapy group by a peer with "How do you feel about that?" He stunned the audience with his flood of responses. "I feel happy, I feel sad, I feel nothing. I don't know if I have a feeling. Thinking about feelings makes me lose them. I felt something before you asked me but now I don't know where that feeling went. Oh, here comes another feeling . . ." and on. Surprise gave way to laughter and joy, as people in the group found themselves mirrored in his comments.

John was referred for therapy because he voiced pain over the many losses in his life. He used the sessions well and gave back immeasurably more than he got. I blessed his nature and congratulated his pain as the perfect expression of the life and the death in him. He was working on how to be, and I helped his essence "be" more brightly. He released me from the clinical nature of my conceptions and drew me to a more transcendent view of how humankind is built.

I would not call John dissociated, nor bring clinical attention to an apparent lack of integration or center. That would be missing the point totally. His expressive skills, his ability to address the obvious and to talk to the white spaces between the words, lead us to a more general principle. It is setting that evokes, not personality that penetrates. As one functions closer to the miasma, one can relinquish fixed character as a defense. One can open up to possibilities, until it is but the celestial gate that separates one from total unity with all.

TEXT ORGANIZES BEING SO THAT CHARACTER EMERGES. THE MODERN CHARACTER IS A CONCATENATION OF TEXTS. SOCIAL DEVELOPMENT REQUIRES A TEXTUALLY CORRECT CHARACTER. TRANSCENDENCE DEMANDS THAT WE PEEK AT THE UNDERSIDE OF THE CONCATENATING URGE.

Is personality too cumbersome, too material a concept? Do we require a tactical over a strategic model, role instead of personality? Do different scenes evoke different roles in those who are done with their initiations and have learned to move beyond the safety of a cohered self? John was able to say that it was the way different parts of him bounded into view with the mildest invitation. I am Proteus. I can be any man because I am Not-A-Man.

We have all kinds of models. How do we say which one is the more useful? Skinner (1976) counted himself lucky for locating a piece of discarded apparatus for his animal experiments, and not bothering to cut off a spindle that was attached to it. Later on, he devised a way to use that spindle as a recording instrument for his experiments. Imagine him finding a pictorial out of the Physics Department that captured events in space-time and fused the past, present, and future in a nonlinear fashion. What kind of science would he have made? Did the contraption he found in the garbage funnel his perceptions away from larger truths? Was serendipity midwife to the operant conditioning paradigm? He conceived a thin tendril of a behavior, in the repertoire but weak, progressively strengthened by contingent reinforcement. Where there was once a little or almost nothing, now there was a highly predictable and frequent behavior. He saw people as shaped by their environments; thus his particular version of all organisms as a tabula rasa.

Harlow conceived of learning in quite a different way. He saw a profusion of responses available to the organism. The person could respond with everything. Learning was not the progressive building up of one behavior from out of a flat background. It was the narrowing down of the whole repertoire to a specific behavior in the evoking context. Learning was not building-up; it was narrowing. It was a case of tabula completa (Siegel and Ziegler 1976).

Gestalt theory, existentialism, and daseinsanalysis, create different versions, further collapsing the linearity of our temporal view of growth and expression. We owe it to ourselves to be in touch with all these points of view and more, in order to grasp the larger and whole truth that seems at some skewed angle, out of full range of our perceptual powers. In that way every patient creates another theory of humankind for us and invites us to see ourselves anew.

Is this not the goal of every therapist, to find within himself something of the patient, to find something of all the patients seen and going to be seen? In our transcendent form, are we not like John? As long as I knew the man, I noted his ability to inspire people and things around him. A xenos became a philos, nursing home furniture became his furniture, the walls his walls, the sky his sky, the trees and bushes his trees and bushes. These acts of inspiration were godlike, because he had defied the patterned need to overinvest in one's family, belongings, and home setting and had avoided the marasmus one surrenders to when taken from one's setting. The question has never been, "Is there a God?" or even "Where is God?"

It has always been, for the contemplative person, "How do I locate God within myself, and then express Him?"

Henry lay quietly in bed exploring his sensitive gums with his tongue. The pizza they served last night was hot and crusty, but the beer was cold and satisfying, and had put out the fire. Pizza always did something strange to his mouth, even when he had all his teeth. This morning it had left an acidic, soreful pleasantness that he mulled over, carefully and pointedly as the foggy air rolled into his room from the nearby lake. It was six in the morning, and from this point on no one was going to get any sleep.

His roommate's oxygen machine was pumping and wheezing with the desperation of the African Queen's tired piston engine, and he imagined himself as Humphrey Bogart far off in the distance, struggling manfully and joyfully to keep his most cherished outward expression of self afloat and alive. The regularity of the machine reassured him, although it wasn't doing much for his roommate, who sporadically gasped in a panic. At those times Henry empathically felt a large mean hand squeezing his own tiny lungs to the shape of a creased onion skin, as he described it. Their relationship hadn't seemed to have advanced to the talking stage. But their camaraderie deepened nevertheless because Henry was there, suffering with Charlie, gasping with him, shivering with the cold touch of death at his shoulder, knowing that Charlie was going to die in a state of total panic. Henry described him as a caged and frightened animal. Even though Charlie was motionless, Henry felt him pacing and clawing and wished only that Charlie did not consider him the jailer. Toward that end, Henry did his best to commune with the man, to be with him, to give up his own needs from time to time in order to be there. He felt that Charlie knew, that he had learned he didn't have to be defensive, that he could be himself. But he stayed tuned-in to Charlie, lest he be wrong.

It was positively bracing, the cool morning air on his ultrasoft skin. A shiver ran through Henry, as he imagined the feel of water droplets on the open shower chair, a plastic toilet-bowl contraption with wheels. It would have water on it and he would feel chilled to the bone until he got under the hot water. Wrapped in a sheet, hunched over, he laughingly described himself as a baby once more. He once saw himself in the mirror, on the way to the shower room, and was shocked to find he resembled the Mahatma that he remembered from old footage in the 1940s. But he was a Gandhi-opposite, rugged and muscular in his youth. He had lifted the front ends of a few cars in his time.

The transmogrification was at first unsettling to the old man, but in the therapy he learned to delight in it. It was his passage. He had seen the Star Wars trilogy in the multipurpose room of the facility and likened himself to wrinkled and stooped Yoda: no hair on top and plenty sprouting out of his ears, slow and hopefully wise. He laughed much of his life, and he found his laugh again in our weekly sessions, as he described each thought, feeling, sensation, and urge. He told me many times that he was not doing it for me, although he might not have been able to do it if I were not there.

He liked the Gandhi idea and he worked it, asking me about the man and what he stood for, studying whether there might be more than surface likenesses. Along the way he decided he had discovered the holy man's secret—he was sure the man had found a way to express pleasure in his asceticism. Henry had not read that much in his life, and he was more at home articulating his bodily sensations than concepts. It was through bodily sensation, however, that he related to the holy man, and now that he seemed to move and sit and be more like him, he felt he had found something out about the universe of pleasure that lay all around him and washed through him.

Henry was still the hedonist, able to find pleasure directly through sensation and perception, rather than secretly stealing some through stoicism or masochism. The pale lighting on the pastel walls, the blank white of the sheets and coverlets, the rough crinkle of the plastic-covered mattress all fed his heart, body, and mind. His realness radiated to the synthetic living space of the room, so it might as well have been a smoky cave with rich-smelling animal furs strewn across the floor, he the still egoless human, the animist who felt and was a part of everything he perceived around him.

There were the fetid, sour milk smells that occasionally wafted in from the kitchen. They sang the conquering song of the nosocomial bacteria that had colonized that area of the building and had survived countless boiling water bombardments. In a take-no-prisoners effort, they came out of hiding after each scouring and multiplied with orgiastic abandon, until the building was theirs. They, too, added dimensions to his bliss after we reframed the smells as cheesy. Disgust gave way to gustatory interest. They were yogurt on top of sourdough on top of gorgonzola cheese on top of baby spit. Hadn't he warmed his own acidophilus cultures overnight on the stove, so that the blanketed pots and pans yielded up quarts of creamy yogurt with its little popped craters along the surface? Hadn't he left his milk crock bubbling on the windowsill for a few days, in order to make sourdough bread? Hadn't he sliced through the creamy gorgonzola, the real gorgonzola, gliding down until he would hit a hairy blue-gray blob, then push through to the bottom, sectioning up the dead worms that formed a carpet there? That stink was heavenly. It filled the room with goat, horse-hoof, cow's breath. Hadn't his beautiful infants burped up their warm spit on him? Two he remembered got him right in the mouth as he held them up to gaze at their perfection. He remembered how he hated to throw up as a child. That disgust dissipated as he had accepted the necessity, the rightness, the beauty of the convulsive act. He learned to vomit during the therapy, when he needed to, taking a protective stand and refusing to swallow everything.

It was warming up outside, and soon the aides would close the windows. He did not mind the homogenized air spewing out of the whirring units. It was just that the outside, stinky, rich stuff was a good thing. But then other smells would come alive later and he knew them all well. There was the barnyard smell of piss in the men's room, as if they were all being kept on a diet of hay—that musty sweet hay smell. There was the rosewater his neighbor sprinkled all over herself. There was the aroma of failed skin, still in place on one's frame, part of the structure of cheeks and underarms and palms and buttocks, not yet dead but not robustly alive either.

He shook the protein drink and felt the graininess of it in his throat, made more distinct by lack of any definable taste. Every now and then a meal would bring with it a great gustatory and olfactory charge, reminding him of how gratifying food used to be. But in general he was not getting what he wanted in the way of "commensibles." I explored what kept him from arranging something special with the staff. After some time he approached the Recreation Department about bringing in restaurant cuisine every six weeks or so, and they accommodated him.

The aide helped him put on his favorite shirt—a threadbare flannel, soft to the touch and soothing to his bony back and arms. The woman spoke rapidly and gaily in French to fellow staff in the hall, and he let her excitement touch and caress him. Music was coming from three different sources and it mixed with the echoing laughter of the aides and housecleaners. There was a sweet clarity to the woman's voice as she reached ever higher notes—he thought of the clear beauty of his wife. The aide's voice was his wife's lilting voice. She was beside him again.

He experienced a remote tickle in his genitals, evidence of his once explosive orgasms, and it all came back to him in a moment, but without the urgency he remembered as a young man. He could surely make love to this woman who was caring for him, who did not seem to notice his thoughts and feelings. Of course he was wrong. I had been talking to the staff for some time, and the aides and nurses were very aware that they were caring for sexual beings. Sexuality was defined as much by what the residents did not say or do, as by activity. Boundaries were in place, because most people did not know how to broach the issue or deal with it verbally.

Henry felt it would be nice to take a good, long piss. He had remarked to me how his friend would always tell him, "A good piss is better than a good lay." I understood the aggressiveness in this: that not knowing how to structure this caregiving period with the young woman in some constructive way led to the desire for a petit mort, an orgasm. Shorn of its romanticism, it was a good piss, an act of tension reduction. I explored with Henry what was the most frustrating thing about dealing with the aides and helped him articulate this impersonal reaction. We got to the issue of hostility and to the pleasure of discharge. Interestingly, he was able to relate this to his marriage also. He had remained somewhat detached from the kind of merger his wife was capable of showing. She had taught him much, although he still recognized the gap between their levels of empathy.

Henry had been referred after his right leg had been amputated. In his own words, he had become "ornery," and he needed help to properly mourn this loss. He had always seen himself as quiet, a man of action, a generous person, one of good humor, but he had never given himself the opportunity to talk. Now he felt forced to. Nearly seven months had passed after the operation and he was still moody and isolative.

It took a few months of talking freely in the therapy to restore his former attitude. Henry probably had never articulated his attitude before, and in lending words to the impalpable, he found he had even more control over his life than before. He decided that the pleasure of discharge was everywhere. The loss of his leg meant much less than he thought it would, and it reminded him of a conversation he had long ago with a close friend, over this very issue. The other's point of view was that life was not worth living without one's limbs. This struck Henry as incredulous. The man simply wanted to die if he ever lost the use of his legs, and he asked Henry to do him in, if he was not strong enough to take his own life. The restoration of this memory in his consciousness helped Henry work out the anticipatory loss of his other leg, should it also have to be amputated. He was grounded once again in pleasure.

Understanding the world through pleasure gave Henry relief in special ways he was able to communicate to me. When the shock waves of phantom pain would overtake him, he would ride them out. He knew they would stop, so they could roll through him, consume him as they wished. He had a life that was longer and larger than any pain. The very act of talking strengthened Henry and revealed to him resources he only felt at the corner of his mind most of his life. He liked what he was finding out about himself, and he wanted to do more work in therapy.

He was sensing a spiritual dimension in his search for a

personality beyond the one that he knew so intimately. Caught up in a search for the transpersonal, he used the sessions to describe the best of all the people he had ever met—really, the best in himself. He became aware of the cognoscenti, men and women who communed at this level and had touched him in business, in social contact, in the mutual practice of religion. They were special in a way that he could now appreciate and reach for himself.

He found the integration he was looking for. As I listened to him, I understood his position as, "I know what you know. I am where you are. We are broken, we are powerful. We are slipping away, we are more *there* than ever. Form is emptiness. Emptiness is form." He found a philosophical position that reflected these ideas clearly. He listened with understanding. He found the aspects of me that were inside of him. He gauged accurately that humankind's condition is an amalgam, a fusion, an allele of power and weakness. He moved beyond the confines of his body and identified himself as other than what his body was. He grappled with theological issues in the sessions and ended up with a sense of whatness that is descriptive of the most integrated and well-functioning elders in our society.

AT ITS PEAK THE EGO OF THE ELDERLY PERSON IS CONTRARILY AN OPEN GATE, LEAST RESTRICTING, THE MOST SUBLIME EXPRESSION OF BEING IN THE HERE AND NOW.

The philosophy of it was simple. He saw it as life against death, the sensuality of the moment, an urge to be one with the universe. He could just taste that oneness just around the corner, and its elusiveness only caused him to pursue it more. He engaged both chaplains in the building, the rabbi and the Lutheran minister. He spoke endlessly with his family and became a magnet attracting them out of the busyness of their own worlds. Near the end of his life he found the great desire to let the family know of his search for integrity. He died a beloved and revered man, a symbol of transcendence to his family, and a positive introject installed into the hearts and minds of his children, their children, and their children.

Elaine had never used the services of a mental health professional. She understood there was need for such people in the culture, but she was proud to say she had managed fine without one. Now in the span of two weeks she was referred to both a psychiatrist and a psychologist. In her late eighties, she was succumbing to cancer and had suddenly become withdrawn. The adult children were worried about her listlessness and general change in adaptive status.

The psychiatrist diagnosed an adjustment reaction with depressed mood. Elaine was not happy at the prospect of being defined psychiatrically. She warned me during our first meeting that if I was going to construe her life in pathological terms, she would exercise her right to refuse treatment. After a few visits she challenged me with her view of my role: "I suppose it makes sense to you that I am depressed, and you will now go hunting for proof that I always had a problem. This is how you were trained." On the contrary, I found her contemplative and increasingly disinvolved. I saw these as maturational reactions to life events. I told her it was the right way to be. If she wanted, I would continue meeting with her so that she could maintain a maturational response to the stressors facing her. She laughed. "I'm depressed, and you'll say anything just so you can stay here and help me."

The narcissistic slight of being considered a patient was intensified by the arrangement of the milieu. Whether Elaine came to my office, or I went to her room, there was always the possibility of a witness. "Elaine, dear, Dr. Bouklas isn't visiting you, is he? You don't need a psychologist!" This sort of nettling was frequent in the building, until the time that I had visited a large number of people. At first the prospect of getting a visit from me was roughly equated with getting a nasty and unsightly rash. "Oh, have you caught sight of Elaine's eczema? There she is. Smile and wave. Poor thing." When several of the most influential people in the facility found my services helpful, then it became a mark of one's wisdom and self-understanding to be arranging sessions with me.

Elaine remained self-conscious on this count, despite the fact that in her professional work she had frequently recommended counseling and psychotherapy to people. Her discomfort was necessary, because she had decided to use the therapy to the best advantage. She was going to go all the way and describe her real self, the one behind the facade. She was going to tell me things she knew of all the time, but had not revealed to a soul. Her professional career, her marriage to a gentleman who was of high rank in his own profession, their wonderful children, and their social standing were one side of it.

Elaine's deprivations and hurts had been deep and pervasive, following her through her mid-teens. Her mother died when she was 6 years old, and it fell to her to care for her younger siblings. Her father could not sustain himself in the little town in Poland that his family had known for countless generations, and he sought work elsewhere. The children were placed with aunts and uncles and saw little of their father. The family that cared for Elaine had a strong patriarchal structure. The father trucked no interference with his wishes, and this heavy drinker soon began to visit Elaine in her room. As far as Elaine knew, no one would even confirm this reality by speaking it aloud, much less challenge him.

The uncle fondled Elaine and frequently tested her, finally achieving vaginal penetration when she seemed able to accommodate him, at the age of 10. Until then, he resorted to anal intercourse. The youngster understood that her survival depended upon cooperation, but it also depended upon her maintaining an all-thereness and mindfulness about her situation. She organized her day around the nocturnal visit and prepared herself for it. Afterward, she attempted to collect herself and rebound from the hurt. Time was spent in planning an early escape, and her opportunity came when she was 15.

Her father located family members in America and arranged for her to go there. It was time to tell her hosts that she was leaving. She remembered the indifference with which her pronouncement was met. No one feared that she would tell of molestation, because it hadn't really happened. No one feared an exposé. There was an offhanded feeling about it, that she had gotten much, much more than she had given—a good bargain. It was as if she hadn't touched the lives of these people in any way. She packed and left quickly, and she vowed this chapter of her life would remain hidden.

With the telling of this story, a great burden was lifted. Elaine got to put the family secret into words, to the molester himself. For, weren't my visits an invasion? Hadn't she been placed into my hands by the attending physician? Hadn't the caretaker given her over to this "nosy" guy, another kind of "poker"? This was how she understood it. History had been repeated. The physician was her guiding light and her source of strength, but he recommended psychotherapy to her and therapy meant traumatically revealing her vulnerable areas to another person.

When the sessions began, neither she nor I directly knew that molestation was going to be the theme. The giveaway question was, "What do you want from me today?" She started every session with this question, and it took on an increasingly sexual meaning each time she asked it. Central to all the therapies is that we recognize the way the person has felt himself damaged by the interpersonal environment. Our work is then aimed at creating a maturational solution as an alternative to the repetition.

Whatever she thought I wanted from her had to be discussed fully. Thus my actions had to remain in the realm of opprobrium. The safety required to share secrets is predicated on the sentiment that we are not going to be acting toward the patient in a way to engender trauma. When she felt she could trust me, she got the whole story out, with its conscious and unconscious elements. Elaine had cancer of the uterus, and she asked me whether I believed that this was in any way symbolic. In the repetition she was inviting me into her womb and showing me the anti-baby that was growing there. It was the hate-baby conceived of her egg and the uncle's sperm. It was on its way to becoming our hate-baby.

Much has been made about the types of illnesses we succumb to. There is a strong propensity to consider a disease or a failed organ a form of body language. The psychosomatic formula places the bodily dysfunction at the end of the equation, as a primitive expression of a meaning that could not find access through talk. Working with so many physically ill patients has helped me shape a different opinion. I believe the disease comes as it comes, and a meaning is later assigned to it. The physical problem is yet another way to achieve connection with the unspoken, so it can be said out loud and examined.

Her cancer can stand for murderous conception, as her cardiac condition can stand for the broken heart of her abandonments and cruel treatment, as her arthritis can stand for the stiffening of the prepubescent child under the crushing weight of the man's insistent cravings. At the same time, a healthy uterus sending forth many children can be a sign of compensating for the hurt, an unusually healthy heart can mean that one learned to steel oneself before the onslaught, and a sinuous body can signal a conquering of the attacker by absorbing the insult.

The psychosomatic equation is real enough, the same as dream content. Both are used by the patient and the therapist to plumb the unverbalized and unconscious material that is seeking expression in some way.

About the same time Elaine made her revelations, she also told me how she felt my presence to be insistent. She felt she had to talk, that my effect on her was somewhat hypnotic. I agreed with her and asked her to describe my Svengali hold on her. In this manner, she talked to the offending uncle and got him to talk back to her. Intermixed in this was conversation with the lost mother, who had achieved a level of aloofness and grandness in her untimely death.

Elaine stabilized in the therapy and returned to a path of integration, her persona beckoning fellow residents and caregivers to her, to give and get comfort, to understand her and themselves, to be touched by great-grandparently wisdom. By the mildest sleight of hand, where a hated part of her history became distinguishable from her self-regard, she was able to accept all of what happened in her and around her. This occurred because I allowed the transference of the hated uncle figure to be brought successfully into the treatment relationship and went along with this process to allow her a fuller dialogue with a part of herself that she had cut off for many years.

4

The Gift of Understanding

Understanding is central to the therapeutic process, and we can only understand of others what is realizable in us. The patients constantly challenge us to resonate with them. During this search for fulfilling timbre, the best fit is found, and this establishes the purpose and reason to go on and establish a treatment alliance. To resonate we must find the like elements and dynamics in us that match the patient's. This is the activity of echoing. Interventions punctuate the resonations. Finding the patient reflected in us, and staying with this newly recognized self-organization through the sessions, gives the patient the experience that we have the right feelings for him. Verbal interaction allows for a more conscious apprehension of what is already there.

To the blind patient, we acknowledge our own blindness. To the anxious patient, we relent in our defenses and acknowledge our own anxiety. To the furious and destructive patient, we bring a self-understanding of our own aggressiveness and impulsiveness. We find in us addiction, passivity, sabotage, collusion, negativity, intoxication with power, sadism, and masochism. Just as surely as the

patient has a transference to us, we accept that we have a transference to him. Just as we know the patient methodically resists forward
movement, so do we know that we develop a hardness within ourselves that blocks out light, understanding, and progress. Just as the
patient wants to live and die, so do we want to live and die. Being to
being, smokepot to smokepot, we talk the language of the patient,
we are where he is, and so we are the hand that unlatches the gate
to the oceanic.

It is the fact that we want to do all this, that we have dedicated
ourselves to such a life, that we persist when everyone else gives up,
that constitutes our therapeutic presence. Will, dedication, and
persistence all exist within a broader worldview, or cosmology. They
are guided, driven, and constantly refocused by some larger aim that
we have embraced in our contemplations. We have chosen to make
the empathic sacrifice that puts us emotionally where the patient
needs us to be.

This is not lost on the patient. He registers his mirror image in
us and mirrors back advanced parts of us with new organizations in
himself. If he is schizophrenic, we are schizophrenic and contemplative too, having reflected on our schizophrenia, attached words
to it, developed its ego-adaptive dimensions, and accepted that it is
a position we ease into as a matter of self-preservation. If the patient
·is depressed, we are depressed and contemplative too, having taken
the first few months of life where the depressive defense is natural
and given it access to a lexicon, aware of its action in us, giving in to
its reflex when its demands overwhelm our will. If the patient is
anxious, we are friends and lovers of anxiety, of fear, of horror, and
of dread.

We bring a certain mindfulness to the proceedings, which
shows Methuselah the way. We always remember, we never forget,
that we are melting into the soil even now, reuniting with the grand
Being that first propelled us into cellular organization. Our personal forays may seem to be hidden from public view, but they all
register on the patient and encourage his progress.

These dynamics in us help all our patients, but the acceptance
of dying is what helps Methuselah the most. Here is where he has

fallen short, where he has no cosmology, where advanced self-organization is yet to happen. This is where our wisdom has most effect. To know that the humus is reclaiming us at this very moment, to accept this and flow with the insistent death instinct, is to have found humility. In this we become the humble warrior. The humiliation of psychological symptoms, of objectionables, of perceived deviance, and of being found out is at base a repudiation of the facts and the signals of dying. The denial of death leaves us humiliated when its workings are exposed. When the action of death is acknowledged, humiliation washes away, and out of its component pieces arises a higher consciousness of the process of ensoiling, of dust returning to dust. Out of humiliation, humility.

When we can be like the patient, the patient can be like us. In melodic interplay with our own mental organization, he sings out a solution for his dilemmas and imprisonment. For as we are resonating with the patient, he is resonating with us. As we make the empathic sacrifice to set aside our aversive reaction to unpleasant thoughts and feelings and organize within us an image of the patient so that we become him, the patient is doing the same. We say that he is introjecting the therapist, but that terminology throws us off track. It is not that the patient has swallowed us, taken us into his body cavity, or absorbed us through the semipermeable membranes. The oral metaphor is misleading, because the dynamics are occurring at a more discrete level than that.

A fitting image would be the way DNA creates strands of RNA. The DNA chemically and electrically attracts to itself, out of the surrounding nuclear soup, the elements to compose RNA that will match it. Our psyche acts in that capacity for the patient. It stimulates and provokes across space and through our individual skins a like assemblage of pieces so that a reflection of us comes together in the psyche of the patient. The part of us that is alien provokes rejection and destruction. The part of us that we have allowed to organize to echo the patient is most recognizable to the patient and easiest to resonate to. It is our resonation to the patient that paves the way for his resonation of us.

In behavioral psychology, we say that when a person is learning a new skill, we can start more easily if we select responses that are already in the repertoire. Psychodynamic therapy works to shape complex mental organizations employing the same principle. By resonating with elements of the patient's psychic makeup, we are setting into motion a shaping program that opens the patient to organizing within himself aspects of advanced coping. The authority of text relaxes and the concatenating urge is once again aroused. Because we have multiple organizations within us, we will offer stepwise opportunities for resonating growth. The behaviorists say nothing succeeds like success, and it is the adaptive dimensions of the patient's behavior pattern that we find redemptive and give the most intimate feedback about, in the form of resonation as emotional communication. Experiencing embrace of a part of himself that has been hated by himself and others, the patient is ready for more success. It is our empathic sacrifice of diminishing the authority of our own textualized self and returning to the concatenating urge that is the action of the therapy.

We set a simple pattern by easing back to resonate with the patient. As the patient finds more of himself in us, his accommodative powers are increased, and he can use us as a sort of DNA to build new, more adaptive parts of himself. If we held ourselves out to the patient without reflecting him in us, we remain alien, unreplicable. The therapist-as-DNA should be considered a limited metaphor, because in truth our psyche is to the patient only one possible future. In our own psychic development, we have prefigured the patient. We are holding out a model for where the patient might be today if he had not been prevented from following his normal maturational path. In fact he resonates with our multimind, finds his, and is opened to many futures.

By resonating with the patient we are providing a preverbal form of meaning anchors, so that our organization becomes more subsumable. Our subsumability is central to the therapeutic process. If we compare the interventions and advice from a therapist who is a recovered addict with those from a therapist who has not indulged an addiction, they seem to be the same on the verbal level. But patients with addictions will gravitate to the person most like themselves, will find his words more meaningful, will hear in them more acceptance, and will feel more cooperative. The resonances are more automatic.

The solution for the therapist is neither to become addicted to a substance or activity nor to stick with only those patients who reflect his personal history and struggles. The solution includes finding the addictive self and stressing the importance of an activity that puts this wisdom above the preservation of the therapist's presently adaptive mental organization. The main challenges in the therapy are to understand what is preventing the patient from getting what he wants out of life and what is preventing the therapist from helping him. The emphasis is put on getting the patient's oversubscribed mental organizations to lose their rigidity, become more accommodative, and respond adaptively to life's pressures and challenges by changing.

We do this by reinforcing the defensive aspects of the organizations. A behavioral principle is that reinforcement of a response sends it moving up a learning curve until it maximizes, plateaus, and becomes more firmly established in the repertoire. But we see in psychodynamic work that maturational reinforcement will cause a response pattern to peak and then to subside as new textual organizations form. The impetus for this comes from Being finding more access into being.

We resonate with the patient's pattern, within a relationship where we put thoughts and feelings into words, and so induce him to sacrifice reliance on an old pattern. With a lessened reflex against damage wrought by uncontrolled entropy from us, there is an organic and physical trust. The structures of text loosen and allow for rearrangement along the lines of increased adaptation. At the same time that Being is given a chance to manifest more of itself into being, the social contract is also being paid heed.

We become the facilitator, embracing the patient's mental organization in the most intimate way we can, by finding it within ourselves. Then we continue to form anew deeper and more primitive organizations as the patient expresses them. Our conscious recognition of this and our contemplative urges are subsumed by the patient, who gains a more coherent subjective identity by observing our reflection. Methuselah needs to see how one solves the problem of regression unto dying, while being asked to respond to the challenge of a transcendent position in the family and society. As we regress with the patient we grow, developing the mental organization of Echo. Our regression in the service of integration returns Methuselah to the path of great-grandparently wisdom. He finds his solution in humility.

5

The Experience of Dying

The old man nudged at the nurse's arm. Before she knew what he was doing, he gripped her desperately. He pulled her to him, squeezing more tightly and imploring her with his eyes. He searched for understanding, drawing her ever closer. She pulled back, attempting to pry free his fingers while talking to him in calm and measured words. He nodded his head from side to side, shaking in a silent cry. She tried her best to disentangle herself with a minimum of fuss and no hint of the desperation she was experiencing from the man.

She spoke softly all the while, patting the man's hand, then deftly freeing herself she faded beyond his reach. The man was left grabbing the air. The nurse made a quiet apology and stepped out of the room. He mouthed silent words after her, beseeching her, his face distorted with a great emotional pain. Upon her leaving, he became terrified, gasping, raising his hands and head as if he were being swallowed up by quicksand.

I was sitting at the other end of the room and observing. He had looked right through me the whole time. All his attention had been focused on the nurse. He had put a special, indefinable fear in her, as he did with many caregivers who allowed the initial, primitive feelings that touched them to grow and register. Most people dealt with him by blotting out the facts of his humanity, and herein lay the answer to what he was doing to staff. The issue was one of obliteration. He set the stage, and they reacted in kind.

I understood this drama as the unverbalized request that he die with company. He did not want to go alone, but the nurse did not want to go with him. Neither openly acknowledged this was the issue, and in my explorations with staff I found that people were not consciously aware of what was going on. There was an emergency of some kind, but they were not able to apprehend its meaning.

The staff had tried everything with him, to no avail. His request seemed to go beyond their ability to calm, succor, and satisfy. There was something happening with him, and the staff needed both to know and not to know. He aroused the greatest disquietude. It took some amount of talk before the staff could assert that he was a yawning pit ready to swallow anyone who got too close. His need was greater than all the supplies the staff could muster. People grasped the situation in terms of an unfulfillable need. It was true, in a way. He had become aware of the experience of dying precociously, way before he was maturationally ready to grapple with it. His need was to get the staff to resonate with him and add their conscious experience. The staff was resonating and acting out with the desire for self-preservation, but was not able to bring conscious awareness to the situation.

He stared at me. Hope was aroused in him, and he reached out to me. His face was frozen in a grimace, and his fingers opened and curled in anticipation of grabbing onto my material being. I let the feeling of his suffocating both of us overtake me, and I met his stare. "I will let you take me with you," I thought. "I will go along." I gave him both my hands. In my gaze I let him know I would not frustrate him. He had fallen through the gate into the oceanic, and I would fall through, too.

By the time our hands touched, it was all over. The demand, as I saw it in his eyes and felt it reverberate throughout my being, shifted. It had been a furious challenge up to this point: "Die with me!" When I answered, "I will experience dying with you" in my resonatings, he became someone new. His eyes softened. He was no longer death personified, but a hungry infant. He gripped firmly and I leaned to him, letting him pull me in, letting him fuse with me, going along, feeling myself wearing his clothing, chafing at the confinement of the wheelchair, squirming in the tightness of the sneakers, itching from the angry cancerous growth on his temple. He knew I was not going to frustrate him.

"Stay," he ordered. "I'll stay," I told him. "Stay," he moaned, crying openly and finally chancing to close his eyes, but still holding me, in fear that I would disappear. "I'll stay with you. As long as you want." He held me loosely, more into himself now, more interested in focusing on his feelings than in riveting me with a hungry gaze. I allowed my own feelings to well up and allowed the fusing to take me over. I let him pour over me, climb into me, get me to surround him, use me to strengthen him.

I could actually stay as long as he wanted, for in real time it was nothing. In fusion time we had already been a unity for years, for centuries. We both found access to a more direct unity with the universe. We stepped into the timeless, so in real time there was the conclusion that satisfaction had occurred.

He let me go. Touch did not matter. I was with him, and he with me. "How am I sure you will return?" A comment like this was obligatory. It was a nod to the ingrained rituals that help the ego hoax maintain. We carried on the sham of separate egos, but at this point with a doesn'tmatterness, with a dissolution of pressure. If I never answered, he would have been just as satisfied. When we looked at each other, he was convinced that he had never been alone. I had always been with him, and I would always stay. He could never lose me again. From now on he would be conscious of the sham of separateness. From being in the most regressed state one can imagine, he magically shifted to a transcendent position.

His voice was normal, the panic dissipated. I arranged a time for us to meet next and left him my card in case he wished to talk before the session. This was, of course, ridiculous. We were bound forever prior to meeting, and our contact only reminded us both of this truth. Our meeting was found to be an incident in a continuous and timeless relationship. All we had to do now was put all of this into words.

I had faced a great turning point in such matters some twelve years before. What I could tolerate wholeheartedly in my late forties, I had not worked out at all in my mid thirties. I thought back to one child who had a head so large she could not hold it up. She was blind and profoundly retarded. She bit herself incessantly and had to wear mitts to control the damage she had done to her flesh. She cried and drooled, material ran out of her eyes, her hair was matted within an hour after her morning shower, and she smelled of decay. She gnawed at herself weakly, despite her mitts, in some faint and diminished expression of the predatory instinct. She was not yet a teen, and the hydrocephaly engorged her head to twice the size of an adult's.

It registered dimly on me that she stank of death, but I wanted to put that idea out of my mind. My reaction was to avoid her when I visited her room and to give my attentions to children I felt could benefit. This was unstudied; I never gave it another thought. My emotional reaction to this child was equivalent to the behavior of the harried nurse. I was intent on disentangling in a way that I would do least harm.

One day my mentor and good friend, David Levinsky, visited the program. He was drawn to this child immediately. Holding her hands in his, he murmured softly and soothed her. To my surprise, she stopped crying, raised her head, and winced to more clearly catch something of Dave's outlines. She cooed back to him. He stroked her hands, took off her gloves, and led her in simple communication. She laughed! The child was possessed of a personality! She had a sense of humor. Dave spent a morning with her, introducing her to the delights of the social world. There was no learning curve here. She was connected and intimate from the beginning. It was as if she and Dave had been old friends from time immemorial and had reunited after a brief separation. They got along famously, and he aroused her appetite for contact with the rest of us.

Where I saw irreparable scarification and blockage, Dave saw an open gate. In truth, the gate had always been open, beckoning me to a place that heretofore signaled danger. Without more sophisticated behavior patterns to get in the way, the child was in touch with the oceanic. To protect myself, I thought of her as profoundly retarded. Dave confronted me with the fact that she was profoundly related. This has been Dave's everlasting gift to me. In that moment, he gave me the universe.

My friend and I spent many evenings discussing this incident, until it became clear that the child represented to me the state of dying. My fear of rapprochement was the fear of being pulled to an ego death, watching my boundaries float off in all directions, relating in the pre-ego way that the child needed. Why was there any fear at all? There were a few things involved, including the fact that I was still in young adulthood, that I was a man, and that I had had few educational experiences to help me properly interpret the incident.

To allow the conscious perception of these facts would bring me dangerously close to acknowledging the siren call within me for self-destruction. The fear was that I would succumb to my primal hunger for the void, the same void I had struggled to build a whole life against. The child was me, when I was an infant, with full access to the universe. More impossible to accept, she was me right at that time, in my thirties. For I was still one with everything, had never left fusion with everything, and did not want to know it.

This was a lesson waiting to happen. As an educator, I had regularly taken on ever more difficult children. I worked with youngsters few other people knew how to handle, and I taught them to speak, to read, to write, and to function. My search for the most challenged students was an effort to clarify the presence of the state of dying. Through them, I might learn more about myself. I chose a mentor who knew more about this than anyone I have ever met. Dave had taken the same path, educating the most hard-to-reach youngsters, and in the process charting the nightmarish depths of the human soul. This had become well-traveled terrain, his terrain, by the time we met.

Watching his direct, revelatory approach, and talking it out, helped me locate the dynamism of dying. The experience of dying is captured as the activity of the constancy principle—a psychological equivalent to physical entropy, ratcheting down, quietude, and descent into reduced energy and organization. It is very hard to experience dying because of the need to preserve the sense of ego. On the way to resonating more fully with the entropic demand, we lose ego boundaries. There is a desperate time where it seems that all is lost, for the focus is on the boundaries that just dissolved, and all attention is riveted on refortifying them. We grab at the ego as we would a life preserver, when we face the ocean.

With the guidance of another who has negotiated this psychic space, however, the fear loses its commanding presence, and you can ease into a state where you and the horizon are joined, where you are the sky, you are the clouds, and you are the objects in between, all of it that goes to complete your apprehension of the animate and inanimate universe. With some exposure, you recognize that the only thing that has changed is your consciousness. You recognize that you have always been in this relationship with everything around you.

You absorb and become part of all there is, the light, the cement walls, the floating particles of dust captured in the shaft of light, the dirt floor, the smells of mildew. You do this not to animate the world into part of your living self. Instead, you become one with the world in all its levels of inanimateness. You see a thick stand of trees, and you can find yourself in its midst, tall and stoic, quiet, bending with the wind. You feel the grass under your feet and meld with it. Any scene surrendered to loses its original composure to find you in it. Once you are one with it, the scene loses its constancies and undergoes a detextualization. What seemed to be immutable is in fact protean; what seemed to be material is mere mirage. You are glimpsing the machinery of textualization itself, as the convincing whole reveals its essence to be subordinate to a greater whole, the greatest whole, the universe and everything in front, behind, before, and after it, the omniverse itself.

This may sound like some technical or occult feat, but in fact, it is all too easy to do. We are doing it all the time. Out of Being projects our small, individual being, and our small being is composed of living and dying. Through the experience of living and dying we are connected to everything and everyone. This whole process is readily available for increased awareness, but for many it represents an intolerable regression.

We are human beings, not human lives. But even though we are beings, we refer only to our life. We allow only the erotic metaphor to capture our experience. To be erotic, living, and building are to be healthy, in the commonly accepted worldview. There is a grave risk involved in giving up this definition of health. For you may retreat to the distortions of neurosis, find yourself shattering under the psychotic process, until you are at the miasma, viewing Being without the guidance of texts. In our youth the devolution to Being is unspeakable; it makes it impossible to talk, to relate what is happening. We do not live in a society that values this regression, and so if a youthful person were to find himself undergoing this transformation or kundalini, the fear and loathing of the society would cause him to turn available aggression upon the self. The defense against such experiences by society would also be a deadly communication to the person, one inflammatory to his self-murderous propensities. Damage would result.

But what youth cannot afford to face, old age cannot afford to deny. The one common thread connecting most of the nine hundred people I have treated is that they have managed to live a long life without registering or appreciating the experience of dying. Old age comes as a surprise. Illness is not so much the progressive breakdown of the timebound body as it is an ambush. The person faces the end of his life with a youthful naiveté. He has not gotten to the point in his development where he can process the experience of dying and, in fact, has erected a seemingly unscalable defense against it.

He is naive but also ripe for knowing, and a good degree of our therapeutic leverage comes from recognizing his emotional position, having worked to contemplate the experience of dying in our ongoing training, and serving as a model with precocious great-grandparently vision. Our precocity is framed in a therapeutic context. We come to understand that life and death, too, fulfill the wholeness of our being. We are prepared for what is to come. THE SPECIAL KNOWLEDGE THAT DISTINGUISHES TREATMENT WITH THE ELDERLY IS HOW THE EXPERIENCE OF DYING NEEDS TO BE SET FREE FROM ITS ENACTMENTS.

Those who frantically grab their caregivers are only the more demonstrative from among their fellows. They are the obvious ones. They capture in overt behavior what is going on everywhere else in a nursing home building. There is an insistent psychological grabbing emanating from the elders, and it is filtering past any ability of others to crowd out the message. And the meaning is evident if we learn to listen.

That man who grabbed his nurse was in the throes of humiliation, his feet and legs melting into the ground-as-humus, he returning to the clay, looking away in horror, seeking another set of eyes that might translate the unspeakable he was experiencing. He was digging his psychic nails into the woman's throat, taking her down with him, so that he would not have to face this melting away alone, pulling her down into the soil, fusing with her, disfiguring her boundaried self, just as he was being disfigured and detextualized.

This is the meaning of many undesirable behaviors caregivers confront in a nursing home. No matter how matter-of-fact and regular these behaviors seem, they beget an avoidance that staff has to fight to control at times. It is this call to merge that horrifies. If this is couched as a parental responding and feeding, then caregivers can be demonstrative and available, but then they feel a burnout whose antecedents are hard to capture. It is only when they understand the wish of the person to reestablish omniconnection, and when they are taught that this is entropic and truly one way to experience dying, that they work better with it.

The experience of dying, integrated into one's perceptions and daily living, is a regression in the service of transcendence. The constancy principle, or entropy, is at work all the time. When it is not understood and recognized, it severely affects maturation in the later stages of life. By maintaining an environment where the patient can adopt a more well-rounded understanding of his being, we return the patient to his maturational path. It is in this light that he can accept the cycle of his life and his mortal features.

ACCEPTING THE EXPERIENCE OF DYING

Donna sat by the window, looking down at the main road beyond the large and ornately flowered front lawn. She refused to leave her room for any reason except lunch. She described fellow residents as boring, and the staff aloof. No one seemed to suit her. Her husband had died twenty years before. She thought of him fondly and described him as fun-loving and jovial, but she showed no interest in finding another person like him. It was as if his presence had been an aberration in her otherwise reclusive and self-involved life.

It was just her and the cars. As they whizzed by, she imagined their drivers free and happy. They were on their way to some chosen place. She hated the nursing home and would just as soon have died in her beautiful, rent-controlled apartment in Manhattan. She missed that full and uninterrupted access to the possessions and environment that she had taken years to invest with the deepest of feeling. The nursing home represented an incarceration. She wanted to be in her old surroundings so she could melt into them and become one with them. If she could have expressed it, she would have said that it did not matter if she lived or died there, as long as she was there.

I had watched people try to cheer her up, to counsel her, to encourage her to attend activities, and to offer her a change of clothing. But she refused it all. She put on the same blouse and pants every day, sat in her chair, and stared at the cars. Efforts to arouse some good feeling seemed to backfire. She became perniciously angry, pursuing the staff, accusing them of delusion. "You must be out of your minds! Everything here is awful. As awful as life gets. It is better to die."

She took to opening the windows. They were locked at ten inches, and she sought some way to open them completely. She talked of jumping to her death. She had one daughter she never spoke about, who moved to California years ago and refused all contact with her mother or the nursing home. She told the staff she had nothing to live for, and she would eventually find an open window to crawl through.

During our first session, my quiet interest was somehow perceived as a pathological neutrality. She felt I did not care, considered me a stupid and lazy doctor, and told me it was about time I looked for a real job. I accepted this, seeking to understand where it came from. In the induction, I concluded this was how she felt about herself. When confronted by anyone who did not resonate with her in a specific way, she felt attacked and responded by attacking. When people tried to echo her misery, thinking that was the route to an emotional connection, she would bitterly accuse them of mimicking her. It was not the misery that needed echoing, but something else.

During our second session, she revealed through her questions what she needed from me. She asked if I worked all week, or if I was semiretired. This was the theme of the first session, but she repeated it in a more benign fashion. Here was an opportunity to mirror her own inertia. Freud told us the dream was the royal road to the unconscious, but here, it was obvious that her question in its glorious revelation was that royal road. I knew what to say: "Oh, I'm all but fully retired." This gladdened her privately even as she registered a public shock. She pondered this for a while and then smiled wickedly, "You made a pile of money and now you intend to live off it." She asked me how I spent my days. I could not explore in the ordinary way because she became enraged easily and had already kicked the psychiatrist, social worker, and other helpers out of her room.

I had to keep pace with her and leave the impression of a conversation. Of course, it was not a conversation in the way we conceptualize one. Some patients have restricted latitudes of acceptance that are so fragile you have to become one with them in order to get along. So this was not always a dialogue. Sometimes it reverted to a monologue with two people in the room. This was all she could tolerate at certain times. Here the call to resonate is seen more clearly, without all the camouflage and distractions of character.

Looking over her situation, I sought to describe myself: "I sit by the window and watch the traffic go by." This brought guffaws of appreciation, although she criticized me. "You? You're not ready to give up." I asked her why I wasn't ready to give up. She could not answer that. I asked why I couldn't watch traffic all day. "Because it's boring!" Why would that bother me? "You don't mind being bored?" I told her it was one of my favorite states, sitting motionless, without a thought in my head, watching the traffic go by. As she responded, she found similar ways to put entropy into words. The more she became aware of the experience of dying, the more she thought about living.

She asked, "And other people? You don't miss them?" I responded, "No. Not at all. I find other people very boring." She laughed out loud. "You too? I find other people very boring." I complimented her taste. "You find other people very boring because they *are* very boring!" I let her know we could talk about living, but we could talk about dying, too. One was as valuable as the other in her integrating efforts.

We went on in this fashion for months. Her suicidal talk stopped and she was able to express her loss feelings more directly, in a way to give up her depressive position and to properly mourn. In the fifth month she demonstrated some worry about my adjustment. "It bothers me that you don't talk to anybody. You sound to me like you have given up on life." She repeated this in different ways until it occurred to her to say this more clearly. In a flash of insight she used the actual word to characterize my behavior: "You act like you have died."

Here I went all the way, echoing with gusto. So what if I died? Why couldn't I be dead and go through the motions? Why did I have to deal with very boring people in a very boring world? The explorative questions were a constant invitation for her to put the prefeelings of entropy into words and so capture them. She decided that I needed rehabilitation, and she used the sessions to explore my antipathy to others. She told me I had hate. I could not carry so much hate in my heart. I had to relent and see the bright side of human relations. "What bright side?" I did not ask this as a challenge but as a part of a continuing exploration. She was influenced to conjure up good reasons for social interaction. She thought I could spend more time speaking to people in the nursing home. I mirrored: "Very boring! Half of them don't even make sense!"

She enjoyed this kind of echoing very much. It made her laugh. Because I so wholeheartedly took this unattractive role, she could safely explore it and stop using it as a defense. By means of this relenting and softening, mutual resonations are phenomenally experienced. She chided me in mock exasperation, "So who says they have to make sense? Who met anybody who made sense? You ask too much!" She worked on me, and I made sure I could be changed. The point was to show the right amount of malleability. If I was a pushover, how could she relate to me? She would not be engaged in the accommodative process of changing her own views, to offer a more optimistic rendering of the social universe. If I was intransigent, I would just break her heart all over again, just the way it happened for her eighty-five years before.

For in the induction I knew exactly who I was. I was her depressed mother who had given up on life. She was the toddler, trying to cheer me up. She was playfully engaging me, and this time the maturational need would not go unanswered. She convinced me to come into the commons area of the home and meet with other residents, and as we completed the individual therapy, we shifted to a weekly social with twenty or more people, joking, laughing, sharing stories, showing tolerance for each others' quirks, and making adjustments for the very needy among us. Donna demonstrated good social skills, and she used them for two more years, until she took sick and died.

THE EXPERIENCE OF DYING IS OUR CLOSEST FRIEND, TO BE EMBRACED AND CHERISHED. IF IT IS NOT, IT IS OUR WORST ENEMY, TO BE FEARED.

When Donna learned that I could acknowledge my deadness and still work to live better, she found the same resources in her own being. Prior to this she had been intoxicated by the entropy she felt, and she was acting on it. When we used me as an object to explore, she could safely discuss the process of dying and accept it in herself. I did not press her to personalize the issues in the treatment. My therapeutic contribution was to echo her and to continue to protect her so that she could stop acting out her experience of dying in alienation, in mental obliteration of the peers, in mental murder of the daughter, and in impulses to suicide. In me she found a twin and was heartened to find her way back to her developmental path. In this indirect way, her worst enemy became a close friend.

Andy ruled among his peers. At 78, he was jaunty, clear-eyed, quick-witted, and sociable. He had an answer for everything. It was said he could arrange for a fellow resident's grandson to get a driver's license even though the youngster refused to take the driving test. It was said he could arrange to get food stamps. He took bets on the ponies. Worst of all, he was the enforcer in his facility. Some nursing homes have highly disruptive residents who do not or cannot care about the needs of others. They may scream at the top of their lungs for hours, spit, threaten, or throw furniture.

In this particular home, people who acted up were occasionally found with bruises. One had pointed to Andy as the assailant. There was an investigation, Andy loudly proclaimed his rights and got a lawyer, and the matter ended in a draw. As a result of his presence, the home was quiet, and Andy had the respect of his grateful peers. One day a nurse observed him draw up the point of his cane and aim at a disruptive peer across the dining room. "Pow," he mouthed.

He was counseled by social services, and the administrator met with him to try to take away his cane. He invoked his rights and called his lawyer again. Once the ruckus died down, there were assurances all around that everyone would behave. He knew how to use his lawyer as a blunt weapon, for the facility even apologized for daring to confront Andy. He refused to see a psychiatrist, and because the staff knew his attitudes, they did not broach the idea of therapy. The facility was working on the situation. The patient bill of rights had just become policy in the state, and the staff was particular about controlling his aggression while preserving his assertiveness and personal power.

He knew who I was, and he bridled at my presence. He would mutter curse words as I passed by. When I asked him about this, he growled, "I wasn't talking to you. You're hearing things!" He had control, but there came a time when this was not enough. He was driven by his destructivity to express more intensely. We watched him become more rageful as he increased the circle of victims to include young and unassertive aides. One day he was standing in the middle of the hall, seething, looking for a young aide to verbally dress down.

I walked by and nodded in greeting. Thwack! He caught me on the temple with his cane. Down I went. He cursed me: "Miserable bastard, I hope I killed you." So much ran through my mind that moment. This was an opportunity I might never have again. So I cooperated with his murderous wish and did not move. A minute passed, and he kicked at me. "Get up! Come on! Get up!" I lay still.

For the first time since any of us had known him, Andy became panicky. He called the nurse, and she ran down the hall. "This man here fell down. He won't get up." She turned me on my back, supported my head, and opened an eyelid. I winked and closed my eyes. She ran to the telephone and called the administrator, who came immediately and surveyed the situation. She ordered, "Get this man into my office!"

Andy followed us down the hall. "Serves him right! Is it my fault if he slipped?" The administrator whisked me into her office and slammed the door. I got up, and we both laughed in surprise. Neither of us had an idea of what we were going to do until we did it. The chance presented itself, and the solution was so economical. Everything that troubled us about Andy was captured in that moment.

The administrator poured us coffee, and we took the time to review the issues of the week. Outside, Andy paced back and forth, calling out, "It's his own fault!" He screamed through the door that I was a clumsy idiot and that my death would not be on his conscience. Just then an ambulance happened to pull up to take a resident to dialysis. The nurse ran to it, jerked the gurney away from the attendants, and ran it into the administrator's office. Now Andy got really worried, and all the cockiness went out of him. He kept asking if I was okay. He knocked on the door. He pleaded with staff to let him know what was going on.

The nurse left the room looking worried. "What's the matter?" he pleaded. She answered, "What do you think?" The nurse said Andy sank into a chair and told himself that if I would be all right, he would give up his cane. They gave me crutches and bandaged my head. I staggered out of the room, staring at the ceiling. Andy cried out in relief, ran over, and hugged me. He threw the cane on the floor and he never used it again.

SOME PEOPLE AREN'T SATISFIED UNTIL THEY HAVE MURDERED. THEY ARE SO IMBUED WITH THE EXPERIENCE OF DYING, THEY CANNOT SEE WHAT IS HAPPENING. ALL THEY CAN DO IS ACT OUT.

I was younger when I met Andy, a lot more physical, ready to take a fall. Over the years I have met a number of savage people who could have benefited from so potent an intervention. Increased carefulness has prevented me from pursuing this avenue more often. The therapist's role is as much defined by morality as it is by effective treatment approaches.

The issue in the facility, however, was more a total misreading of Andy's situation. We do not want to admit that people can enjoy such murderous impulses, and the reaction of most nursing homes is to block such knowledge, to find a way to arrange psychiatric hospitalization, or to finesse a transfer to another home. In my experience, these approaches solve the problem for the facility, but leave the person with his destructive pattern intact.

For years, I ran schools that were the last stop for students who had exhausted every other venue. Some had even been rejected by psychiatric hospital day programs. When there is no place left to go, then you and the student have a chance to focus on his destructive behavior. It is no longer some side issue that keeps the student from functioning academically and socially. It is the behavior of concern. I have had knives pulled on me, I have been spit on and kicked, I have had bats swung at my head, and I have even faced a youngster with two large shards of glass in his hands, looking to sink them into someone's flesh. I am convinced of the human capacity to destroy.

Polite society with its measured emotional responses acts as one grand empathic failure for such people. You have to be willing to look into the abyss with the other person and accept the incipient horrors that are threatening to break through. This is echoing at its most frightening, and this is why such people do not receive much help in our society.

Years before, a couple brought their teenager to an evening program I added at my high school. It was an alternative for students who could not cope with the daytime social environment. He hated school and had been kicked out of every one his district sent him to. At home now, he was methodically ransacking each room, hitting his siblings, and so threatening his parents that at least one stayed awake each night. It was dark when they brought him to the school, which was at the other end of town and had no definable markings over the front door. They told him it was a library.

After a few minutes in my office, he growled, "This isn't a library!" It was full of books, everywhere he looked, so I asked him what was the problem? "This isn't a library!" He transformed into a brute, and his seemingly frail body rippled with muscle. He flipped my desk over with one hand. "This isn't a library!" He ripped fixtures out of the wall as his parents scooted out of the room.

He knocked over every piece of furniture. He ripped books off the shelves. He stomped my belongings. He raged and raged until he was exhausted. Then I growled, "You missed that picture there! Get up!" He ran over and smashed the picture. I bellowed, "Some more books! What are you waiting for?" He knocked them over. "The desk! What about the desk? Are you done with it?"

Spent, heaving, he put out his hands in surrender. He stared at me in new recognition. "Are you nuts or something?" In a voice that rocked the room, I answered, "I'm not nuts! No, I'm not nuts! I just want to know if you're done! Or is there something *else* you'd like to do?" We had an understanding. He took the next two hours to clean up my room, and I never took my eyes off him.

For our next year and a half together, he was not physically aggressive either in school or at home. I had joined him in the abyss. We faced the horror of detextualization together. All the people he had known adjured him, "Out of chaos, cosmos." This drove him to greater extremes of destruction. The call in him was, "Out of cosmos, chaos!" He experienced the lack of resonance with his entropic demand as a stifling, choking death. He needed a therapeutic presence who could function in society and could be willing to communicate that cosmos could turn to chaos in a flash, and the chaos could be felt and not acted upon. I was his model.

He saw behind the mirage of acculturation and was horrified. I understood this mirage and taught him how to live with it. If I had to pick one central theme in my twenty years with severely disturbed children, it would be their precocious and unprotected exposure to the facts of entropy. Not able to bear the dying they had unluckily uncovered in themselves, they used every resource available to try to control the horror.

This is what the severely disturbed child and the significantly maladjusted elder have in common. For in his seventies and beyond, the person is feeling the unbearable pressure of entropy to make itself known, to find a place in his active repertoire, to be hailed as an equal to eros, and to be given its rightful place on the dais. For being seeks its fullest expression in both the activities of living and dying. With such people, there may be no return to the comforts of the neurotic defenses. They need a cosmology and a pattern of social action that can let them live with the true knowledge of the impulses that go to make them up.

A teaching nursing home was conducting grand rounds for doctors who were in residency at the local university. I was invited, along with other therapists, to add a psychological dimension to the proceedings. Of particular interest to this assembly of staff and visiting residents was a younger woman who was refusing a life-sustaining treatment. Although she was depressed, the psychiatrist had found that she was competent to make up her own mind on this matter.

The attending physician was interested in everyone's thoughts, and he went around the room until he had polled all thirty people.

As the exploration continued, more attention was paid to the patient's therapist. She had met with the woman twice but seemed to have made no progress. The nursing home resident felt there was no purpose to living, and she told the therapist to face the facts of her dying process. The therapist reached out to the group for feedback. The attending physician also felt hamstrung by the patient and concluded he had gone beyond his usual ministrations to get her to change her mind. He urged the therapist not to take it so hard.

The staff members and visiting doctors gave the therapist a great amount of support. It seems several people had tried to counsel the woman, but she would have none of it. A deep feeling possessed the group, and there was anticipatory mourning for this mother of three who was soon to succumb. People seemed transformed by this story, moved by the youth of this person, having found a theme that touched their essence. Here was every person's nightmare, played out in the drama of the patient's brave confrontation. Every dream contains within it a wish, and the nightmare is an effort to grapple with the experience of dying. It is a wish to integrate the experience of dying with the experience of living, to give greater access to Being in being.

The physician continued polling the group. "Let her go," was the unifying theme. This sentiment grabbed the group and took on a life of its own. Let her go on to her own reward. It was my turn to add to the gratifying solemnity of this shared occasion. But one simply does not echo destructivity with anyone who is likely to act on it. So I looked into the eyes of my fellow therapist to hold her close in this way until she was going to listen. "You should make every heroic effort to get this woman to cooperate with her treatments."

Those words shattered the group's blissful merger. "You go in there. If she gives you any baloney, bring in her aides. Bring in the nurse. Bring in the supervisor. If she still won't listen, bring in the administrator. Bring in the family. Bring in the priest. Bring in her neighbors. Bring in people she likes. Bring in people she doesn't like. Tell her you're not going to stop. Tell her you're going to get the Commissioner of Health. The Governor. Tell her you're going to bring in *the President of the United States!*"

There were howls of disbelief from the group. An enraged person leaped up and yelled that I was crazy and ought to be locked up. Others argued heatedly, accusing me of being out of touch with modern ethics. I sat quietly, for I had achieved my goal. The therapist had been grabbed by the notion. I resonated with her wish to help the patient live.

The group tried to ignore the therapist's abdication from her morbid role in this drama. They did what they could to revive that utterly fulfilling experience I so rudely disturbed. They tried to continue as if I had not said a word, but it was not the same after that. It has been said that an interpretation is much like spitting in someone's soup: the person may continue to drink from the bowl, but it will never taste quite the same.

The therapist recognized the intoxication of the group. She gently suggested to this irascible bunch that she was going to follow my advice. This aroused a furor. "Why?" a number of people shot back, incredulous and confused. She took her time to answer. "It just feels right to me." Well, it did not feel right to the group. To them I was fighting a rear guard action for the old morality. Today people had a right to choose their fate. In fact my immorality was astounding, and the group proved quite adept in exhaustively describing it. I took a good pummeling for the rest of the meeting. People were outraged. Some lined up at the end to give me a more personal lambasting. I took it, understanding that it was better to experience the murder in this group than to participate gauzily in an infanticide.

The therapist pulled me aside and thanked me. She said she was not too concerned with explanations about what happened in the group, but she felt everyone had been lulled into misreading the case entirely. Thereafter she approached the patient with such a clear will to see her live, that the woman went along and accepted the life-sustaining interventions.

My fellow staff members felt differently about me from that day on. There was wariness and an uncomfortable respect, and I was never going to be their "buddy" anymore. It was an important day for me. I had been forced into a corner, to finally become a therapist worthy of people's negative transference feelings. Even though I would continue to function in this world, I would no longer be of it. I would make a conscious effort to locate the experience of dying in all of its guises. Analysis would be silent, so that I could continue to function in the world. I would look for ways to resolve people's resistances to seeing more clearly.

MURDER, DIRECT OR DISGUISED, IS A GRATIFYING EXPERIENCE, AND LITTLE CAN COMPARE WITH IT. IT GIVES DIRECT AND IMMEDIATE ACCESS TO THE EXPERIENCE OF DYING.

Man has been murdering with reckless abandon over the millennia and looking to society to protect this right. Maimonides said that the world would never forgive the Jews for censuring infanticide; herein lay much of the world's fury against the people of the Old Testament. The group was acting out the experience of dying in the form of a murder. This case had given people more direct contact with the experience, and the large group process intensified it to the level of art. When we live, we only exercise half our being. The other half needs its outlets, too. This patient powerfully portrayed needs that had built up in the participants. over time. Her story represented a compression of that need to special heights, and people reacted accordingly. Their intoxication was literal, in that what they could not consciously grapple with acted as a poison in their psychic systems, reducing their sensibility.

The therapist was changed by the intervention. She was strong enough to appreciate the intoxication but then to go on to do what the patient needed. The chaplain was also changed. He recognized the necessity to ferret out these impulses and over the years became skillful at "finding the murder in the room." The attending physician, who was intelligent and probing, asked for a full explanation of what had happened. He needed to grasp this rationally. A number of self-referrals came out of this group. Stunned by so clear a demonstration of the presence of an unconscious, people wanted to learn more.

Months later, a few of the medical residents and their supervisor invited me to lunch. One of them described how an elderly resident reached out in an inconsolable panic. The young woman was shaken by the incident. She had brought this up at school, where she was advised that her intellectual powers would eventually overcome any unwanted emotions. The feelings would go away and she could be an effective practitioner. She looked to me for confirmation. This aroused the small gathering, and they looked for me to give the resident a dose of what I had given them earlier. To the surprise of the group, I told her that intellectual powers were highly desirable in the field of medicine, and her supervisor was right. She glowed with the satisfaction of a good feeling. Being therapeutic to her was a better way of initiating her in the process of resonation, than being didactic about her patient.

Joann subjected the staff to a barrage of demeaning comments. The withering fire of her criticism seemed endless, and it was even excruciating when she stopped for a while. The staff could be sure of a destructive ambush and was put more on edge. "You tied my shoe too tight. Are you stupid? Of course you are. Who takes such a menial job?" It was best not to answer her. "You're talking back? Your stupidity is evident in your dumb gaze. Who would ever be interested in such a cow?" Protecting oneself would not do. "Just tie the shoe, idiot. Do as I say. Why, if I spit on the floor right now, you'd wipe it up. You were put on this earth to clean my spit. If you didn't, I'd have you fired, and you know that's true." She knew what to say and whom to say it to. If self-pride was an issue for the caregiver, she went after that person with a vengeance.

The family members ran interference for Joann. They pointed to failures of the staff and cited these as the irritants that provoked their mother. Meetings designed to help Joann adjust better ended with the family calling the state adult abuse hotline. This set many an investigation into motion. The facility was never censured or cited. But neither were the family members, and they saw this as a vindication. As far as they were concerned, the perception of the nursing home as ineffective and substandard persisted, even though it was well-run and without deficiencies during its decade in existence. No one ever seemed to be able to get through to this family.

Joann's adjustment was complete, in its own way. This was how she had spoken to people throughout her professional life, which had extended into her early eighties. Her hegemony had gone unquestioned for all those years, so from her point of view she was dealing with "lazy, incompetent fools whose parents would have done best to abort them." It was surprising that the family accepted the physician's referral for psychotherapy and encouraged Joann to see me. It seemed that the attitude was that even though therapy was not needed, it could not hurt to have someone from a higher level of society to talk to about the "third world staff."

Joann needed a cohort, so she prefaced all her comments with "doctor" and did her best to exclude me from the categories of people she hated. She soberly described a portion of the populace that was subhuman, that could not survive on its own, and that certainly ought not to be encouraged. She was not suggesting eugenics. She seemed familiar with this concept but preferred not to air her thoughts on its successes or failures. "Just don't encourage them," was her stock answer.

Her hatred was strong, and I reflected it without saying a word. She felt she had a partner in me, and her attacks on staff eased. They were not an operant behavior that needed extinction. They were expressions of a discrepancy between her superego self and her ideal self. They were outward manifestations of an inner war. As she behaved better, caregivers were more relaxed and therefore less attackable. Now her critiques were sporadic and followed on the heels of some verifiable empathic failure of staff. On the other hand, the sessions became a panegyric of mass murder, accomplished through an active boundarying off of the untouchables and imposing on them a slow and torturous death.

She became cognizant of me as a separate person somewhere in the second year of treatment. "Bouklas. What kind of name is that?" The ethnicity of it no doubt grated on her sensibilities. I asked her what she thought it might be. The exploration pursued for a few minutes, but then she grew more irritated. "Are you going to tell me or not?" I told her I was considering it. That did it. She screamed at me, told me she never liked me from the first, that no matter how obliging I seemed, I was no doubt a bleeding heart liberal who could not be counted on to see things clearly.

Then a change came over her. I had slipped over some internal line, where I accrued an alien coloring. "If I spit on the floor, you would clean it up," she enunciated slowly, as if driving a nail into me. "Of course I would," I answered. She was taken aback. "You would? Why would you do that?" I responded, "What could I possibly have against it?"

More slowly, she ordered, "If I threw garbage on the floor, you would pick it up." As before, I agreed. "Of course I would pick it up. There's no question." This was not going predictably for Joann. Her attempts to humiliate me were finding acceptance. She was not used to this. "If I vomited food all over, then you'd clean it!" I told her I would do it without a moment's hesitation. She was furious. I was more like the hated caregivers than ever but still important to her as a mirror, for she accused me of having no pride. "How low would you sink?" she cried, imagining herself talking as I had talked. "Lower than you could possibly imagine."

"Then you and I have nothing in common, nothing at all!" We sat silently, while she composed herself. "Give me one good reason to keep seeing you." I told her that was easy. "I have sunk lower than you could possibly imagine." She, who was in the last stage of her life, felt echoed and could not say why.

I could accept any dead matter flung at me because I knew I was dying. My conscious knowledge immunized me against any shock. I faced the fact with humility. After all, what were spit, garbage, and half-digested food to a dying man? They were all parts of me. I could not reject that very stuff I was turning into. And since she and I were joined anyway, I could not reject anything coming from her.

Joann had spent her whole life evading death. She practiced murder by economic strangulation, by humiliation, by rejection, and by mental obliteration. Anyone unlucky enough to find himself in her employ was going to have to die one way or another. Each death was just one more she did not have to feel within her. It was like the Hawaiians feeding sacrifices to hungry Pele. Keep him sated, and he might not cast his eye upon you. But their stratagem was conscious, whereas hers was unconscious.

Her repetition also bore a communication. She was dead matter and would tear people down until they were dead matter, too. This would continue until the anxiety surrounding this hidden knowledge was dealt with. Everyone conceived of her as a powerful entity. They went to their metaphorical deaths reminded of the earliest Other in their lives against which they could never mount a suitable defense. She was being misunderstood by everybody. All they could react to was her sense of raw power, every infant's terror—the parent run amuck. They could not follow through and see that her action against them was designed to arouse a therapeutic action back.

I understood her, so our relationship was reversed. It was I who was being wicked toward her. As she continued to talk, she accused me of dark intentions because I was arousing in her a hunger for merger whose erotic proportions she had repressed and had sent over in the service of psychic murder. The eros had gone a long while with no gratification. She was convinced that the closest she was going to get in having any needs met would be in controlling and savaging others. My interventions were stirring an eros she did not trust, but also missed. They aroused an old hunger and she sensed a possibility of gratification. But to have her hopes dashed would be a great cruelty and dishonesty.

In her own mind, she was the most honest person who ever lived. If she was cruel, she was open about it. People knew right away where they stood with her. If they could take the "real" Joann, fine. If they could not, they could leave. The centralization of aggression in her emotional life had been, and continued to be, an effort to repair a more deadly experience. Aggression clothed in eros was the ultimate prison for her, and it seemed I was choosing this path with her. It seemed I would sweet-talk her until she dropped her guard, and then I would administer the coup de grâce.

She developed this theme for months and was able to give up

her poor treatment of the staff as she intensified the search for words in the sessions. I continued to echo her in the specific way that had evolved in the treatment. I acknowledged that everything about her was embraceable, which was a core sentiment that she silently held. This can be seen too easily as a process of repair. In the repetition, the therapist fully experiences but holds back the destructive elements that created a fixation in the first place. Then he makes emotional communications that help the patient relive early experiences in a maturational fashion. In such constructions, the emphasis is on the reparative process.

In work with the elderly, it becomes evident that an equal emphasis is required in understanding the destructive elements themselves. My understanding in this case was that Joann's early entropic urges were met with an overstimulating entropy from the parental environment, but were clothed in eros. It was a sickly sweet kind of murder. Joann considered herself morally superior by letting her own personality show through directly. It was the best repair she could make on her own. The ongoing action of that repair was in destroying others while being proud that she had written a new chapter in the family history and had dealt with others honestly. Now as she was approaching death and the true nature of her behavior was threatening to shine through the thinning veneer of her defenses, she redoubled her efforts to externalize the deadness within her.

There was some unwelcome personal work to do in these sessions. It involved tracing aspects of my own punitive superego and the self-hates that founded it. These objectionables were nothing more than early indulgences that had been confronted with the murderous responses of parental figures, and these indulgences were entropic. The focus has always been, and still is, on the effect parents have on the psychology of infants. In the worst cases, there is a Witch in the Nursery who is conceived to be the mother. But I have discovered a more disturbing truth over the years: there surely is a Witch in the Nursery, but it is not the person of the mother. The Witch is the combined entropic demands of the child and the mother, and the child has much to do with setting the undercontrolled entropy of the parents into motion.

The infant is a murderer, more murderous than he will ever be the rest of his life. His entropy shines almost as brightly as his eros. It is pure, direct, and sustainable in a timeless fashion. The grown killer is the one who has tapped this early infantile experience and is one with it. It is not dulled by any ego accommodations. In him we see the intensity of the infant's entropy potentiated.

OUR CHALLENGE IS TO BECOME MORE CONSCIOUS OF THE ACTION OF DEATH INSTINCT IN EVERYDAY LIFE. FROM NOW ON LET US MAKE IT THE PRIME FOCUS OF CONTEMPLATION IN OUR MIDDLE AGE AND BEYOND.

The therapist who works with the elderly will feel a pressure to embrace the entropic demands within him—an actual dialogue with the early lethal strivings and how they play out in his present personality formation. I kept this at the forefront in my sessions with Joann. The entropic embrace was required to return my own objectionables back to their earlier state as indulgences. To work with cruel and destructive people, we have to locate it within ourselves and love it. If we hate it, then no matter how kindly we attempt to be, we will communicate that rejection. If we do not know it as our closest friend, then we can be lulled by it so that it shows up in our behavior or in the behavior of the patient. This is the meaning of all iatrogenic contacts. We run the risk of making the patient sick when we have not carried out a sustained exploration of entropy—we do not know where the murder is in the room.

As long as Joann and I met, she remained under control, kept her angry retorts in the sessions, and continued to improve. She learned that there was no deadly sting to my approach, and her paranoia subsided. Without warning, the family decided she would move to California to be close to another of her children. I heard that she returned to her former patterns, and on the day of her death she fought and screamed to stay alive, damning everyone around her. She screamed until her last breath.

6

Entropy: The Dynamic Action
of the Death Instinct

During my senior year of college, I worked as a therapy aide with elderly men in a psychiatric hospital. For my initiation, my co-workers directed me to change the diapers of a certain man who lay in bed. Young and inexperienced, I showed no hesitation, and even as the man reached inside his diaper, I made no move to protect myself. What was he going to do? Hit me with a handful of excrement? Luckily, I chuckled with my mouth closed, for he did pitch a handful and got me square in the face.

The aides thought this was great fun, as I made for the open toilet area, groped the wall, and found the sink. It was messy stuff, but the soap they used in the hospital was strong, and soon one could hardly tell I had confronted such a stinking menace. I returned, ready to dodge this time, and completed my task. The co-workers, a rough bunch, were uncomfortable that I had taken it so well, and there were grunts of apology. I had not taken it that well. On the other hand, they knew nothing about my past. I had been raised on a farm with two brothers, and to ease the boredom of long days and backbreaking work, we found all kinds of interesting uses for manure. Getting hit by this man was nothing compared to strolling along a back field, hearing a faint whoosh, and looking up just in time to see a hardened cow chip explode into view, lobbed from some fifty feet away with the precision of a howitzer shell.

Once christened by the elderly patient, I was accorded all the rights and privileges of the aides on the floor. There were about a dozen aides, most in their forties and fifties, and to me they seemed to have a glorious passion. They were loving, kind, and dutiful in caring for the elderly men. But there was also a free expression of any and all feelings, especially frustration and anger. The workers seemed to have found a balance that worked for them. In this era when there was no patient bill of rights, the geriatric ward ran more like an extended family.

Aggression did not come in the form of abuse. The aides were simply direct about how they felt. When they were loving, they were loving, and when they were "pissed," everybody knew about it. A loud, "Don't be pissing me off!" was enough to straighten out any agitated gentleman. Voices were raised with no thought of consequences. The results were refreshingly benign. What started out looking like a problem quickly evaporated.

When the mental health professionals would come on the ward, they were viewed with disdain. It seemed these people never got very far with the patients, and the reason was their good manners. The patients came from rough and tumble situations and were largely unfazed by the contacts with the professionals. They sensed the aides truly loved them. The aides were willing to show all their feelings about their charges in a most demonstrative and real manner. In screening out the anger toward the patients, the mental health professionals inadvertently screened out the love, too.

How different was this exposure from the one I had experienced as a research assistant in another hospital the year before. On the day my supervisor left the grounds for a meeting, another doctor asked me to interview four women. This was an unusual request and came from someone I had no contact with. I entered the room and the door was locked after me. The women looked at me with smiles that created a strange, unreadable feeling, but I made allowances. After all, this was a psychiatric facility.

I had brought paper and pencil tests, and I did a group administration. The women were cooperative and even cheerful. As they finished, they asked to stay and talk. I held my first, impromptu, group session at the age of 20. The interchange remained animated, and everyone got to say something. Then my supervisor peered through the wired glass window on the steel door. He was angry and was telling the aide to hurry with the keys. The door flew open and he whisked me out of there.

He was upset about something. He brought me down to the doctor's office, and there was a heated exchange between the two of them behind closed doors. Without further word, we returned to our own office. Later in the day, he told me that all four of the women had murdered. For some unfathomable reason, the doctor had collected the women in the room and put a youngster in with them. My supervisor would never have agreed to this, so the doctor never checked with him.

As far as I was concerned, the aides knew a lot more about life and about their feelings than the professional who was conducting a little science on the side. Yet both the aides and the doctor were acting out. There was a strong focus of aggression in both incidents. I had no context for understanding this kind of behavior until I received my first assignment consulting in a nursing home nine years later. The administrator of the home had worked with me in special education and had come to my in-services. Special education teachers were being exposed to a great degree of frustration and anger and needed to develop a repertoire for using the feelings that were created in them.

First, we became comfortable with the idea that the feelings the students were arousing in us were natural and that anybody in our shoes would feel exactly the same way. Next, we practiced a host of interventions that allowed us to properly use our feelings. The students actually functioned better when we not only provided good educational programs, but made emotional communications based on the feelings they induced.

The administrator remembered all this and called me to speak to his staff. He had a wonderful, pleasant, devoted group working with his frail and ill elderly. But unfortunately, it was alleged that a worker had sought out the local apothecary for a poisonous substance and had attempted to force it down the throat of a contentious resident. The staff took it a lot worse than the community. There was no system of thinking that would account for this heinous deed. The staff was there to be loving and responsive. It would never cross anyone's mind to feel aggressive. The residents were to be dealt with compassionately, even when they hit, scratched, and punched. The very notion of a staff member having a "negative" feeling was scandalous.

People put distance between themselves and the accused staff member. They saw her as having some kind of severe breakdown that made her so different from them that there was nothing to learn from this incident. People sat through my inservices on induced feelings. They smiled and nodded in the right places, and they agreed such phenomena might actually occur—to other people. Their caregiving reached greater heights as they intellectualized negative feelings and did all in their power to conjure up affection and compassion.

This incident taught me a lot about what a staff member has to do in order to function in a prosocial manner in a nursing home. The angry side too easily threatens to destabilize the person. It cannot be dealt with, so it is denied and repressed. Any effort to create conditions where staff members integrate all their thoughts and feelings must pay great respect to such dynamics. In many cases, it is better for us to echo the angelic organization of the person's psyche, until that resistance runs its course and relaxes. For to mention anything about the natural feelings of anger, frustration, patricide, and matricide is automatically construed as an accusation of the person as demonic.

Behind all this lies a faulty belief on the part of many people. They are convinced that if they have such feelings, they will be compelled to act on them. In my twenty years of training and giving in-services, I have not seen this happen. The analytic dictum has held: what you can put into words you will be less likely to do. The cure is talk. The more access impulses have to our thinking, judging, integrating part, the less access they will seek in the musculature and in action.

Probably the most foolhardy thing I ever did was agree to appear on a cable talk show with a therapist of great renown. He is a genius. I know this not only from his writing, but from the excellent training he gave me when I was a young man. He did not remember working with me, and we sat in the green room as strangers, awaiting our cue to take the stage. He asked me what I did for a living. When I explained my therapeutic sessions with staff members, he showed his disfavor.

I told him the effort was to make sure staff members learned how to have all their thoughts and feelings so they could truly be integrated in their approach with their clients. Because the most difficult clients had angry and hateful feelings, these were the ones we talked about a lot. He scowled at the idea of my legitimizing the "negative" feelings. He made an unkind remark about my ideas, we were called to the stage a moment later, and I said little through the whole debate. He made clear what he was going to do to me if I strayed far from the regular experiences of people.

The aides who put me in harm's way with the aggressive patient wanted me to face up to the fact that we are all made of shit, that we are decomposing all the time. They wanted me to react with horror, so they could feel joined and laugh in relief, but they would not have been able to own up to their dynamics. The doctor who locked me in a room with four murderers wanted to see me lose my life. He wanted to have the four women get up, knock over their chairs, raise their arms, corner me with their hypnotic gaze, and tear me limb from limb. He would not have been able to say this. If he was asked, he probably would have said he wanted to know how a murderer's profile is distinctive on the paper and pencil tests. He just put them all together in the room to make it easier for me.

The staff that withdrew from the allegedly homicidal caregiver had been resonating with her for some time. The anger and frustration were split off and fomenting below the staff's level of recognition. The alleged attacker was the weak link. She acted out the group's frustration. Having done so, she relieved the press of the whole staff. People were then able to comfortably shine in an angelic fashion. To say this to the staff would have provoked howls of displeasure. If they had stoned me in response, it would only have been my fault because angels never stone without a reason.

As concerns the renowned therapist, some helping professionals are actually quite angry and cross, but if you would have the audacity to mention it to them, they would say, "We are not here to work on my feelings. We are here to work on yours." And the truth of that reaches beyond the words. Every person needs his defenses, until he does not need them anymore, and it does not matter if he is an angel or a devil, the helper or the helped, someone "in the know" or not "in the know."

THE CHALLENGE IS NOT TO INTRODUCE PEOPLE TO THE EXPERIENCE OF DYING. THE CHALLENGE IS TO RESOLVE THEIR RESISTANCE TO THE SELF-INTRODUCTION THAT DEVELOPMENTALLY AWAITS THEM.

The experience of dying is discovered by contemplation. This contemplation can only occur in an ego syntonic environment where some guide knows where the murder is. To know its whereabouts is to establish the toxipsychological focus necessary to learn about this other half of being. For if we risk having an iatrogenic effect on the other person, we also work on avoiding such errors through a toxipsychology. Echo is not iatrogenic. She does not act on her murderous impulses. She brings Methuselah into the garden by integrating him enough so that he can contemplate. She is him, within her, and she supplies her own self, too. Thus strengthened, he can begin the self-study he has managed to evade his whole life.

A DAY IN THE AVERAGE LIFE

As Gerald stirs to consciousness, he is bereft of any will to move. His mouth is ajar, he is breathing lightly, and he is comfortably nestled in his covers and pillows. It takes some moments before he finds the energy to rouse himself. It is seven in the morning. Gerald has lain in a dreamless state, and this morning-awareness of quiescence, as it slowly suffuses him, is one of the joys of his being. He just wants to lie perfectly still.

He draws toward this same state about three o'clock every afternoon, as he is working at his job, de-energizing and drifting into a mild half-somnolence. He wishes he were a citizen of Florence, Athens, or Rio, in a culture where an afternoon respite would be sanctioned, so he could give in to the swoon and drop back into a large and fluffy couch for a siesta. He feels the call of entropy strongly, and fighting against it to partake of the world gives it only a minor gratification.

He switches on the television. The commentator is reading off the latest figure for the national debt and discussing Congress's growing intent to increase personal taxes. This news rankles him, and why should he subject himself to it? If they are going to screw him, they are going to screw him, and he does not have to endure a detailed description of how long and how hard. He does not have to subject himself to anything that is going to ruin his momentary experience, not if he has anything to do with it. He does not think all this out in some logical way we could directly tap; he is invoking a procedure of general protection against bad news.

Another channel has news of an incipient crisis that requires our volunteer army to mobilize. Young men dressed in camouflage, with earnest faces, paying no attention to the cameras, march by in full battle gear, the sounds of transports firing up in the background, tanks grinding toward their cargo bays, helicopters slamming the air just overhead. Gerald is mesmerized. His martial spirit is aroused, and he has visions of fighter pilots wheeling, spinning and dodging, angling to find the offending bug of a lesser pilot in their sights and blam! Satisfaction in a clean hit. He stretches and feels an equal pull into the living room and back onto his pillow.

He puts on his socks, working around the hole in his right one, so his big toe does not stick out. There is a faint worry about taking some time to darn the sock, but he lets it go. He likes these socks. They are comfortable just the way they are. They will do just fine.

No, in fact they are perfect. How could he show any pretense with a holey sock? It's real.

Breakfast is a cigarette and two cups of coffee. He takes in the burning smoke, watches it dance in front of him, and washes down the brackish taste with very sweet and very light coffee. He is able to return in these bodily senses to the moments prior to full awakening. Eros and entropy have shown themselves in every way possible, in every act and every moment of just these few minutes.

Reaching for his newspaper on the stoop, he sees the neighbor out of the corner of his eye. "That guy never shuts up," he mutters, as he works at putting on just the right face. If he smiles or looks too long, the sonuvabitch takes it as an invitation and saunters over. This is a fate worse than death. "Shoot me! Kill me! Bury me in the backyard!" he thinks. He would have to grimace through the man's nonstop blabbing and find some way to excuse himself. Torture. So he does not encourage the man. He gives a quick nod in his direction and wipes him out of his mind.

He withdraws from his wife and his boss, too, in the same fashion. His day in the object world is negotiated through many small acts of obliteration, some noticed and purposeful, some reflexive. That is, as he has been growing and developing he has learned something about the process, and has some contemplative grasp of the situation. Because no one has made an issue of it, however, he has not gotten past a rudimentary examination of who he'd like to wipe out of his mind and why. It just works, and it feels right.

Starting up the car, he listens intently for those ominous pings. He has images of vital engine parts burning out and remembers the absolute fury he was in when he was caught upstate, miles from anywhere, his last clunker dead as a doornail, he getting overwhelmed with catastrophic ideas. He would do anything to avoid such a replay, he thinks, but each day he passes the service station, and he decides he is running late and a ping is not a breakdown, anyway. The dissolution of his car is strangely satisfying, and if he could say it, he would describe the sublime torture of nudging something dead to life each morning, seeing it in the process of expiring.

The parkway is crowded this morning, and he has to wait on the ramp for a bit. There is no sign that anyone is willing to let him in. He guns the engine and, as the pinging turns into muffled banging, he roars onto the road. He nods his head back and forth in unison with that of the irate driver he spies in the rearview mirror, mocking her. "Yakkity yak, yakkity yak," he fills in, chagrined over the woman's lack of charity. If she slowed up a little, he could have eased in with no problem. But no! She thinks she owns the road! He hates her for her easy obliteration of him, treating him like he was a bug, trying to ram through and crowd him off the road.

Just a mile ahead is another ramp; an elderly fellow tries to nudge his behemoth onto the parkway. Gerald guns the engine again, unperturbed by the gacking sound the car is now making, gliding by as he shoots the man a nasty look. "Oh no you don't!" He stares the man down in his rearview mirror. What is wrong with people? Can't they wait a minute or two? Does he have a big magnet on the front of his car that pulls these people on top of him? The car is now smoking, but Gerald has decided he must make a stand. Charity cases should get off the road. The old man should drop dead anyway. Why the hell is he still driving?

He pulls into the service station by his place of work. The car is wheezing now, and the mechanic listens to it. He pops the hood and feels around. He tells Gerald that his computer is not working correctly, and he is getting an incorrect fuel–air ratio. Gerald digs in for an argument that will sway the mechanic's thinking. He begins to share his pet theory, based on a 1972 Thunderbird that made the exact same noise. The specialist will hear none of it. He repeats what the problem is and stares at Gerald. Suddenly feeling very stupid and abashed, Gerald blushes and retreats. He cannot handle confrontations and usually ends up attacking himself. He rages the rest of the day about backing down, hating himself for it. In brief glimpses, he even wishes he were dead.

The day passes slowly, and work has been marginally satisfying. There have been a lot of things he has not wanted to do, and he has put a lot of time into getting them on someone else's desk. A lot has been repetitive. That is comforting for a while, but it lulls him into fantasizing. The only problem is that there is even some novelty in the repetitive, and he has to be on guard. That ruins the fantasies. By the end of the day, he just wants to be left alone and notes that just about everyone he works with is a horse's ass.

On edge, he returns home to find his wife's things all over the living room. He registers resentment that she has disturbed the orderliness of the house. He repairs to the den, where his socks are mixed in with the newspapers and magazines, one slipper is visible between his soiled garden shoes, his unopened mail is sandwiched in the *TV Guide*, and the remains of breakfast remind him he needed to stay in bed this morning, or at least fit in a siesta.

It does not matter if Gerald is 21, 37, or 55. It does not matter if he is working on a cure for cancer, piloting a commuter train, or adding up numbers in an accounting office. It does not matter if he conceives of his life in a useful vein or lives it out in a useless manner. It does not matter if he loves his wife or hates her. It does not matter if he is validated in his work or not.

Gerald is totally within the experience of eros and entropy, and these two forces play themselves out in his being throughout the day. He rests and climbs out of rest. He feels body rhythms that call for a return to entropy. Because the culture is not going to allow that, the entropy comes out in other ways. He blots out the existence of others as reflexively as he blinks his eyes. He feels a joy about war. He feels the greatest comfort with deterioration, whether it is represented by holey socks or deficient car engines. Reality creates aggression, which he all too frequently turns on himself.

While he progresses enough to keep pace with the pressures of the real world and so play his part in the mirage, he also does not progress. He is in a continual activity of canalizing. He is pursuing patterns that avoid the transcendent because the invitation to disorganize in the service of transcendence creates too much entropy. He could just lose "him," float away, and he will wisely not risk that. His entropy is most comfortably exercised in quiescence, withdrawal, blotting out, dying down, getting angry at being trifled with, and wanting to see the other guy get his. Provoked by the possibility of transcendence, Gerald remains within the limits prescribed by his entropic patterns. In this way he fulfills his social contract. He builds buildings, he raises children, he contributes to the common weal. He does what he can do, and that is fine. This is what is.

Entropy as a psychological principle found its way into Freud's theories after World War I. Up to that point, he identified eros and self-preservation as our two basic instincts, which drove our behavior, required the baptism of acculturation, and figured in psychopathology if the baptism was severe. The mass carnage of World War I could not be accounted for by these instincts, and he was pressed to find an explanation.

Adler had brought up the centrality of aggression in human life over a decade before, at the Wednesday night meetings Freud hosted at his apartment (Spotnitz 1985, p. 46). Sabina Spielrein (Kerr 1993) had more recently written on the urge to death and may have speeded Freud's inquiries along, although he made no specific reference to her work. Nietzche and Schopenhauer had addressed the issue long before Freud, but he seemed to purposefully steer clear of their presentations.

The impression given is that he wanted to be original and to put such ideas clearly in his own terms. Authorship was an issue for him. Just as he may have not wanted to bow to other writers on this subject, so too was he jealous about his own material. In 1918 a student and analysand, Tausk, seemed to be listening to him too closely, interpreting ideas Freud was still formulating, and passing them off as his own in lectures (Roazen 1969). He sent Tausk to be analyzed by a colleague, and the student subsequently committed suicide. We can suspect he had a very immediate experience of infanticide but wrote nothing of it.

In "Beyond the Pleasure Principle" (1920), Freud discussed a number of phenomena, which called for a new explanation of how we are built. Why did people have nightmares? Why did they repeat traumatic interpersonal experiences in their new relationships? Why did the infant risk separation anxiety by initiating and pursuing the game of peek-a-boo with its mother? These questions took on new significance as the modern world faced the possibility of war so total it could lead to extinction.

Why would people engage in behavior that was aversive? It contravened their obvious hedonism—seek pleasure and avoid pain. What intrapsychic process demanded compulsions that acted beyond the pleasure principle? In an act of genius, Freud (1920) posited that the two basic instincts were eros and the constancy principle. Eros sought to increase tensions. The constancy principle sought to reduce tensions. Later these were called the life and death instinct, or eros and thanatos. He identified an intrapsychic demand to return to a more inorganic state, working in concert with the urge to develop and to complexify. These were our foundational processes.

This greatest of formulations has gone all but unheeded by most therapeutic schools and by branches of psychoanalysis itself. Yet there is nothing more evident about our being than the presence of these dynamics in our life cycle, in our physical bodies, in our coenesthetic experience, and in our advanced capacities. The omnipresence of these dynamics in our psyches is apparent to all of us.

Life surges up, death dissipates the surge, moment by moment, in the white spaces between moments. This death is more accurately the action of entropy. Our personal being achieves a discrimination of experience by the ongoing contrast that eros and entropy continually create. There would be no experience of being were it not for its separation into these two contrasting phenomena. Just as it takes a background to identify the foreground, it takes entropy to identify eros. But this background is not empty. It is formative to the foreground and then shares with it equal powers.

Death precedes life. The organic springs out of the inorganic. An energy hike is measured against a background of stasis. If there were no stasis, how might we we know about energy? So many processes proceed in a wax and wane, but hidden behind the words "wane, stasis, empty, nothing" is another truth. Entropy is a process as powerful as eros and works in its silent way as eros works in its flourishes. Its power is evident in the infant, it is observable all through our lives, and entropy overtakes eros in our final seconds.

Freud's metaphysical theories retain their merit because we need a metaphor that will capture our plight. We are beings aware of the transitory nature of our existence in the corporeal. We face the cruelest truth moment by moment, and we never get away from it. This is the truth of mind and body. We have a mind that can soar beyond our skins to caress the span of the universe in its fifty billion light years. We can turn inward to imagine the dance of atoms designed like solar systems. We can see deeply into protons and neutrons, to find they are composed of little solar systems themselves. And those littlest of solar systems are teeming with solar systems of their own. We can conceive of all matter being a mirage, of all the distances in the universe being equivalent to one dimensionless point, of all time past, present, and future colliding, frozen in, never having escaped from, the tiniest piece of a second.

This majesty of comprehension, of reach, of appreciation of every kind of stimulation, is encased in a body of clay. Just as sure as another day will pass, our bodies will proceed through a pattern of growth and disintegration, until our mortal clay is joined with the larger clay that first gave us form. This is beyond reckoning in the first half of our lives. In order to function in our youth, we must hurl such ideas far beyond our intellectual or emotional reach, or else we will remain in the all-consuming mourning of depression, or the symbolic self-sacrifice in schizophrenia, until the entropy fulfills its promise and we die. There is little that is redemptive in an entropy that never finds a voice. It is conceived as pure pathology in this society and it is reviled. Thus to know early is to die early.

The blanketing force against such knowledge is the denial of death. People want to feel alive. They will run from dying into the arms of living with everything they can muster, splitting being so that one half of it seems to magically disappear. Living an adventurous life, taking chances, partaking of the world in large pieces, exciting the sensorium, pedestalizing youth, letting others suffer for one's excesses, dominating others, or partaking of an in-group that extols its virtues to the detriment of an out-group; there are many ways to try to feel alive. Yet death is given its due in each instance.

Adventure finds its outlines against the homeostatic background of boredom, as entropy takes back from eros. Taking chances is a way to mix dying with living. The brinksmanship contains within it a brush with death, one designed to make us feel excruciatingly alive. The incorporation of the world is the infant's incorporation of the mother. There is no other instance of aggression being so total without the presence of hate, because of the lack of an ego to express or experience it. The sense modalities only register peaks against an entropic background. To love youth is to despise old age and to seek to extirpate signs of it in the self, hating the facts of death. Any suffering that is put on others is the activity of entropy sent out toward the object world.

There is no way for the population at large to undergo a transformation where such understandings would be accepted and woven into the daily fabric of life. This is because the intervention required is not educational, in the sense of placing some new foreign idea in one's repertoire. It is formative, something that has to be eminently available in the child's environment, something he can internalize and make part of his personality. If anything, it is cultural, and the culture is at present channeling people toward the direction of splitting being into only one of its components—life.

The experience of deadness is lost in a society whose paradigm relentlessly presses for the experience of life. It is the eroticization of being that we have all submitted to in our acculturation. This paradigm seems to do its job credibly, until we reach old age and late old age. Then it is recognized as sadly wanting. There has been a whole side of our being that has gone unrecognized, and now it crashes down upon us. All we can think is, where did the time go? When did I become an old man? How did this happen to me? In more extreme situations, the facts of dying go to provoke defenses that rob us of any gratification during our last years.

OUR ROLE IS TO EMBRACE THE RESISTANCE AS IT PRESENTS IN THE TREATMENT RELATIONSHIP, IN ORDER TO ENCOURAGE THE PERSONAL GROWTH THAT WILL ALLOW THE PATIENT ACCESS TO FULLER BEING. THERE

IS NO EDUCATING PEOPLE ABOUT THE EQUAL EXPERIENCES OF LIVING AND DYING.

Elizabeth was haunted by terrible nightmares where she confronted a sinkhole and vanished in it. It swallowed her up almost every night, and she spent each day dreading the return of the darkness. She shared her agitation in the sessions and was greeted with my continuing equipoise. What she saw as horrible I saw as benign and as formative to her being as eros was. When the nightmares subsided, the new theme that replaced them was the alienation she felt toward her peers. She put aside her grapplings with an overwhelming truth and found something in the textual world she could handle. We worked on understanding what it was about her peers that aroused this reaction. As we came up with solutions, she found her peers somewhat more accessible. The nightmares did not return.

Ida gasped with blinding panic attacks, describing a dark cloud coming over her to engulf her. She shook in her wheelchair, pitifully alone and cut off, looking this way and that, hyperventilating, crawling out of her skin. She portrayed this painful experience in the sessions, where I sat calm and still. I became the dark cloud, presenting a serene and encompassing side of it. She confronted the source of her panic, and it turned out to be a friendly force that resonated with her. In her core she learned the cloud was really she, as was the light. What she experienced consciously was quite different. She concluded I did not have much interest in this particular symptom. She understood this as the source of her subsequent relaxation. She turned to a more textual theme: her difficulty getting what she needed from her cold and unreachable family. She was helped to say everything about them, so we could better understand the nature of their resistance.

Ann was frightened and angry during our first meeting. The caregivers were out to poison her, she was sure of it. She had a lot of evidence pointing to their intentions. She picked through her food looking for foreign substances, checked under her bed for killer radiation, and kept the telephone on her lap should she need to dial 911 right away. Medications had failed to curb her paranoia. Her accusations were met with a homeostatic calm, which quickly damped the extremes of her presentation and influenced her affect. I accepted her murderous feelings and loved them directly. The sessions continued weekly, she sharing her paranoid ideas and checking with me to see which of them made sense. After a year these also subsided, and Ann focused on the little things the staff members did that proved they were thoughtless and distracted.

Martha raged at the staff members, vilifying them for their lack of generosity and empathy. She shouted out her condemnations during the early sessions, but then became aware she was in the room with a composed and attentive person. I resonated with the gratifying infanticides she was conducting in her mind's eye. She put aside her complaints and focused on responding to the demand characteristics of the treatment relationship. She dressed for the occasion, controlled her behavior, and sought to be the lady to my gentleman. In the process, she revived her premorbid work persona, arousing dormant aspects of the successful salesperson she was for most years of her life. The therapy became the support for this professional in her, which gave her an ample repertoire for dealing adaptively with her pressures.

Harold ruminated over his impending death, crying at the sight of his wrinkled face, at the numbness in his feet, sure that he was emaciated and on the verge. What he sought to escape, I embraced, so filled with the truth of entropy that I was dying for him. He discussed these issues for only a few sessions, and then became very interested in my life and how I conducted it. He told me he had never met such a calm and happy man. The more he focused on me, the less he talked about dying. Soon it was as if he had never had mortal fears, as he asked me questions about how I would do this or handle that situation. He tolerated long explorations that allowed him to project all his inner resources onto me and practice them in that way.

Julia was despondent over the loss of her home, her belongings, her close friends, and access to her community. She had lived in one place for thirty years, and the move was traumatic for her. She experienced the placement in the nursing home as the death of her normal way of life. She withdrew from company, refused to eat, had the television and radio removed from her room, and took to sitting in the dark with her hands folded, staring at the wall. In the sessions she described herself as dead. She was just waiting for her body to find out and catch up. This theme continued for a month. I sat with her, becoming one with the room, the furniture, the curtains, using myself to connect her to her surroundings. As far as she was concerned, the consistency of my visits and my accepting demeanor drew her into conversation. In a matter of weeks she put the loss feelings aside and asked me to escort her in the building. She took my arm, graciously introduced herself to her peers, and strived to act with the same skill she had brought to her first days in her brand new apartment in the 1960s.

Oscar attempted to leave the building, so distressed was he about the deaths in his room. His first roommate died on May 16 in the morning. By midafternoon a new, sickly roommate was lying in bed. That man died on June 10 at night. After a day's hiatus, a third man occupied the bed. He died in November. Oscar had had enough. Everybody died in this place. He was going to escape this fate. However he never brought any of this up in the therapy. Where he registered distress, I reacted with calm. The dying he rejected, I accepted. I never had to say a word about it. He stayed in the room, no longer attempted to elope, and sought to establish a relationship with me, where he brought up topical conversations and engaged in light talk. As long as we met, he did well. If we missed two or three sessions, he returned to his former patterns. The therapy was aimed at maintaining his functional adaptation.

Each of these cases had in common a breakdown in the denial of death. As soon as therapy was offered, the patients found a way to shore up the defense and to experience relief. There was resonation to their entropic demands, but this did not lead to verbal–level acknowledgment. There was repression that led to milder, derivative themes, such as alienation or emotional abandonment. This textu-alized way of talking about the experience of dying gave it enough access to consciousness and also provided protection in the deep encoding. There was reaction formation, in an all-consuming interest in my life and the life of others. The patients used the therapeutic relationship to turn away from death and to negate its presence.

Such solutions are necessary for people, even those who are chronologically in old age. Developmentally, they are not prepared to absorb what would be the full body slam of mortal facts. The goal is to support the defenses that they need at present, and not to investigate more totally ideas that are already frightening them and disrupting their ability to function. To pursue rather than subtly invite consciousness about the experience of dying would have an iatrogenic effect.

7

Primitive Defenses That Affect the Working Alliance

The oracle at Delphi told the pregnant woman whose son would be Narcissus, "He will live a long life, as long as he ne'er knows himself." Patients will retain the unreflectiveness of narcissism during our time with them, and we will need to play our part. We will find our ways of helping them misunderstand themselves, so they can return to a life-affirming denial of entropy awareness. Our clinical decision to do so is based on their reaction to directness, which ranges from ignoring us to toxic recoil.

As we study whether the patient is going to benefit from directness, we come upon an important distinction in psychotherapy. Patients respond to us in two ways. There are times they will process and assimilate our clarifications and interpretations, and will cooperate with us in working through what they have learned, so that it affects their life both in and outside the sessions. But they can also respond to any new ideas with a mobilization of resistance. This resistance may take the form of acting out, somatizing, denying and repressing, or attacking the self. Clearly, directness can be iatrogenic, creating more problems than it could possibly alleviate. The first reaction is referred to as oedipal-level. The second is described as pre-oedipal, or narcissistic.

If our approach is more behavioral, there are also two reactions, but they present in a somewhat different manner. There are times the patients work closely with the therapist, cooperate with in-session activities, role-play, and do their homework. There are also times they cry out for relief but do not cooperate readily with any of those aspects of behavioral work. If pressed, they are likely to leave the therapy and not benefit at all. None of what is presented to them feels right, and they do not put faith in the precepts of behavioral change. Here again, there are oedipal and pre-oedipal dynamics at play. On the one hand, the focus is on behavior, and there is less stress on the ego, so that pre-oedipal defenses are less likely to be aroused. But another set of problems arises, because even well-defended patients come to therapy to receive a certain kind of emotional communication, and behavioral interventions can be experienced as empathic failures too great to tolerate. We all have a core of narcissism, and it will be readily pressed into service as a defense, given the right conditions.

So if we attempt to deal too directly with the analysis of meanings, a good percentage of our patients will feel attacked. If we attempt to exhort and encourage behavioral change, a good per-centage of our patients will feel misunderstood, underestimated, or undernourished. Either way, we have played our part in bringing narcissistic dynamics into greater relief. These two approaches are predicated on a frequently unannounced assumption—that the average patient is willing or able to organize his resources to react with progressive talk or movement toward a goal.

Psychoanalytic theory has extended diagnosis below this level of functioning, to make clear that two distinct phases precede mani-festly progressive behavior, even for people who present in a progressive fashion. Before external and obvious progress is re-corded, some patients must resolve a status quo phase where they seem to go around and around in a broken–record fashion, repeating the same material to no apparent end. Underlying this circular behavior is the integration of the ego. Just as in the case of socially adaptive progress, the ego is integrating in order to handle more of the realities that confront it and to still find ways to bring more Being into being.

Before the status quo phase there is a treatment-destructive phase. This is marked by alienation, low frustration tolerance, acting out, a wish to withdraw from the treatment, and a marked sensitivity to the presence of the therapist. This is the patient most at risk. He cannot bear to live with his symptoms, but he cannot bear the invasion of an Other into his life. He comes into the sessions testing his unstated but ever-present hypothesis: surely the cure is worse than the sickness. During this phase, being is making a more adaptive effort at letting Being shine through, but at a more primary level that uses even less verbal fluency and more body talk (Spotnitz 1985).

By adopting a certain point of view, the therapist is more likely to avoid the troubles inherent in facing these phases. He simply asks what has prevented this person from getting what he wants out of life. Shorn of its contemporary meanings, the question is more directly asking: What is preventing this person from experiencing the most of Being in being? Having asked the question, the therapist pursues his search along the same lines. He does not analyze meanings or exhort behavioral change as his primary intervention. He analyzes resistance and takes a complementary position to the oscillations and emanations that bespeak of stasis.

The resistances can be characterized in this way:

Treatment-Destructive Resistance
Status Quo Resistance
Resistance to Progress
Resistance to Working Alliance

They suggest the chronological order in which the most regressed patient will advance. They reflect what potential range we all have in ourselves for responding to treatment. They are a measure of how progressive or regressive any patient is during some phase of the therapy. They describe what can happen in one session.

Although they are not equipotential, they can be equally accessible. They frequently show up during each session, although one of the resistances may seem to be the commanding theme. Their ratios change with progress, and the intensity of the first two resistances lessens. Movement backward on this list asks that we be aware of possible iatrogenic effects or stressors in the environment. At times a patient comes to treatment making progressive communications and then regresses as part of his repetition.

THE TREATMENT-DESTRUCTIVE PHASE

The treatment-destructive phase can last for a brief time, a month, or a year. It is the urge to detextualize, due to the strangulating confinement of character armor on Being, played out on many fronts. In the parlance of relations, it presents as the patient's attitude: "I do not recognize your existence." It is an obliteration of the Other, with the dual consequences of the narcissistic pattern. The Other has been done away with and disappears, to allow the disturbed infant within us to return to blissful sleep. At the same time, it is a profound declaration of the unity with the Other that pre-dates separateness. "I do not recognize your existence because we were never apart. There is no you or me. To recognize *you* is to give up the paradise of omniconnection."

In the treatment-destructive phase, the patient is irritated by Other-ness. Thus, in our handling of the treatment, we reduce this Other-ness. The patient considers our presence noxious and we respond by flattening up against the background as much as we can, losing our distinctive relief. We echo Methuselah and become a viable mirror. We do so by responding to his entropy and by magically destroying our Other-ness, bringing into relief the Methuselah in us.

At the level of self-study, the patient cannot tolerate becoming aware of the meaning of his behavior. He finds acting out a preferred mode of expression. In this way entropy is channeled and controlled. If he were forced to recognize and reflect, there would be a danger of damming up the entropy and forcing it to express bodily, in the form of somatizations or in some act of murder. In depression we murder our feelings and in schizophrenia we murder our minds. Finally, there are homicide and suicide.

The patient will not come to sessions, he will get up and walk out of the room, he will yell and threaten, or he will talk nonstop with no nod at all to the reality of our presence. He will spit on the floor, talk to himself, masturbate. Textual meaning can provoke damaging insight, so he strives at the pretextual, focusing on what it will take to manage his tensions. He feels the search for structure will kill him. We understand the toxicity implicit in meaning, and we use the sessions to study our resonations and to find suitable words to join the resistance.

At the level of adaptation, the treatment-destructive phase is wreaking havoc with the patient's life. This activity designed to keep tensions within a manageable latitude has ecological consequences. The patient is not showing up on time where people expect him. If cooperating with time schedules would further disorganize him, he will stick to his inner clock. He does not stay on task. Inner modulation is more important than responsiveness to the environment. He has trouble organizing his thinking. Primary process material is breaking through or is forcing defenses to redouble their efforts and to throw a pall on his creativity and cognitive processes. He has to organize where he needs, and disorganize where he needs, to give threatening Being access where it needs. His emotional miseducation has left him without the skills to parlay the press of the inner into a viable lifestyle.

This phase of the treatment can be a trace reaction to a stressful situation or to perception of upcoming stress. It can be a characterological pattern that prevents an easy working alliance throughout the therapy. It can be in the form of addictions that open the gate to the oceanic. It can be aggressiveness or a psychotic break. Where therapy is concerned, this state is perceived as a healthy disdain for the helping professions, supported by fears of potential iatrogenic damage. Our role is to help the patient put the disdain into words, join the disdain, or mirror it. The hope behind the fear is that we will do this without harming the patient.

Often a treatment-destructive position is held by people who do not see therapy as an issue in their lives. Their families, fellow workers, and colleagues may wish therapy for them, but they seem content with their situations. They create dysfunction, pain, or disaster all around them but magically float over these problems. They find their behavior ego-syntonic and are so comfortable with destructive discharge that to see a therapist would equate with taking a vow of poverty. They are rich beyond measure, it seems to them. They have found a way to bring more of Being into being. However, they have not broached any encounter with the social contract. Their refusal to do so reveals the tremendous vulnerability underneath their sentiment of indifference.

Responding to the social contract would reveal a still-nascent latticework of early character formation. The bonding, trust, and mutual merger that form the base for epigenetic development have been left weakened by early events that were experienced as major empathic failures. Relatedness remains a frightening proposition, because it beckons the experience of dying in the form of rage. This is central to antisocial and criminal dynamics but is also accessible to the practitioner as an organizing principle, one of our many sides in multimind. These dynamics are more evenly distributed throughout the populace than any of us would like to admit. They bespeak of our potential to react to the resonating needs of others in a way to inundate their self with our entropic demand.

If we read up on interesting clinical cases, spectacular scandals, or tell-all biographies, and watch investigative people "dish the dirt," it is only to reintroduce ourselves to our own potential. We do not have to follow sensational stories of murder, mayhem, incest, and rape to know of these things. They are in our heart. Everything that everyone else has ever tried, or dreamed of trying, is also within us and we are capable of resonating with it. This is the part of people that keeps them away from therapy, but it is also the part of us that sends people out of therapy. The culture has not yet found a way to capture such experience in a therapeutic manner, so it remains hidden, just in the way that people with such character formations remain hidden from the therapist.

Of course, the acclaimed response is to reject activity that goes against the social contract. Such renunciation is important for the social glue to work. But the transcendent response is to hear what society would judge to be the most egregious or obscene story and acknowledge, "There go I." For those who work with us, we respond with the utmost understanding and acceptance, even when their counterinstinctual defense is overwhelming. We think, "Poseur, let me embrace thee."

The patient in the treatment-destructive phase is us, in our early infancy, first broaching textualization as an ego response to challenges from within and without, dropping back to pretextual nakedness, loose from fetters, freer to express yet also locked in this Eden by organizing principles that establish a fixation at this primitive level. Entropy must undergo the same careful training that eros must, in the development of a healthy personality. This is no more evident than in the treatment-destructive resistances, which replay the early damage for us to see.

We use the contract with us as a re-educational exposure to the larger social contract. And just as acculturation gives rewards, but acts upon the individual hatefully with Procrustean limitation, we also show hate within the contract, expecting the patient to come on time, to be with us, and to pay for the session. We calm and redirect worrisome urges by resonating with the patient's chaotic urges and by offering up our own organizing principles as adaptive alternatives. We show the patient how to bring more Being into being without risking decompensation. We have all our entropic feelings without acting on them.

We need to recognize that we are going to see the most primitive aspects of personality with Methuselah. He is already exercising them with everyone around him. Either he is going to repress such dynamics upon meeting us, or we will be using the sessions to draw the transference onto us and to reduce its coloring of all his relationships with caregivers. At the earliest level, he is saying, "I am alone in the universe." He reacts with a sublime indifference to the object world. This indifference is defensive but also contains the complacence of omniconnection. If we look through the large end of the telescope to microsize the field, the indifference is an escape back to an organizing principle where there was no threat to the immature system of an invasive Other. If we look through the small end of the telescope to capture the grandeur of the universe, it is the connection to everything animate and inanimate, and this first statement of "I" signals the consciousness of being and the corraling of Being.

From indifference comes the uneasy recognition of another presence, just beyond the horizon of awareness. This is unsettling, causing the infant to seek homeostasis once again and to avoid the object world. Awareness is burgeoning, underscoring a separation between the archaic "I" and "not I." Eros provokes tension increase in the form of new stimulation; entropy provokes tension reduction and a return to the inorganic. Eros creates unwelcome opportunities for stimulation; entropy reacts with a strength of its own.

As awareness grows, the Other becomes more distinct. It is recreated in the mind's eye, and so the Other is not the real person out there, but an object representation within the infant, called the object. It is seen as a looming Other cresting the edge of the horizon and threatening to destroy the infant. The archaic ego, or pre-ego structure, registers alarm and hate. What is so awful about this Other that arouses the hate? Freud felt it was due to the disturbing of the infant's homeostatic Eden. This has been a fine working hypothesis with much support in clinical observations. It tells us that before love, there were indifference and hate. Entropy precedes eros. The problems that plague mankind are less in the sphere of loving and are more concerned with hate and homeostatic indifference. Underlying all the cases we work with is a substrate of entropy that has to be addressed by the therapy in some way, silently, aloud, by modeling, or by resonating.

We have since learned to see that which the world would rather leave unknowable. It is the infant's entropy that is used to limn the character of the Other. He uses the parenting figure to create a demonic version of himself in the ego. Who he sees in the mind's eye is his own entropy brought into structural view. If he perceives a Witch in the Nursery, that Witch is more his own incorporative and destructive being, brought into the ego and more directly perceived. It is he who wants to devour and obliterate. The Witch plays a diminutive part in his adult character if her features did not find added completeness in the response of the parenting figures. Aspects of the early Witch, informed by entropy, can meld with the later Angel, informed by eros, to integrate the object and lessen intoxication.

When he is older, this entropy is going to repeat, taking a variety of forms. At the second year of life it becomes the Elf King at the Window. The child will project his entropy onto a looming Other who threatens his sleep, and he will respond with night terrors. Then it is a Gremlin Behind the Door, as the monster who will molest him. It is the Virago in Front of the Classroom, who kills his joie de vivre and sets dynamics into motion that will forever ruin the chances for success in his life. It is the Medusa in the Bedroom, the poisonous spouse who has perverted the merger experience so that it is ruled by hatred and anger rather than by love. It is the Monster in the Boardroom, who turns his worklife into a living hell and makes him rue the day he was born.

Our early, unfettered entropy is potent, creating organizing principles that defy accommodation to later benign learnings. As the entropy undergoes a structuralization as part of its education and miseducation, the person's views of the object world reflect danger, instability, and darkness. The distinction between victim and victimizer has furthered our confusion about what is really going on. One is seen as all-bad and one as all-good, but as we know already such thinking harkens back to our earliest perceptions of objects. We use our most primitive form of perception to conceptualize the hurting that is done among people.

The victim is radiating entropy, just as the victimizer is. Both are victimizing each other, but in different ways. Psychiatry spent its first hundred years cataloging human ills within the framework of the caregiver's effect on the infant. Now it is quietly steering in the opposite direction, to lend some balance, with the infant's effect on the caregiver. The morals of larger society preclude the investigation of what the role of the victim is. This is because as a culture we are experiencing each other at the relationship-destructive level (the larger category in which treatment-destructive behavior is found). Attorneys are able to blame the victim and to obtain freedom for clients who perpetrated terrible damage. Our moral outrage has to do with how poorly ensconced controls against our own entropy are. We think that to understand the victim's rightful role in fomenting attack or damage on himself will loose even more destructiveness. We are too ready to take the weak victim and finish him off. If society is ever able to develop to a point where hateful feelings against a victim can be felt but not acted on, we will better understand human relations when they go awry.

Adults are therefore infanticidal, but infants are eminently killable. They have drained the mother of nutrients, loosened her bone, weakened her, stretched her and, with their arrival, no one is going to be getting any sleep. They are demanding and needy, but more to the point they radiate entropy more strongly than they ever will the rest of their lives, and they invite damage. They call to be overwhelmed, and it is an act of empathic sacrifice that people raise their children with good will and honest effort. It is a credit to eros that there are just as many organizing principles for seeing the world brightly, bringing the best out of each other, acting altruistically, loving, and seeking the transcendent.

THE STATUS QUO PHASE

Overwhelming entropy is the hallmark of the treatment-destructive phase, and it needs to be resonated with so that the patient recognizes he is in a holding environment where his needs are going to be taken care of. He is not going to be murdered off, but he is also going to be educated not to murder us. He is not going to be drowned in a loving kindness he would only experience as murderous as a hammer blow. We are going to listen, understand, and take a complementary stance. We are going to introduce the contract as a most minor corraling of freed entropy. The resultant furor will prove that the contract provides just enough corraling of the acting out. More would be perceived as strangulation.

Resolution of the treatment-destructive phase leads to the status quo phase. This is an especially hard one for therapists. Progress can be quantified during the treatment-destructive phase, as the patient comes under control, becomes consistent, gives up certain aestivating patterns, and responds to the therapeutic contract and therefore to the social contract. But the progress that is occurring in the status quo phase is hidden from view. The ego is involved in a preverbal project, seeking to fortify its earliest channels against future regression-provoking circumstances. Verbal equivalents of primary circular reactions, which were more physical and muscular in nature during the treatment-destructive phase, now dominate. It is reenactment at the verbal level, seeking to get resonation. But it is primitive talk, because of the pressure of certain organizing principles.

The person has been prevented from following a maturational path by the early organization around distinctive themes. The entropy sent out and overly responded to has aroused structures. These have calcified the dynamism of the growing ego and have trapped its expansiveness within an extruding plate. Being is trapped, and resonations out to us are designed to invite us to turn time back, to melt the hardness of the plate, to release entropy into its free state again, and to allow development to go forward from the time that it became set in stone. In the repetition, the patient is asking to be damaged all over again, it seems, but in truth, he is communicating the entropy that begs to be educated.

The status quo phase is one in which the holes in the colander are widening, and rigidity is giving way to flexibility and accommodation. The threshold for the colander refreezing and recasting itself is very low. Extrapsychic aggression—our aggression—threatens to mobilize resistance and to materialize entropy as structure. This is a time to be careful, but we also get chances because some error is allowed in the status quo phase. It is also a time where the patient is not going to bolt out of the room at the sight of empathic error. He will close up like a flower in the rain but will open again when he feels sunshine.

In attempting to describe what is therapeutic, I am using a host of models. I say hold on to them all and add them to the armamentarium you already possess. Put them all together. Take the mask, the colander, the DNA, flowers, hands opening up to warm touch, the traveler taking off his cloak under the warm rays of the sun, and extrapolate beyond them to sense the majesty of the human heart and mind. We were brought up with one religion and had a set view of God, but as we grew older we found out about everyone else's view. At some point in our life, we realized every view of God was a mask, and behind all the masks lay some grander reality. The prolific quantity of masks suggests the grandeur of what lies beyond. On a lesser stage, let this be true of man. Let the numbers of metaphors multiply until we have enough to make a sensible extrapolation.

There is a movement afoot to integrate the psychotherapies, at least by adopting a technical eclecticism. That is, students would best be exposed to a number of approaches during their training, which include psychodynamic, behavioral, humanistic, Gestalt, and existential techniques. Beyond this there has also been a call to find a unifying model of humankind that would predict why techniques drawn from over three hundred schools of therapy work. On the way to doing this, it is best to expose ourselves to more schools rather than to fewer. There is a refreshing panoply of models that suggest our rich complexity, far beyond anything we have ever built or can imagine. It is a sentiment in psychology and in physics that the mind is always going to end up being more than anything it will conceive. Toward that end I do not take an orthodox view, even though I am talking about an orthodox worldview that has been largely inundated by other, milder points of view about humanity. Therapists are not hearing enough about eros and entropy, and this model extends their view of how to best treat Methuselah.

In the status quo phase the infant is communicating, "Now that I have gotten used to you, don't go changing on me!" It is a protracted test on one level and, more dynamically, is the searching out of resonations within us that are going to continue to provide the patient with maturational stimulation within the deep structures of character. That it appears so predictably, that it has a season, just like the phases before it and after it, that it begins and ends lets us know it is an organic development in the therapy. The resistances that arise within this period are to be understood, loved, and embraced, as we offer within us the self-control of entropic acting out and teach the patient to do the same. We echo Methuselah with a sureness, we allow him the phenomenal experience of tying us into knots and bringing the therapy to a standstill. We allow the family and the caregivers to criticize our inability to generate observable progress in Methuselah.

During this time we are going to make best friends with the family members and the caregivers. They confront the person's status quo resistances all the time and are totally befuddled. The patient refuses to talk about anything new. He refuses to take a shower on a new day or try a new medication. He hates the idea of a new roommate. He drove his 1975 Oldsmobile for twenty years and by God he would have driven it another twenty if the children had not hidden his car keys. He eats overdone toast with strawberry jam and weak tea with a lot of milk every morning at seven. He has overcommitted to schedules, patterns, and habits that have taken on such meaning that they define him.

He will not try anything new. He will not wear the new clothing the children have brought him, he will not watch cablevision, and his old wheelchair was working just fine. He likes people who look and sound just like him, and everyone else deserves no more than a quick glance, just enough to decide he will have nothing more to do with that person. He repeats the same stories and seems to be doing so in order to drive the family to suicide. He asks the same questions even though he knows the answers. He makes the same critiques again and again. He goes over happy memories, and he goes over rotten memories with the same loving touch as he applied to happy ones.

The staff is sure this is a sign of dementia. Most people do not realize that this is how they themselves would present in therapy.

There would be a flurry of activity in the beginning, but then they would settle down to this status quo process, which Freud experienced as the stone wall of resistance. Direct interpretations about what is going on do not have much effect. Most interpretations are not armor-piercing bullets that smash anything. They are fashioned out of the entropy of the therapist, and so are a bolus of aggression flung at the walls of the patient's character. It is a matter of aggression in response to aggression. Interpretations only mobilize resistance. That is, a bolus of aggression lobbed at the patient's defenses only promotes automatic wall-thickening.

The therapist does best to wait out the patient. He tries not to make any false moves and corrects for those he does make. While he is seeking to resonate with the patient, he is building the trust that will allow the patient to take him in as an advanced form of reality. The colander holes are opening. During this phase, entropy has been seen in its structural form, thick, seemingly immutable, an impenetrable armor.

RESISTANCE TO PROGRESS AND RESISTANCE TO WORKING ALLIANCE

These two phases follow the resolution or repression of the status quo phase. During this time the patient is asking, "Can I trust you enough to open myself to change?" and "Is it possible you are the person who will ally with me so I can make the greatest change?" The patient at risk is in the treatment-destructive phase. Once he calms down and reasserts his character armor, he is in the status quo phase. Most of the patients referred to us in crisis are at the former level, and most other people are at the latter level.

The magic in treating Methuselah is that his treatment does not involve the ego complexification sought after by the younger person. While in the treatment-destructive phase, he is letting the self go because he cannot stand the horrible reality of dying. Of course what he cannot stand he is acting out. By resonating with his entropy, he is able to risk letting the self go to more directly experience and appreciate entropy's foundational character. What was treatment-destructive behavior turns into sentiments and attitudes at the level of working alliance. The way we resonate, join, mirror, and echo Methuselah takes the most horrible thing about his existence and makes it acceptable in him as it is in us.

During the status quo phase, the self-as-possibility is locked behind rigid mortar, a castle keep that has been erected out of the very stuff that Methuselah cannot know about. The dying is portrayed in the deadness of the character armor. As we echo in all our ways, Methuselah is invited to step outside the keep, to look back, to admire its architecture, to know what it is and what it is for, to know he can go back to it when he needs, and to take some time before re-encapsulating himself. He has stepped in a magic way out of deadness into being, and he experiences the working alliance.

During the resistance to progress phase, entropy is aroused at being caused to learn a new pattern. There is a hate unleashed in the disorganization of the textualized character. As we echo this as utterly natural, expected, admired, and embraceable, Methuselah loses his fear of dissolution and returns to the concatenating urge with a motivation akin to ours. Along the way, whatever seems to be the worst objectionable of the patient, when echoed, turns out to be a source of power and growth. Entropy acted on or structuralized presents as maladjustment and regression without redemption. Found, loved, and articulated, entropy creates access to transcendence.

8

**Aestus of the Mists:
Molestation Reports
of the Frail and Ill Elderly**

Over time Aestus coalesced out of the mists, to show himself to me, Aestus the roiler, who I had only known in more distinct form as the molesting Gremlin. I was not expecting Aestus. He caught me by surprise. Soon he was materializing in more places. When I learned to look for him, I realized he was in places I never expected.

A clear majority of the female patients I have treated have reported exposure to the aestivating effects of an older man. If I were to give the percentage here, it would arouse cries of "foul play!" The angry response would not be directed at Aestus, the roiler of young children's developing egos. It would be leveled at me, for pulling back the bedsheets to reveal how many males are touching children, rubbing them, poking them, having orgasms on them and in them, taking them over, threatening them, and bending them to their wills as well as bending to the children's wills, resonating with their entropy and eros, to envelop them like a mist.

Molestation has taken the place of infanticide and is practiced by young men and older men, fathers and uncles, neighbors, friends and boarders, rich men and poor men, men under the influence of something they have ingested, and men "under the influence" even if they have not ingested anything. In fewer cases it has been practiced by men on boys, and in a few cases by women on both sexes. It is so consistent a part of the patient's history that it begs investigation.

Not once in twenty years have referring physicians suggested molestation was involved in the patient's history or presenting problems. Only infrequently have I formed an impression in the first few sessions that molestation was an issue. Not once have I ever suggested to an elderly person that molestation was in her history, nor have I steered her toward such talk. But I do try to resonate with everything coming from the patient, and this includes sexuality, while many caregivers and practitioners are likely to regard this as a taboo area.

I did suggest molestation as the core issue once, treating a young woman who had turned to prostitution early in her life and who seemed to be acting out a childhood rape many times over. She was so shocked at my interpretation that she fought me and worked to preserve the honor of the men in her life. She described my ideas as inaccurate and eventually helped me realize it was not necessary to make the interpretation. All I had to do was accept the roiler. Aestus has gathered up and given himself material form only as I have taken the attitude of embracing everything in the patient's life.

There can be no doubt that aestivating is an inviolable perquisite for society, a steam valve for infanticidal impulses that enough people go along with to ensure its continued presence. It is a more economical activity for expressing Being in being, because it incorporates both entropy and eros. Cultures are not going to give up this behavior any time soon, and the more critical scrutiny that is given to it, the more it fades into the mists so there is less and less evidence it occurred, in the mind of concerned parents, the victim, and even the victimizer. Recent efforts to pursue this phenomenon in court have aroused a professional backlash that people have applauded.

Aestus is a collective presence, and we all share him in some way. He first achieves his gauzy form in the early sexuality of the child. He exists prior to the crystallization of personality and frequents the interstices of texts as they are being molded together by the ego to form a credible and adaptive response to the pressures from within and without. He lives among us as a transpersonal ghost, easily fading from view but ever-present. He finds camouflage in the early mind and is more obvious in a dissociated part of the self.

Aestus is us at 3, 4, and 5 years of age. At these ages, the child can atomize without effort. He is himself one moment, he is someone else the next moment, and he can be no one in particular. He has mobility and strength, and he can express his entropy more clearly in action upon the world. He is experiencing a focus of his previously diffuse sexuality in the genitals. All this is happening in a character that easily atomizes.

The entropic and sexual pre-selves are aching to be fixed in place, to be given a center of organization, and Aestus is thrown into activity. He is exercising both aspects of being and ought to retain the privilege of aestivating his social world without being over-whelmed by an intense version of his own seekings in response. The child has a right to roil. Young Aestus is at risk. The people around him have to be able to keep an eye on the murder, so it is not used against the child. But when murder is enacted in erotic form, Aestus's character fixes. He grows into adult Aestus.

An evasive adult this Aestus is. He is so well hidden from prying eyes that he himself hardly knows he is there. A "complicitor" within his hazily boundaried self, he is more the virtuoso at inviting complicity in all the cultures of the world. He is among us, and most of us claim not to see him. If he is fervent in his desire, no one knows. If he plans his life out so that he can find stolen moments with the infant version of himself, no one suspects. How would he sneak around, act suspiciously, if he does not suspect himself?

Aestus of masterful intelligence, at work his whole life on a singular project. He manages to put himself in the company of a child and exclude all watchful eyes from the unfolding and working through of his project. Is it possible that the part of him that acts is dissociated in the same manner as the part of us that does not see? Aestus who works the cracks in the system—an apartment base-

ment, an empty hallway, woods that surround the elementary
school, his child's bedroom, any room next door to where all the
adults are, his brother's trust, his appointed role in the community.
He is as goal-driven as any man will get; this project gives form and
urgency to his being. He comes alive out of his malaise as a force in
the mists.

How do we look for someone who can take on every other
contour with such ease? He will look like Narcissus, a self-involved
person who has annealed love and hate and seeks to enforce the
same annealing in the child. He will look like Oedipus, a man on a
mission to sexually conquer. He will look like Ulysses, neurotic
modern man who has to investigate new thrills before he settles
down to conduct his more pedestrian affairs. It is easier to locate the
Invisible Man, who at least is painfully aware of his state.

Aestus is not pained and he is not aware. He does not seek to
know. He wants to complete. In pursuit of his project, he has invited
levels of cooperation rarely seen in any other human enterprise. He
encourages an eerie onemanship: no one ever heard of him, he
does not exist, he remains the dissolved phantom. No roomful will
be moved to acknowledge his presence, although on deeper inquiry
we will find that close to a third of the women and a fourth of the
men have been engaged by him in their youth. He is right there in·
the room with us, and he is not going to say a thing.

Masson (1984) told us how Freud discovered Aestus, but then
lost him again in the mist. The first psychoanalyst discovered him in
the lives of his patients and reported on his findings to fellow
physicians. But his findings were rejected. Subjected to criticism, he
repaired to his office to rethink his position. Once the bad publicity
died down, he came upon an elegant solution that would forever
quiet the Aestuses in his audiences. It was the child's fantasy that was
being reported as truth. The mnemic trace of an actual event and a
fantasy were equivalent. He claimed that this was how he had made
his first error.

What is one to do if one has apprehended a fellow who society
prefers remain free? The detective is damned as a false accuser,
entrapper, projector of his own private feelings. Freud turned his

back on Aestus the adult and let him waft back into the mists. It was political genius to focus on Aestus the child, who was in no position to act on his entropy in any decisive way. The adult version could make him a pariah. The child had no such power. Freud created the oedipal situation to re-explain the data gathered in his treatments. He used the truth of the oedipal drama to disclaim the presence of adult Aestus, as if both the acts of the adult and the wishes of the child could not exist simultaneously.

Freud let Aestus go and instead mystified us with a powerful Sophoclean metaphor that has still entranced us ninety years later. But he is not the architect of our blindness, only a propeller of it. Our reliance on his ideas is an example of the limits to which the artistry of blindness will reach. It was precocious to inform society of what it was up to in 1900; it will be no less precocious in 1999. We are dealing with half-realities that go evanescent as we reach for them.

Aestus is not so much dissociated or in a kind of fugue as he is nebulized. He is not fragmented into constellations of the ego as much as he is a profusion of droplets up from the smokepot's first condensations into textual form. Aestus is the part of us that nebulizes the best. He can look us in the eye and tell us with utter conviction that he has not betrayed our trust. He can forget in a flash, in a way more effective than repressing or dissociating. He de-concatenates.

A great number of my elderly patients have reported being molested. If the average treatments lasted longer than forty or fifty sessions, perhaps more would have added their own stories. Women have raised their hands in sudden recognition, bounded out of their chairs, suddenly sat up, gasped, or cried out. Their voices have frozen, broken, become strangulated, slowed tremendously, or gathered up in an explosive assertion. The idea has dawned on them, hit them like a sledge hammer, snuck up on them while they were talking about something else, or been given as an association to a dream. Or it was something they always knew but never talked about.

Rape has not figured as largely in these stories as have shaping phenomena, penetrability being evoked with more mutuality. Perhaps it is the advanced age of the patients. It is no doubt their experiences in the sessions that nothing they say is going to be criticized. It is certainly the free resonating with a host of tension songs that ordinary society would not put up with for one minute. In most cases a story is told of older men insinuating themselves into the lives and bodies of the young women or female children. What is hidden in these stories is the insinuation of the children into the poorly boundaried selves of the molesters. It comes out as the patients keep talking.

The more aware patients talk readily of their shame. It is specific. They went along with the seduction and cooperated in keeping the incident or incidents a secret. More to the point, they registered excitement. Even if the results were traumatic, or if the repetition was an unpleasant one, the stimulations are more often than not remembered as exciting. Such shame and recognition of complicity may figure in the frequency with which women recant their testimony before the bench. Behind the admission "it never happened" may lie a truth laced with shame, "it is not that *he* did something to *me*."

The resonation in the sessions frees the memories. The patient is experiencing all sorts of things that he has regularly reacted to with the suppression or repression of taboo. As the taboo is lifted, the story of aestivation is discussed openly or is brought into the treatment relationship and acted upon. Erotic transferences most frequently reveal themselves to be based on molestation experiences.

Edna told me, "I have an itch, right here, between my legs. Marry me, so you can scratch it." I explored why it was necessary for us to marry. What did she have against illicit sex? We discussed this for some time until the excitement died down and she was able to more fully describe her fantasies. Within the fourth month of such explorations she blurted out in one session that her brother had come into her room and seduced her when she was 8 years old. She described his sexual precocity and his habit of lying with older women. She never told anyone in the eighty years that had since passed.

Janice eroticized her view of the sessions, believing me to be hopelessly in love with her. She decided my sessions with other patients were perfunctory. With her, I came alive. She felt encouraged by this view and had the confidence to offer a liaison. "I never did it with anyone but my uncle and my husband. You'll be number three." I explored if she would rather I did it like her uncle, or like her husband. This led to detailed descriptions of the uncle caressing her, beginning with oral sex, and first entering her when she was 11 and large enough to accommodate him.

Louis used the sessions to describe the miserable sex life he had with his wife of sixty years. She was horrible on their wedding night, and things just got worse over the decades. Then he fell silent during the sessions, and in the induction I felt the eroticizing of our time together. Finally, he asked: "I never went for homos that much, but it's different with you and me. Here we are, all alone. What do you say you play the flute?" I asked if he preferred I blow one note at a time, or a whole chord? He was surprised at my generosity. He had been sure I was going to retreat in embarrassment. We discussed how he liked his oral sex, and he eventually made the association that his piano teacher had done it the best. He was 13 at the time. When he married at 20, his wife never had a chance. She did not even come close. Only men knew how to do it to men.

Marlene was referred for sliding her dress up to her groin and getting the cognitively impaired men to stroke her genitals. The facility wished I would teach her self-control and self-respect. But I did not bring up the incidents. I just met with her and helped her put her thoughts and feelings into words. She hiked up her dress for a number of weeks, showing her diaper, but eventually gave up that behavior. She felt absolutely no criticism from me. One day, she asked, "Good-looking fella like you must do it all day. Mind if I watch? I'd like to see you do it with a blonde." Mind? I told her I would find it highly gratifying. I asked for her various scenarios and resonated with her excitement. She volunteered one week that she had watched her mother have intercourse and she had reacted by masturbating. She left the room to find a boarder who had just moved in. Without a word, he invited her into his room and they had intercourse. She was 12.

Wilma described herself as a one-man woman. She used the sessions to tell me the great fealty she had for her husband of forty years. When he died, she remained celibate and never touched herself. It was over twenty years since she had even had a sexual thought. The intimacy of the sessions was arousing erotic excitement. "You're the only man for me. I dream about you all the time. Never another." I told her she had better not think of another man. I was a jealous lover. This immediately aroused a memory of her father telling her the same thing. She distinctly remembered him coming into her room and having intercourse with her nightly. As the sessions continued, she came to believe that he visited her much earlier than her eighth year. Now she remembered peeing freely whenever he touched her genitals. She placed this memory at the third year. Near the end of the therapy, she was reminded how her mother had always been cross with her. She accused the child of having night terrors to seduce the father coming into the room. Those events were described to her as beginning when she was two. The mother was especially upset that once the child started having night terrors, the father ended up staying in her bedroom until the next morning.

Eunice was upset that her marriage had never worked out. She spent a lot of time describing what was horrible about it, vainly hoping that she might still rescue some piece of it. The husband never seemed to touch her emotionally. On the other hand, she found me dashing and full of energy. If only he were more like me. She could take it no longer, and she propositioned me with as much directness as she could muster. "I've been married sixty-two years. Do you understand? When I hold my husband's hand, I think of you. Do you understand what I'm trying to say? I'm embarrassed." I only wished her imagination would be as rich as she could possibly make it. It was her private domain. She reacted by sharing a fantasy. As soon as she started, she blanched and covered her mouth. She had a clear memory of her father returning home from one of his drinking bouts and lying with her. They kissed most of the night, until she was beside herself with excitement. Nothing would do but intercourse. This happened when she was 13, but as the therapy progressed, she concluded there was evidence of prior incidents. The husband had been competing with this experience, and as she put it into words she integrated him into her sexual life and more fully enjoyed him.

Hilda explained that as the weeks went by, she became more intoxicated with my presence. My reactions to her comments made her conclude that everything she was feeling was wholesome and womanly. "If you don't find us a bed," she warned me, "I'm going to scream my head off! Because I can't take it anymore!" I told her I could hardly control myself and I was going mad. This aroused a memory of someone telling her, "I must have you." Out of the mists came a memory of her father putting her on his lap and stroking her genitals while she had a series of small orgasms. She thought she was 7 or 8 at the time.

Toni had a full and varied sexual life. She had been married three times and made sure she had time for consorts. She could not say she had ever had an orgasm with any of these men. Self-stimulation was the closest she came to experiencing any gratification. She noted my reactions to her confessions, hoping to excite me. In an effort to seduce me, she confided, "I put things into myself. But I would rather have you." When I explored this, she felt my reaction fell far short of what she was looking for. "You're a mean bastard for torturing me like this." I agreed that I was a mean bastard for denying her. She volunteered that her uncle was also a mean bastard, hurting her with his forced intromissions, but never taking the time to make her feel better or to give her any pleasure.

Lori Ann declared during the first month of treatment, "I would like to do all kinds of things to your body. But I would not like to ruin it with your wife." I was incredulous. "My wife? Why bring her up at a time like this!" An explication of her fantasies led to a dawning realization that she was more sexual, womanly, intense, and attractive than her mother and had taken her father away from her.

She could not explain it, but she had forgotten how she had sex with him from the time she got her period until after she got married.

Many more patients coalesce a memory of molestation out of the mists and do not necessarily configure their realizations within the treatment relationship. The information was not there, and suddenly one day it is there. It is tied to their sadness, to the weight they feel on their shoulders, to the failures of empathy they experience in the social environment, to the pervasive sense of punishment they are being subjected to in old age, where nothing is turning out as they hoped.

I am one of very few professionals with whom these women have had protracted conversations. Our relationship is sanctioned as medically necessary, and my behavior remains beyond reproach. Knowing what intense feelings can be aroused in the treatment relationship, I do not casually hold or touch the patients. I keep to the dictum of putting all thoughts and feelings into words. When the patients ask what the larger goal of the therapy is, I tell them that it is for us to learn to say everything to each other. Thus the patients feel a closeness that they have only had with their husbands, if they were lucky. Therapy with a man arouses dormant memories that were simply waiting for the right stimulus.

It is hard to generalize and conclude how widespread these experiences are. Because my purpose has been to conduct therapy over research, I can only report on my limited experience with almost a thousand patients. But I will say that Aestus has used the sessions to allow himself to be discovered. He is shy and needs the right invitation. Hatred aimed at him drives him back into the mists. The cultures seem to conduct a resistance movement to hide him in their cellars and attics, away from the prying eyes of superegos that would seek to crush him. So he knows he has support and will therefore materialize if he feels empathy.

He dies with the same urgency that he lives, seeking to bring his tensions to unbearable highs and to quench them with total release. He is the early genital child, whether he inhabits the body of a 3-year-old or 30-year-old. He is more often a merged creation of the victimizer and victim than we care to admit. He is a steam valve for society, which for some undiscovered reason has the unspoken belief that he must be allowed to roam free. He is an expression of relationship-destructive behavior, inheriting his aim from the Witch in the Nursery. He is a way that children get what they deserve. He helps in the effort to sublimate the murderous urges of adults. He will continue to enjoy his existence until society decides to curb him and teach him how to put his thoughts and feelings into words.

First of all, we would have to admit that this apparition is part of all our psyches. We would have to accept him as a bona fide reality. Our institutions would have to reflect a knowledge of his hungers and his ways. It would be better if we knew we only beg him to act out, with the way we structure adults' time with youngsters. We adjure him to be proper and we leave him in his own recognizance hoping for the best, but he cannot help himself. It would take a bill of rights for children, where we would actively limit their exposure to psychological hurt.

Then what would we do with our murderous feelings? Aestus continues to exist because he is important. I see him in the lives of my elderly patients and my youthful patients. Renouncing him would be a great act of cultural maturation. An adult in a lethal relationship with the world would realize what he has been doing, and he would have more boundaries and self-control as a result. An adult who knows where the murder is in the room is one who outgrows aestival gratifications.

9

Inviting Movement with the Regressed Patient

The surest and quickest path to wisdom for Methuselah is in contemplating the equal roles of eros and entropy in his experience. Put at risk by illness and the facts of advancing old age, he redoubles his eroticizing of being. It does not matter if it only worked marginally in the past. It is what he knows, and he relies on it more than ever, to his detriment.

He seeks to be young again. He wants the pains to go away. He arranges consultations to medically block or neutralize the insults against his body. He becomes terribly self-involved and is in no mood to adopt the great-grandparently position with family members, no matter how needy they may be for such leadership.

He reveals that he lives in the phenomenal world of the 26-year-old. When talk comes around to this theme, he realizes it is his twenty-sixth year that he never left. That year created a powerful avenue for Being into being. There was an intact marriage, money was coming into the household, and there were children to capture and portray one's own hungers for expression. Life was as close to perfect as it was ever going to get.

He has spent his private moments in that year. It is his secret garden, and if he is not too depressed, he can nourish himself with visions from that time. He had an active love life, he surrounded himself with material things he could finally afford, and he acted decisively and forcefully on the world to shape it to his needs. He felt most *alive*. The years twenty-one, eighteen, and thirty-five come up too, although less frequently. There is no other time for Methuselah besides his mid-twenties for the fullest efflorescence of Being into being. So he lives in the past and is haunted by it, unable to face the present and to learn to derive sweetness from it.

He is employing all sorts of remedies to avoid awareness of entropy. He controls the world around him with imperious force; he withdraws from it into empty indifference. He hates the people around him and the setting he now has to consider "home." He sabotages efforts to induce him toward a path of maturation. On the other hand, he locates the entropic demands of caregivers and resonates fully with them. He knows who is alienated, disgusted, beat, beat up, miserable, and in a rage. One sour look from one caregiver is of more import to him than twenty loving ministrations. The sour look remains with him and renders anything else meaningless. It puts a face on his own entropy.

He seems to be as far away from wisdom as anyone can get, but it is a peculiarity of old age that he is also closer to it than ever. For he does not have to press forward toward wisdom. He can regress into the more fully integrated position that underlies it. He does not need ego complexification to deal with his miseries. He may seem to be hell-bent on completing the ego project begun in his youth, but this is a ruse. He only needs to ease back to the quiddity of his situation to find a greater relief than any young or middle-aged person could ever hope to achieve.

Errol was referred for ripping his colostomy bag off when it was full and spreading its contents across the room. He had never accepted the operation or the device and after weeks was still not able to direct his attention to the facts of his postoperative condition. He acted as if the bag were not there, and even as he was ripping it out he would ask the staff what the fuss was about. He was diagnosed with dementia, but this seemed to be a very selective type of dementia. For he remembered much and his cognitive grasp was still adequate.

P: How ya doing?

T: How do I look?

P: Whatta ya mean, you look fine! I don't get this, I ask how ya doing, and you answer with a question!

T: Right. I want to get your ideas.

P: But what the hell do my ideas count, when I ask *you* how *you're* doing? I want to know how you feel. You might *look* okay, but not be *doing* well. See?

T: Do I see?

P: You ask the stupidest . . . listen! I was only trying to make a little conversation, to be a gentleman, see, but you have to turn the whole thing into a f— federal investigation!

At this point, the reader putting himself in the therapist's position is likely to become edgy. This may sound like the destruction of any chance for therapy. But in fact, things were going fine. Errol was acting out the entropy in the most direct sense. He was spreading his dead matter all over the room, while continuing to eroticize his relationships with staff. He remained untouched by their upset and only registered contentment and a blithe sort of blindness. Right away in our first give and take, he brought the entropy as anger into the interaction. Not only that, he used me as an object of study in order to rationally cope with his own situation: He might look okay, but not be doing well at all. During our next session he was able to be a bit less oblique.

P: How's your ass?

T: What do you want me to tell you about it?

P: Does it hurt? Does your ass hurt?

T: Should it hurt?

P: Maybe it should hurt. A lot of people have problems with their asses. Why the hell am I talking to you about your ass? Do I care?

T: What do I think?

P: What do *you* think? There you go again, asking questions about yourself. Always thinking about yourself. I'm just saying, do I care if something is wrong with your ass?

T: Do I think you care?

P: Heh, heh. This is some kind of game, isn't it? Yes, *you think I care.* You think I'm like you, and care about people, when in fact I don't give a shit about your ass.

T: What's blocking you?

P: I have bigger things to worry about, so your ass no longer appeals to me as a topic of conversation!

Errol was getting closer to the awful realization that he had been cut apart, his rectum had been sewn up, an orifice had been opened on his belly, and a tube had been inserted into him. He did it through me, carrying on in the most primitive way we can imagine, seeming to be far away from a mature response to his circumstances. In the third session he personalized his struggle.

P: What are *you* looking at?

T: What am I looking at?

P: I guess you're looking at me. Are you?

T: Let's say I was.

P: I'm not bad to look at. Not bad at all. The women *and* the men had a thing for me. So, how's your ass?

T: What do you want to know about it?

P: I want to know how it is. How does it feel? How does your ass feel?

T: How should it feel?

P: It's *your* ass! You tell me! Well, I haven't got all day! Give me the news! Does it hurt?

T: What if I said it hurt?

P: I would believe that. Your ass has been through a lot. It should hurt like hell. It should be sore as hell. Well fer chrissakes, you don't answer the question! Answer it!

T: Sometimes it sure hurts like hell.

P: Does your ass hurt as bad as mine does? Boy, getting anything out of you is impossible! You don't give a thing, do you!

Errol threw in the pronouncement about his own condition as an aside. He also let me know the narcissistic mortification posed by this operation and its aftermath, and he recognized that I was willing to look at him and find him attractive, shit and all. He also projected onto me a retentive value. I didn't give a thing. He was resonating with me, as I was with him. By the next session, his behavior came under control.

P: I stopped spreading shit on the floor.

T: (silent)

P: *I told you,* I stopped spreading shit on the floor! You act like that doesn't matter! Well, does it matter to you?

T: Should it matter to me?

P: I thought you might be proud. The room doesn't smell like shit anymore.

T: What's wrong with the smell of shit?

P: You mean you liked it?

T: I like everything about you, no matter what it looks like, what it sounds like, or what it smells like.

P   (crying): You sonuvabitch, if you're lying to me I'll kill you.

T: If I was lying I would deserve it.

Thereafter Errol cooperated with nursing with the same doesn'tmatterness he showed when he was flinging the contents of his colostomy bag around the room. He told me he realized he was dying, and he wanted the sessions to be an autobiographical report of where he had been and where he was now, to give to the grandchildren and for them to give to their grandchildren.

ACCEPT THE PATIENT, IN HIS LIVING AND HIS DYING, AND HE WILL RESONATE WITH YOUR ACCEPTANCE.

GOD'S PRESENCE

This following interchange has occurred often enough to require mention. It makes the religious sentiments of certain patients come alive with immediate import and produces a great degree of relief and composure. It deals with the concept of relief from suffering, which is central to our work as therapists.

P: Oh, doctor, I want to die. If I could, I would drop out of bed on my head and kill myself.

T: Why do you want to kill yourself?

P: I can't take the pain any longer, don't you see? I can't take living.

T: What will happen if you die?

P: Then I will get the rest I need.

T: What rest is there in death?

P: Nothing happens anymore. There is no more pain.

T: You would like to die to get rid of the pain.

P: Yes, so let me die now, please. God, take me now.

T: You're asking God to take you.

P: Yes. He can do it. He has the power.

T: Why hasn't He taken you?

P: He is not listening to me.

T: How do you know that?

P: Because I pray for relief and I don't get any.

T: Then your prayers are not heard?

P: He is not listening to me. He does not care.

T: Why doesn't He care?

P: He is not bothering with me.

T: How can you tell He is not bothering with you?

P: Then where is He? If He heard me He would do something.

T: How do you know He isn't doing something?

P: It's obvious, isn't it? I'm still here and I'm suffering.

T: Your life and suffering prove God doesn't listen?

P: He's abandoned me.

T: And when you die and pass to the other side, then He has listened?

P: Yes.

T: Why can't He be listening and watching over you right now?

P: Because He would know my suffering and take me.

T: Why can't He know your suffering and take you when He takes you?

P: (At this point the patient usually falls quiet to process this.) Why does He want me to suffer?

T: Why would He want to end your suffering?

P: If He loved me, He would want to end it.

T: Do you suppose God could love you, watch over you, prepare for your passing over to the other side, and yet not stop your suffering?

P: It's not what I want. I just want to stop suffering.

T: What if God wants to be with you, in suffering and in pleasure, in this life and its aftermath?

P (processing): You're saying I must suffer?

T: I'm suggesting God may be with you right now. I'm asking myself, why don't you know this, if it is true?

P: God would not care. (Or, God would not take the time; I just don't feel His presence; I haven't believed that much in God; Maybe there's something wrong with me.)

T: So you have a belief that prevents you from noticing you may be one with God right now?

P: Are you saying He is here?

T: Isn't He?

P: Wouldn't I know it if He was here?

T: Isn't it possible He is here right now, and you don't know it?

P: It is possible. Can't I get a sign that He is here?

T: How about our conversation?

P: What do you mean?

T: The fact that we are talking the way we are. The fact that I am here. The fact that you are surrounded by people who could give you solace. Aren't these signs that God is watching and He is with you?

P   (pondering): But I want him to take me.

T: What if He has already taken you?

P: What do you mean? I'm dead?

T: I mean, what if you are cradled in His arms right now? Then what does it matter if you are alive or you are dead?

P: He is here, right now?

T: Why not?

P: Do you notice that every time I ask you a question, you answer me with another question?

T: Is that what I have been doing?

The patient is acting out entropy in the form of emotional suffering. He does not want to acknowledge the experience of dying and is so avoidant of it he would rather just be dead. Hidden in the paradox is an important truth. In an eroticized culture, entropy needs justification of its own. The tremendous weight given to suffering relates to its lack of incorporation in the values of society. Entropy finds expression through suffering, throwing this most natural reaction into imbalance, and making it the bane of our existence.

The patient has intuited if he is to accept God in the way he was brought up to, the distinction between living and dying becomes muddled. As soon as he does that, he comes into awareness of the process of dying and balances himself. He experiences it through the infant metaphor, that he is in God's arms and can rest. He does not have to cause himself any undue suffering. In this he rediscovers the infant part of him that can return to homeostasis. I am resonating with his suffering and showing him how to accept it. The entropy can be freed up from its duty to suffering and can be experienced directly. The wisdom is in the patient articulating the worldview that has been ready to explain how this is done, the worldview offered him by his religion.

When I would take my infant children for a stroll outside, I would note how the fresh air, the sun, the birds, and the mild commotion around us put them at utter peace and helped them drop off to a happy sleep. I was in my twenties, and my worldview admitted a benign characterization of childhood, with the infant's nobility as yet unscarred and untainted. My children were one with nature around them. They found their deepest connection in such a bucolic setting, just as I did.

I raised more children in my forties. I noticed how the infants reacted to the blast of stimulation by responding to an entropic demand and retreating to the homeostasis of sleep. The days were just as beautiful and replenishing, the infants were just as cute and winsome, but my understanding of the process had altered. What gave my complex and multiply reacting ego peace and comfort was an overwhelming wash to them. The light shone with an intensity I had not realized twenty years before. The sounds of dogs barking, cars passing with a Doppler echo, and birds vying for territoriality, announcing their availability or warning of hawks, the air heavy with honeysuckle and rose, all together assailed the senses of the infants, and they promptly shut themselves off. As they become older, they add my response to theirs, but I realize we all share the legacy of entropic connection to the buzzing, booming cacophony of the world around us.

Alicia cried. She wailed and she prayed. She raised her voice above all others in the wing. Conversation was obliterated, nerves were frayed, radios went unheard. She cried so loud that other residents blared their televisions in challenging counterpoint. The noise was awful. When attention was brought to her behavior, she said nothing but cried harder.

I closed the door during our first session and watched her cry. She was oblivious to my presence. It was the same through the first month. I looked for some opportunity to break in; she gave me none. Her granddaughter, who was the last family member in the area, had repaired to South Dakota months before. No one called her, and she made no effort to call anyone. She just cried.

So I cried. I sat in the room with her and we both had a good bawl. I did not outbawl her, but I also went beyond sniffling. I sought within myself her level of grief, anger, frustration, and need for expression. We went on like this for the hour. My reaction captured her imagination, and she talked. No one had known for sure whether she could talk. The general feeling was that she had severe dementia. She had not talked to anyone since she came to the facility.

"You're crying," she remarked. "Most people can't stand to listen to me. You sit here and cry." She stopped and told me about the death of her only daughter, in a car accident, and how the granddaughter had moved away. Her husband had died twenty years before, and she had outlived all her friends. "I am crying about death," she concluded, and she used the sessions to describe what she meant. It took very little clarification for her to understand that her state of crying, unchanged as it was, represented a death of sorts. She had been playing dead. She was encouraged to talk about it, and she cooperated.

Many issues take on existential proportion in old age and late old age, and the clarification must also be along an existential dimension. Entropy takes center stage, having waited in the wings too long and now wanting its expression. It shows up in the maladaptive patterns of the elderly with consistency.

Ferdinand so bound himself in his son's death that he died in his mid-forties, right then when he lost the boy. He captured and recaptured the melding back together with the son in his alcoholism. Now, even though he was not active, he still spoke with an alcoholic drawl and thought in an alcoholic haze. *Death as merger.*

Ernie in his wilder fury killed a man and then spent his life subduing that fury, turning himself into an automaton, a slow-speaking, emotionless being who only reacted to life and brought no center to it. *Death as murder of the soul.*

Martin, whose aggression was substantiated in the cruel, deadening piecework job he held for fifty years, sitting in one spot, repeating the same hand motions minute after minute, year after year, furious at his job, himself, and his family, now in his eighties, reverberated still with that canalized fury. *Death as the job from hell.*

Frances, whose family were all lost to the concentration camps, was alive only for her children, but at all other times was dead for her vanquished family. Her feelings so consumed her they tainted the care she gave to the family. *Death as evocative love.*

Ann killed her life by controlling her impulses, and then worked to ruin the lives of the nurses and aides in the same manner. *Infanticide.*

Bill looked to sexually enslave his wife, his daughter, his granddaughters, and the women who gave him care. *Libidinized murder.*

Gwen subordinated herself to her husband with vicious intensity, awaiting his every command, spoiling him so that he became a monster of control, further allowing him to direct every part of her life and her every action when they were together. *Murder of the self.*

Perry saw every caregiver as a poisoner, had his food tasted by his wife before he would touch it, slept with the light and television on, and catnapped so he could be ready for the inevitable onslaught. *Death as the looming Other.*

Helen, fuming at the housekeepers, furious with the aides, red-faced over having to wait ten minutes for her medications, sent each meal back to the kitchen and yelled to the staff what an abomination they were, wishing the evil eye on everyone she knew in the home. *Death as rage.*

May floated into confusion, showing no interest in the time or the day or where she was. Content with reacting to everything around her but nothing in particular, she seemed to lose her identity. *Death as dis-integration of the self.*

Elma spent hours on the toilet each morning and each afternoon, mentally picturing the compacted detritus built up in her large and small intestines, claiming to feel it backing up into her stomach if she did not evacuate at least a few times a day. Speaking to no one, doing little else, she structured her day around the toilet. *Death as obsession.*

Entropy leaves us aghast. It is a fact we cannot countenance. If we understood how our material firmness was constantly seeking reunion with the soil, we would be able to mouthe nothing but a permanent scream. The young ego cannot respond with humility to the presence of death. It can only muster humiliation at its fragility and all the little ways that fragility gets found out. The echoing environment creates the potential for a transformation of our relationship with entropy. The contemplation that has to occur is given an avenue. The person can take a rest from incorporating large amounts of entropy in defense and can see more clearly. He rests from defense, and the very resting suggests to him silence, breaking down, reduction, and a proper exhaustion.

The elderly person is ripe for this knowledge. The very essence of echoing suggests to him the exhaustion of the object world. It is not going to fight him anymore. In the person of the therapist, it is going to show its entropy. It is going to deaden anything distinctive about itself, and re-form itself to be the body and mind of the patient. If the therapist can be so comfortable with his deadness, so can the patient. It is the therapist who invites the patient to become aware of the experience of dying, by modeling just that, week after week, over and over, until the patient can take it in and make it part of himself.

10

Merger and Autonomous Merger: Adaptive Use of Primitive Feeling States in the Session

Our greatest fiction, which we promulgate with a certain fierce intensity in this culture, is that we are separated and individual. The ego goes to spectacular lengths to create a distinguishable identity, but as the ego ages and nears the point of facing the completion of its transitory existence in the death of the physical self, the hoax can be laid bare. Merger can be rediscovered as the elementary condition of humankind. For we begin our life in closest proximity to another, fused at the center of our spirit, to the center of her spirit, given our nourishment in the most intimate way, our life fluids communing with our mothers', totally surrounded and held close. We are immersed in an ocean we have no way of differentiating, so we are mother, we are ocean, we are universe, and through this experience we find within ourselves the path to the oceanic and the capacity for universe-making. Our quest for spirituality and transcendence reaches back to this time of our lives. For at this time we are one with the way.

It is a timeless time, and so it may be that we have lived eons before we are born. What is a mere eighty or ninety years as an individual, compared to an eternity as the fluid, the ether, the energy of an ever-expanding universe? Where does the real part of us lie, before or after parturition? How apparent can we ever be to one another, when we enter this world in a condition so full with the universe and begin a lifetime of constriction and funneling of being?

What if time is urgently registered within our cells' rhythms, from conception on? In eighty or ninety years we have increased our height fourfold, our weight twenty-five fold, our brain fivefold. But in the so-called "nine months" of gestation we have increased our height by tens of thousands, our weight by half a million, and we have seen the DNA of the fertilized cell explode into a trillion neurons. In a riotous period of expansion, we have developed thousands of times more than we will after birth.

If each stretch of growth merited its own relative time, then we will have lived millenia before we are born and will live another ninety years after we are born. The clinical analog of this presents as a heavy and gyroscopic pull to the primitive, preverbal, prefeeling level in each session. We are all resonations in the end, just like the observable universe is probably all fields whose materiality is an artifact. We need a talking cure to find tolerable ways of resonating with others and finding better ways to puncture the walls of deadness that smother our own resonatings.

This is not how we were taught to conceive the give and take of interpersonal relations. Our rational side in the act of self-observation is the ego in its role as arch trickster. It is a minor crystallization of all we are, pretending not to recognize its proper place. The ego convinces us it is equal to our whole being. It inflates itself to dominance, and its project is to assert and reassert this dominance through each developmental period of our lives. We are caused to believe the ego project is the only serious activity of our being.

The time from departing our mother's body to departing this world amounts to the punctuation marks and editorial alterations to a roughly finished epic poem that is us. What we carry through us from Being is the larger part. Interaction with the immediate environment determines how we will generally think, talk, and function. Our legacy, having come up out of the oceanic into our present material form, is of tension patterns that uniquely color our perceptions, feelings, and joie de vivre and bring a spectrum of color to thinking, talking, and functioning.

Love, work, play, and contemplation have their energetic sources in Being. When they are in balance, there is most opportunity to express Being in being and also to fulfill the social contract. These values already have a ponderous structure of an iceberg by the time of our birth, submerged and overpowering, and are equal to the hull of any manufactured reality we send venturing in its path. The therapist pays attention to the ego and to the foundational energies behind it. He looks to keep his perceptions in an accommodative state so he can be open to experiencing the patient in the way he needs.

The research and observational methods of the physical sciences reached deeply into psychology in its last hundred years. The field of human study has built its reputation on seeking causes for effects, determining laws of behavior, and seeking to predict outcomes. On a macroscopic level, the physical laws give reliability to constructs of psychology. We use this science metaphor to process our perceptions and ideas, to create a functional model of reality.

But physics has continued its search for a theory of everything, which would even account for human behavior, and has passed startling milestones that have brought it away from science as we know it, turning the old metaphor on its head (Wolinsky 1993). It will take another hundred years for recent physical concepts to find their way into our lexicon, our thinking, our perceptions, and our mental constructions about the universe, and therefore about ourselves.

In the utilitarian physics we inherited over the last century, an action is responsible for its reaction. If you do this, then that will happen. A stimulus creates the occasion for a response. But now we know that this is only one way that the universe can be considered to be organized. The physicists have told us for the last thirty years that reaction also comes before the action itself. The flotsam of high-energy collisions mysteriously appears microseconds before the crash that is supposed to create it. There are small places within many particles where time can and frequently does seem to proceed backward.

Rents appear in our space that allow sister particles from another universe to join up with those of our universe. The subject and its antipode then either stay here or go back to the other universe before the rent closes. The elementary act of determining how the scientist will choose to measure a stream of light—as a particle or a wave—then seems to determine how the light acted for the last million years on its way to us. The movement of one subatomic particle in one laboratory can be seen to match the same movement of another particle in another laboratory. Across a seemingly empty space there is some way that the stuff of the universe connects (Capra 1985).

In this cosmos, where we try to stretch our present concepts to account for such apparent realities, things happen before they happen, time has lost its meaning as a fixer of events, more than one thing can occupy the same space at the same time, the act of human observing has the pretensions of godliness, and possibly every place in this space around us is in touch with every other place. The nature of Being lies beyond the structural properties of our perceptual and thinking systems to directly apprehend, and this requires that we ease out of the ego state to pay more attention to the miasma that feeds our being and creates tension songs and dances. We have to be open to a new view with each new patient and to the new possibilities therapy creates for the individual patient.

In the wellsprings that feed our being, everything may end up being possible. Freud told us there were no negatives in the unconscious. Everything was possible. Could it be that this is true of the universe, too? At least more is possible than we presently admit. Merger surrounds and infuses us and others. "I feel I've known you all my life" can gain literal as well as fantasy proportions. The physical space between patient and therapist and the containments of both bodies may be properly ignored someday, as distractions to the reality of shared experience.

Enough data exist for us to consider a shift of metaphors, but there is not sufficient motivation. Humankind is in the period of the lionization of character. This is the age of the individual. Little respect is paid to the possibility of shared experience for economic man or political man. All is laid on the individual and his ability to compete, to increase his autonomy, to reinforce his dominance, and to prove the superiority of the way of the ego. Little will happen until this defense heightens, achieves further focus, works out its need in utter satisfaction, and finally exhausts to let something more advanced take hold.

It is with such inklings about the more encompassing nature of the universe that we as therapists ought to consider our fused relationship to others in our ground of Being. With each new patient we are challenged to give up our set patterns and to relax with an evenly hovering attention, in order to become aware of the pre-aware, to perceive the paraperceptual, and to verbally proceed with the preverbal.

Each patient presents us with an epic poem, part conscious, part unconscious but able to be verbalized, part unconscious and unutterable, part organic from the prenatal experience with the greatest part proceeding from larger Being. The English language seems concept-starved in describing Being. So much of our perception has been put to the work of denying its presence in favor of character and erotic experience. Reductionism does not help, cutting and whittling away at phenomena. In the hopes of revealing the bare mechanics of a particular dynamic, scientists can turn a beautiful animal into an anatomized corpse. Only through the death of art does our present science lay claim to a separateness and individuality. We await a renaissance in our thinking, in the verbal capturing of what it means to be human.

Fusion, merger, oceanic bliss, Nirvana, and resonation are ideas that come close. They describe a place where time has lost its authoritarian hold, where everything is in touch and commerce with everything else. When we attempt to stretch our present psychiatric constructions to this area of our emotional being, we end up with offending terminology. This is the province of the primitive and psychotic, and very un-Western. But this is just fine, because Methuselah is very un-Western, as he is transcending his isolation and putting a name to his merger. He finds the will to lose himself, so that regression becomes regression in the service of transcendence. He finds the will to broaden his involvement with us and engages in the act of knowing it. He blends with us and appreciates the eros and entropy of it.

Methuselah feels our depathologizing influence, and in a magical turnabout, glides toward the fusing vortex he was originally fighting so hard to escape. With our resilience to give him support, he can stop being stuck in his twenties and can look to the end of his life with acceptance. His fearful mergers, made all the more upsetting because he has not understood them, are revealed to be part of the whatness of being. With our help he can learn to seek what he only recently feared. He becomes capable of autonomous merger through the repeated support gained through mutual resonations. Methuselah absorbs our great-grandparentliness. He has been aching for it all his life, and now he has found us, who will share it gladly.

The patient complains that fifteen hours in bed do not suffice in giving relief, and the therapist, accompanying the patient in the soft swoon of relaxation, worries whether the patient is getting enough sleep. The patient is confused and asks the therapist if he knows the time. The therapist mirrors the confusion, slipping through the arms of ratiocination, and asks how one might go about finding the time. After the staff counsels the resident against scratching irritating and offending peers, the therapist is able to explore how irritating and infuriating such people can be, and to join the patient in his efforts to survive.

Forgetting one of the children's names is enough to throw the patient into a panic, until the therapist confesses that the large date book he carries contains the names, ages, and birthdates of his own children—information he forgets on a regular basis. Every loss or impairment is the occasion for the crystallization of entropy into self-abasement. The merger-inviting role of the therapist allows the entropy to be brought into the relationship and reconceptualized in a manner to augment Being in being.

We merge autonomously, while the patient is merging in a self-limiting, dangerous way. He is doing it in a way to act out the entropic demand that goes to make him up. We model a better way to handle the entropy, while offering ourselves as attractors of the patient's entropy in a way that will give him relief. On the behavioral level we are demonstrating grace under pressure. When the patient sees how we handle situations, he receives exposure to new options. When we see how he observes us, we work to offer a model more achievable within his present repertoire.

At the psychodynamic level, we are shifting the terrible onus of entropy. The patient's preferred method of discharge is to attack the hated internalized object. Because this is occurring in the patient's merged state, he only ends up attacking himself. Echo interposes herself, becoming that internalized object and accepting the entropy. Over the course of the therapy she achieves more distinct self-ness in Methuselah's eyes. As his monologue with an internalized object turns to a dialogue with a real and accepting person, grand changes take place in his structures.

At the miasma, where *being* is tolerating the alterations, blockings, distortings, and stepping-down of energy, Methuselah finds Echo merging with him in the ultimate way. She is in touch with the Being that has created and defined her being. Being is the same for all. She finds the shared Being that defines her being and Methuselah's. It is here where they and the omniverse are one, and it proceeds in the therapy out of an "at-one-ment."

P: Excuse me, doctor. Can you tell me the time?
T: Do you suppose I can do that?
P: Yes, I suppose you can. It is a reasonable request. So what time is it?
T: What time should I tell you?
P: The right time, of course. The wrong time wouldn't do. I'm waiting. What's the matter with you?
T: What do you think?

P: It cannot be that you don't know the time. Look at your watch. Come on, what time is it? Cat got your tongue? What is wrong with you? Are you mental?

T: What if I said I was mental?

P: If I were you I would not go around bragging that I was mental.

T: Why not brag?

P: It's a terrible thing. I mean, this place is full of mental cases. Are you mental?

T: What impression do I give?

P: You get dressed in the morning, you drive a car, you talk for yourself. You don't *look* mental. But then, who can tell? You *might be* mental. Are you mental?

T: Let's say I'm mental.

P: Then I would not want to speak to you.

T: Why not?

P: Who wants a mental doctor?

T: Who wouldn't want one?

P   (who has been softening, feeling more at ease, feeling more self-confident): You're no good, a piece of dirt, a thing to throw away. They would throw you right in the garbage.

T: It would be their loss.

P   (Alarmed and surprised at the discovery of the mirroring, the patient laughs): Yeah, you're right.

This is a common interchange. It is often the way nursing home residents reach out to anyone who is passing by or visiting. It seems perfectly innocuous, just a factual question. But I have observed this behavior for years and have watched how the sharing of such information renders the resident more helpless and tentative, and how it feeds self-attack and does not seem to alter the behavior. A therapeutic interchange involves mirroring, which recognizes the resident's invitation to tranform his primitive merger into a transcendent one.

The second most common interchange I have encountered in the nursing home is, "Are you the eye [or foot] doctor?" This interchange occurs in hallways, dining areas, lobbies, with residents who are not patients, but it is important to persist in the interchange in order to model for the staff an attractive alternative to ignoring, avoiding, or becoming unnerved by the resident. We model for the staff how one person reacts to the merger invitation as quite apart from the manifest content of the conversation.

R: Are you the eye doctor?

T: Why do you ask?

R: I need an eye doctor. Are you the eye doctor?

T: How shall I answer?

R: You should answer *yes* and check my eyes. I've been having such trouble with these glasses. I can see some, but I can't read at all. Are you going to fix these eye glasses? Are you the eye doctor?

T: What if I say I am?

R: This would give me a great deal of relief and I could look forward to maybe seeing better. Are you the eye doctor?

T: What if I told you I wasn't?

R: I would be disappointed. Very disappointed. I'm having such trouble with my eyes. You don't know the half of it.

T: Tell me.

R: My eyes have been getting weaker and weaker and I can't stand the darkness. I'm very fearful during the day. I won't go anyplace.

T: Why not?

R: Would you go places if you couldn't see so well?

T: What would stop me?

R: Maybe nothing would stop you. Maybe you would still go here and there, but I'm afraid I'll lose my way. Should I be afraid?

T: Should I be afraid?

R: Sure, you should be petrified. I know I am. We would both be in the same boat. After all this, I still don't know if you are the eye doctor. Are you the eye doctor?

T: I wish I could be the eye doctor for you, now. Unfortunately,

I went to school to study in another field. I wonder what kept
me from studying eyes.

R: So what did you study?

T: How people think and feel. I'm the psychologist.

R: So who needs a psychologist?

The resident has been sitting in the hall for hours, waylaying
staff and visitors alike with this expression of need. Our conversations invariably end with the resident feeling more connected, more
insightful. A peace comes over him. His eyes are failing, and the
doctor is also failing. Eyes are the conduit for many of our powerful
pre-feelings through sublimation. With the loss of sight comes the
loss of this outlet.

But Echo molds herself to the tolerances within Methuselah's
character: as the power to *see* me wanes, there is a growing opportunity to resonate. The *me* that is being reached out to is the mirror.
So when the resident cries, "I am losing my sight and therefore the
ability to retain equipoise," we use ourselves to sustain the equipoise,
and we teach everyone in the milieu to do likewise.

Verbally attacking or devaluing the Other who has offered
himself up for merger will occur with more regularity than people
realize. This option for direct expulsion of poison onto a resonating
person is the sweetest one for the distraught and frustrated person.
Some of the best therapy is done in the dystonic mode, where the
entropy is acknowledged and dealt with directly.

Mantras sound up and down the halls of the nursing home,
filled with rhythmicity, a sign of the willingness to merge totally, to
find at-oneness in Being. These sounds are disconcerting, stressing,
and even poisonous to staff, because they beckon a regression most
people cannot afford to entertain. The regression they call out for
would be a cascading, uncontrollable one, without autonomy, which
makes them off-limits for everyone.

"Aah . . . aah . . . , aah . . . aah . . . , aah . . . aah . . . , aah . . .
aah . . . , aah . . . aah . . . , aah . . . aah. . . ." The beat captures the
rocking and breathing of the resident and becomes as nutritional. It
is the expression of Being in being and is giving the resident

satisfaction even as it expresses pain. The more direct acclamation of entropy unnerves most people, who devote a good part of their psychic energy to hiding theirs. They are resonating to the aggression and are becoming uncomfortable in the countertransference. We mentally move with the beat and adopt it as our own. Whatever powers the resident has to inhibit this behavior become more accessible.

"Mommaaaaaaa, mommaaaaaaa, mommaaaaaaa, mommaaaaaaa." The plaintive cry for sustenance reveals the infant in all of us and works directly against the defenses of the staff, who are forced by exigency to frame their services as professional rather than personal. They must follow strict rules of engagement, and in order to so wholly cooperate with the Resident Bill of Rights, they resort to a superego reaction. Some people can use this reaction to moderate their behavior and still empathize with regressive material, but most people cautioned against instinctual expression must respond with an equally forceful counterinstinctual response. They hate the "momma" because they disallow it in themselves. We jump to the insistent call, both as mother and as fearful infant left in the void. We take the fear and anger and we respond.

"Aiyeeeeeeeeeee! aiyeeeeeeee! aiyeeeeeeee!" The aggression is more naked here. Its primitive and direct appeal cuts through the defenses of others. It is tantamount to the old war alarum, "Cry havoc!" and calls up Awa and Ok, the male and female deities that held sway millenia before the conceptualization of Yahweh, Isis, or Tiamat. It threatens our texts as the old gods threatened the newer ones. And just as the newer gods destroyed the old, so do the textualized selves that work in the building want to erase the generators of the war cry. But we don't mind the old gods. We can go farther back, before texts, so this is nothing to us. Our approach offers the greatest potential for rapprochement.

"Unh, unh, unh, unh." The sound is unseemly, capturing the work of coitus. It is embarrassingly satisfying, an accompaniment to the anal sphincter at work. It reveals the erotic dimension of chthonic activity, the extraordinarily sweet pleasure of doing the same thing over and over again, giving in to *being* more fully. It drives the listener to distraction. We become the lover receiving the beat, the loving mother receiving the child's precious stuff.

During my Gestalt training many years back, a group participant let out a full-bodied, drawn-out, from-the-belly moan. The group leader encouraged us to join in. We moaned, repeated the initiator's rocking movements, scrunched our faces in pain, like his, and "got into it." That technique proved too active for me, because it invited a regression I was not about to risk. But we learn and grow and one day we find that we can get into it. To the extent we can regress in the service of integration, we silently adopt the person's mantra, rock back and forth in our mind's eye, and fully apprehend and appreciate what is happening, what is being communicated, what tensions are being kindled and neutralized, what force is being deflected, and where in the music the record needle has begun to slip, to create such a repetition. We allow Being to flow through us.

The great anger that is in regression reveals itself. "Martha! Martha! Martha!" the mother would call out, close to fifty times a minute, every minute of every waking hour of the day. "Martha! Martha! Martha!" until her throat rasped and her face grew red. "Martha! Martha! Martha!" until she found just the right intensity and force that would punctuate her presence into the larger reality around her without exhausting her. "Martha! Martha! Martha!" fourteen or fifteen hours a day. "Martha! Martha! Martha!" until Martha showed up in the late evening for her daily visit.

Then the mother would stop. Martha dared not look away. She described herself as totally captivated in her mother's orbit and unable to break free. If she broke eye contact, even for a moment, the mantra would ensue, a stolid, hammer-hitting, affect-blunting, obliterating, half-mesmerizing bark, until she was captured again. What Martha did not realize was that she was the sun to the mother's planet, not just an orbiting moon. Only through Martha could the mother find sustenance. Only through her did Being get some access to being.

The doctor diagnosed her with significant dementia, but due to the terrible effect she was having on the environment, he was willing to have me treat her. He did not expect much, and asked that I work on some way to calm her down. Everyone had behavior modification in mind, but I took a different route, seeking to resonate with her and to communicate at the level she needed and wanted.

P: Martha! Martha! Martha!
T: Why do you call for Martha?
P: Martha! Martha! Martha!
T: (silent, waiting for contact)
P: Martha! Martha! Martha!
T: What is it she ought to know?
P: Martha! Martha! Martha!

It did not matter what I was going to say. I was not resonating with her. I had to hunt back in the collective unconscious for my reaction to a total eclipse. I had to imagine what it would be like to have the sun get blotted out. I had to imagine myself as a mythopoetic being who felt at one with the sun and who felt its godlike presence, too. I had to sink back to the miasmic center of entropy, eating up everything in its sight. I had to feel that entropy of mine and sense the eclipse as my own obliteration. The next session went better.

P: Martha! Martha! Martha!
T: Should I call for her, too?
P: Martha! Martha! Martha!
T: (silent)
P: Martha! Martha! Martha!
T: Where *is* she?
P: Martha! Martha! Martha!

This time she included me in her mantra. We could both look for Martha. During the first session it was a defense against recognizing my presence in the room. She admitted that I was with her the second time, looking over and beckoning me to go along with her. Things went slowly for the next month. The staff considered the woman's presence on their floor as cruel and unusual punishment, and care was taken to respond to the nurses and aides in a therapeutic manner. They hoped for some behavioral influence over her and tried many things. But rewards, praise, encouragement, begging, prayer, social gatherings, firmness, hugs, and distractions did nothing to help her abate. They needed a chance to talk out their own frustrations.

When I sat with the patient, I could hear the underlying commentary. "Martha! Why did you leave me? Hateful thing! Martha! Sadist! Martha! I gave birth to you! Why hast thou forsaken me, Lord?" When I steeped myself in this dimension of her communication, felt the mother's anguish, the daughter in her mind, them-in-me, myself-as-them, I was able to intervene to encourage progressive talk, to bring the patient out of helpless merger into a building and transformative merger with me.

P: Martha! Martha! Martha!
T: It is now time to stop!
P: Why? Why do I have to stop? Shut up! Just shut up! (silence)
T: (Respecting the request, I remain silent.)
P: Where is my daughter?
T: Why would I want to know?
P: I need her. Can you get her?
T: How would I go about that?
P: Call her. I have the number. Take the number and call her.
T: What should I tell her?
P: That I need her.
T: After I call her and tell her you need her, then what?
P: She'll come.
T: How do I know she'll come?
P: She'll come, you'll see.
T: When should I ask her to come?
P: Tell her to come right now.
T: Okay, I'll call, tell her you need her and that she should come right now. What answer will I get?
P   (silent): She'll tell you she can't come.
T: Why not?

P: Because she works for a living. Her husband is on disability. She needs to work to hold onto the house.

T: But what about visiting her mother?

P: That's what I want to know.

T: What's more important, the house or her mother?

P: Her mother is more important.

T: How do we get her to understand?

P: *You* tell her. She never listens to me. You tell her how much I need her.

T: Why doesn't she listen?

P: Oh, she cries about John and the kids.

T: How old are the kids?

P: In their twenties and thirties.

T   (letting the feelings build, the same ones I heard underlying the mantra): Let me get this straight. She has a mother who needs her, yet *she* has to go out and *work* to take care of a *shiftless husband* and two *shiftless* children? What *is going on here?*

P   (sitting upright, focused, transformed, verbal): Doctor, I ask myself the same question. What is going on here? Just what is going on?

T: Yes, what the *hell* is going on here?

P: Exactly what I think to myself! What the *hell* is going on here? That little bitch put me through hell all my life. I almost died giving birth to her. She was sickly; I put my whole life on hold just to take care of her. Doctor, you don't know what I did for her. That man she married. He's never made a decent living. She married him and took care of him. Who takes care of me?

In the moment, I was taking care of her, showing her how to put her feelings into words to more fully appreciate them as an integrated being. Echo listens and understands. She does not fear angry talk, has no taboo about what can and cannot be said, accepts accusations against others regardless of their veracity, and accepts murderous feelings with the same grace as loving feelings. The patient can be more of herself in the sessions. She can bring more of Being into being.

Uncontrolled merger with the image of her daughter was symbolic of such a union with the universe. "Martha!" was equivalent to "Mother!" and through the small mother who gave her birth loomed the oceanic mother she felt calling to her. Her yells were tiny echoes of the pervasive voice of the oceanic. Eros and entropy were equally felt although not represented. The patient's call was erotic. She was not aware of the entropy except for its iceberg tip in the form of frustration. She needed support to say, "I feel isolated and alone! And full of hate!"

The analytic therapy process worked in a predictable fashion. The patient had strong feelings she brought into the transference relationship with me. Soon I was the same as she. She could exemplify through me what difficulty she had expressing herself and moving forward. I reacted with countertransference feelings. My original feeling was to hold her and hug her, rock her, steady her, give her a bottle, croon to her. But these responses were the form my resistance took, and there was no resonation when I was resistant this way. It was the miasma she wanted to take me through. She was dismantling character, going back in time. She was detextualizing, nebulizing as being, seeking to drive backward and downward through the miasma to pure Being, in her search for the oceanic.

I went with her, and it was there that I saw the cataclysmic rage, first in my self, and then in her. The emotional communication to her arose out of an understanding of my resistance. I did not want to feel the rage this woman felt. I only wanted to feel loving. This was precisely the way she had imbalanced herself, and she communicated it in the transference. Capturing the entropy was the way to restore balance. Angry words offered in the spirit of generosity allowed her to find her own way of saying what she had been yelling and screaming for weeks. Once she was out in the open, reality principle could have some leverage in getting her to organize mentally and further appreciate the oceanic. For she had found a satisfying bit of it in my echoing.

It turned out the patient's dementia was not as significant as others had supposed. There is copious literature on how depression acts as a pseudodementia. Researchers have yet to comment on how regression and psychosis also act as pseudodementia. In this patient's case, a severe regression that had not been tended to shifted over to a psychosis. She got lost in the regression until she lost her self. She fragmented and lost the ability to talk to anyone, even her daughter. All she seemed able to do was yell.

Most literature on depression as pseudodementia focuses on how to differentiate between the two. In the real world, the mild to severe dementias of elderly intensify and take on a more worrisome hue as a result of the simultaneous action of depression, regression, and psychosis. Almost all the patients I have dealt with who have a dementia diagnosis remit to varying degrees. Echoing them gives them the experience of integration, and accepting the primitiveness of their activity depathologizes it in a way to release progressive talk. What seems to have happened is that mild cognitive impairment and mild memory loss work together with emotional disturbance to lend the appearance of dementia, a comprehensive loss of ability.

11

Managing the Treatment

Echo's labors restore Methuselah's binding to the social contract and allow him to alter in a way that more of Being can be reflected in his being. She helps him figure out humankind's most vexing puzzle. She may find the old man in the corner of the garden, lost in the agora, at the head of the household, or standing by the celestial gates. She takes him as he is and works with him where he is. They go along together a little, or they go for a lot. They stay close to home, or they go far. Echo may leave Methuselah on his chosen path but more secure. Depending on the evolution of their relationship, she resolves his resistance to finding the pathless path. She resolves this resistance a little, or she resolves it a lot. By following certain benchmarks in her work, she increases her influence.

REVIVE THE PREMORBID PERSONA

In many cases all Echo has to do is offer a relationship. Her very presence evokes old organizations that were fragmenting under various pressures. Some medical illnesses have a direct effect on emotional stability. Hypothyroidism requires medication that may create emotional disturbance. Cerebral vascular accidents may leave the person with a loss of inhibition, self-control, and social antici- patory skills. Heart problems and heart attacks may do the same. Urinary tract infections disturb equanimity. A number of them in a row seem to create longer-lasting effects, much the same as a number of individual regressions, each reversible in its own right, can have a more serious additive effect.

There are over eighty causes for dementia, and mild forms of this disorder are enough to create the appearance of disintegration when we first meet the resident. Frequently, the motivations aroused in the treatment relationship are enough to deliver the resident from his seemingly disintegrated state. He makes sure he looks good for our sessions, he puts some thought into what he wants to say, and he shifts back to repertoires that stood him in good stead through- out his life. He becomes the doctor again, the sharp-witted salesman, the union representative, the troubleshooter of his engineering department, or the librarian who memorized most of the titles in his building.

Successful and adaptive behaviors that were nowhere in evi- dence become reintegrated in the holding environment of the therapy. The alteration from dysfunction to capability is so fast as to suggest this is behavior in the repertoire. There is no learning curve. If the patients were younger we might call these *transference cures*. With younger people, textualized experience is still whole, so the emphasis is on the affective realm. With the frail and ill elderly who are in the process of losing their textual puissance, we see changes in both the affective and cognitive realms. This is frequently how far such patients can go in the therapy. They use it to strengthen the control of the old, effective repertoires in their new situation.

The work or avocational persona has the power to provide needed inhibitors to maladaptive behaviors. Its built-in social antici- patory dimension is linked to a new situation. We find that the person had a long history of closing deals and employed a compre- hensive understanding of the other person in doing so. This ability seems to have gotten lost in his present milieu. He does not know how to talk to staff, he is angry and cross all the time, he approaches each situation with a sense of entitlement, and he withdraws. Some physical processes are at work to decrease the easy flow of ideas, memories, and feelings. He presents as passive-aggressive, depressed, and with a mild dementia.

Within a few sessions a significant number of these patients arouse dormant coping skills. The intensity of the treatment relationship is experienced as sharply real, in contrast with the many and fleeting contacts the resident has to tolerate within a facility that is trying to keep services high and costs down. The patient finds the will and interest to showcase his talents and rather effortlessly bridges past and present in a way that quickly subdues his maladaptive pattern.

In the countertransference this feels much different than other forms of healing. The resonations described with other patients do not seem to be as pivotal. The patient has received an emotional communication that we are going to be there fully for him, and that we enjoy him. This arouses the will to give us the gift of the premorbid personality. The sessions are spent further establishing the preeminence of this behavior in the patient's daily give-and-take. Missed sessions are an opportunity to gauge the hardiness of the behavior. It may remain without continued therapeutic support in the short term, or it may require treatment for more practice.

MAINTAIN THE COMPLEMENTARY POSITION

In any bid to stabilize the ego, this strategy is the most helpful. The ego is supported, and entropic magnifications of defense come under control. The activity of the ego is depathologized. It stops working against potential insult. It reacts with increased assimilation in the presence of a more responsive environment. This becomes less a strategy and more a way of being as the therapist uses his resonating self to listen to the patient (Margolis 1994b). This self gets very good at renaming the patient's self-pejoratives. WEAKNESS

BECOMES THE HUMBLE WARRIOR'S STRENGTH, AND FRAGMENTATION BE-
COMES LETTING GO. DECOMPENSATION BECOMES REGRESSION IN THE
SERVICE OF TRANSCENDENCE. We leech the self-attacks of their uncon-
trolled entropy through our enlightened view of the world.

The environment is pathological to the patient. We avoid adding
our voice to the stimulus barrage that heightens defense precipi-
tously, hardens it, and throws the ego off balance. DEPRESSION BECOMES
A NATURAL REACTION TO LIFE'S STRESSORS AND HOSTILITY AN INDISPENSABLE
BUILDING BLOCK TO ALL PERSONALITY. We are not sugar-coating reality for
the patient. We are introducing him to aspects of our worldview. We
embrace him as he is in order to set the stage for growth. We control
the enactment of our own entropy, which could be discharged easily
just by maintaining a painful discrepancy between the patient's position and ours.

This is the sadism of the social environment. Others around the
patient can barely corral their own impulses and must devote a good
deal of energy to that end. They pay a price for containing themselves in the arousal of aggression. This is easily aimed at the
regressed person in society. Iatrogenic righteousness reveals itself as
a wish to keep the other person regressed so he can remain attackable and at the same time act out the hidden impulses of the
converted. If anything identifies therapists, it is a hardy insistence
against this easy solution for ourselves. We are complementary even
before we learn echoing in its various forms and under its different
names.

Resonating is the ineffable substrate giving support to the
complementary position. Joining or mirroring prepares a path for
the primal experience of resonating, so that it can find a tongue in
response and flower forth in secondary process. It becomes the best
way to avoid mobilizing resistance that will freeze all therapeutic
activity. And it ought to continue deeply into the therapy. With the
elderly there is rarely a need to take an anticomplementary stance.
Supportive therapy will provide results as good as or better than
those of insight-oriented therapy. The shift from a complementary
to an anticomplementary stance at the proper time is supposed to

encourage insight, but Methuselah will develop all the insight he needs given the holding environment we maintain for him.

Eight out of ten people coming to our office stay no more than a few sessions. In the nursing home, we get to have continued contact with these eight people. Owing to the medical necessity ascertained by the physician, we get to deal with their treatment-destructive resistances. The resistant patient has a right to refuse treatment and can continue in behavior patterns that create suffering for himself and others, destroying the nursing home milieu. Those of us with the most complementary attitude achieve the widest cooperation among such residents, and we find all kinds of ways to express our wish to echo.

1. We respond to the transference issues as they immediately present in the therapy. The patient may resist transference feelings and may need us to erase any sense of a power differential. He may have strong feelings he is already acting on, and he may need us to be a worthy transference figure.

2. We enlist the staff and family as supporters. The referral has been generated between them, and they have a stake in the patient's success. When the patient's motivation may flag, there is continuing encouragement from important people that he continue. When he states that he gets nothing out of talking, these important people are instructed to persist, "Go in there and tell the doctor what you think!"

3. We check with the more destructive patient frequently, to see that the sessions are going to his satisfaction. We tap entropic tensions before they build to intolerable levels and the patient has to act out by firing us.

4. We engage in pre-therapy meetings of varying durations to develop the very sensitive patient's tolerance for our presence. We inform the physician of our activity and only shift to formal treatment as the patient demonstrates a readiness. This allows us to work with populations who we rarely see in our private office. These people are too frightened of contact, or the potential of revelation. The very thought of

therapy is an invasion. There are also those people who are content with their maladaptive behavior and would not want to give it up.

5. We work with the milieu prior to referral, to increase its therapeutic dimensions. We engage the trust of staff, residents, and families through our proactive interventions on behalf of all of them. Against this backdrop, referrals are more likely to be understood to be good things, rather than insults.

6. Most importantly, we never forget that entropy is the basic issue of management. When we know where the murder is in the room, the patient is less likely to act on it, and we are less likely to make iatrogenic gaffes.

BEHAVIORALIZE OUTCOMES

Structure the diagnosis and goals around a behavioral model. Provide clear examples of the effect the therapy is intended to have, and update every quarter, until the patient has achieved a functional adaptation to his circumstances. Focus on the diagnosis that will provide goals in line with ecological needs. For example, the patient with a history of major depression may not be experiencing problems in that realm. The passive-aggressive personality disorder or adjustment reaction with mixed emotional problems may be the pattern more aroused by the milieu. Pay attention to these and generate appropriate goals. Observe baseline performance of targeted skills and make a reasonable judgment about growth over the quarter. Examples follow.

1. *Adjustment Disorder with Depressed Mood:* The patient is depressed, anxious, withdrawn, and fears contact with peers because he might regress like them.
   - Increase antidepressive skills; practice 10 minutes+/session.
   - Practice relaxation skills 15 minutes+/session.

- Increase positive interactional behaviors 10 minutes+/ session.
- Verbalize thoughts and feelings about loss, air fears about fellow residents, and develop insight about anticipatory loss reaction.

2. *Adjustment Disorder with Anxious Mood:* The patient reports high levels of subjective distress, is uncooperative with staff because of invasive fears, repeats her upset over the loss of domicile and possessions, and feels abandoned by the adult children, who she cannot get to call her.
   - Increase self-control of distress; Subjective Units of Distress decrease from 80+ to 25-.
   - Practice cooperative skills in role-playing situations 5 minutes+/session.
   - Verbalize thoughts and feelings about loss; increase assertive skills 5 minutes+/session.
   - Report at least two gratifying calls or visits from family weekly.

3. *Adjustment Disorder with Mixed Emotional Features:* The patient seems unable to talk more than a minute or two. He is compliant and quiet, but has periods where he becomes agitated and labile. He shows little relatedness to anyone in the building.
   - Increase basic interactive skills 10 minutes+/session.
   - Increase self-control over labile and agitated behaviors; practice 15 minutes+/session.
   - Practice assertive skills 5 minutes+/session.
   - Increase relatedness skills; practice 5 minutes+/session.

4. *Adjustment Disorder with Mixed Conduct and Emotional Features:* The patient strikes staff and residents. He does not understand the effect of his behavior on his relationships. He is very upset about having no one to talk to in the facility. He is frequently anxious.
   - Increase self-control over physically aggressive behaviors; practice 20 minutes+/session.

- Increase social anticipatory skills; practice 5 minutes+/session.
- Maintain peer interactions in group with moderate therapist supports, in four out of six ten-minute intervals.
- Practice relaxation behaviors 20 minutes+/session.

5. *Passive-Aggressive Personality Disorder:* The patient refuses to take a bath or wash with the help of the aide. He attempts to leave the building with his wheelchair to find a ride out of the area. He hits peers who irritate him. He pulls his penis out and waves it at staff when he is angry.

- Practice cooperative skills 10 minutes+/session.
- Practice self-control over physically aggressive behavior 20 minutes+/session.
- Increase assertive skills; rehearse 15 minutes+/session as alternative to acting out.
- Report on progress with behavioral contract worked out with staff and family.

Such descriptions help others know where we are going with the case. They do not limit us. They only give the broad outline of our work in understandable parameters. Within our weekly notes we define our terms and give examples of how the patient is moving toward functional adaptation. Once we have addressed these concerns, we can go on to communicate the qualitative aspects that render each treatment more unique. Interestingly, even those of us who employ the most dynamic of techniques find it is easy to also follow the behavioral dimension of treatment.

DETAIL INTERVENTIONS FOR TRANSDISCIPLINARY PURPOSES

Use the notes as an opportunity to let other practitioners know the activity of the treatment. During discussions, consultations, and in-services, others will show an interest in what they can do to maintain and enhance the progress of the therapy. We can select ethically acceptable aspects of our interventions, for sharing among our colleagues, to be used with all the residents in a nursing home.

I differentially reinforced assertive (antidepressive, cooperative, relatedness) skills 5 minutes+.

I reinforced basic interactive skills through the use of evaluative feedback on Joan's progress.

I differentially reinforced positive interactional dimensions in her presentation.

I cued and reinforced self-control skills during 10-minutes+ intervals.

I provided significant (moderate, mild) therapist supports to evoke adaptive behavior.

I provided therapeutic supports to give Jenny the experience of integration.

I joined the patient's defense in order to mitigate its effect on adaptive behavior.

I sided with the patient's defenses to augment their coping dimensions.

I engaged the patient in the process of catastrophizing in order to reduce unrealistic fears.

I mirrored the affect in a move to provide therapeutic support.

I reflected the patient's resistance in an effort to attenuate its hold on adaptive functions.

I helped the patient talk freely.

I helped the patient talk freely and share all his thoughts and feelings on the subject.

I helped the patient have all his thoughts and feelings on this subject.

I helped Norman verbalize thoughts and feelings on this theme.

I helped Mr. Smith articulate his more intense feelings on the matter in order to reduce the press to act out.

I helped Marie more comprehensively express her thoughts and feelings.

I encouraged Jack to elaborate on this theme in order to shed light on its influence in his life.

I worked with the patient to facilitate the internalization of my accepting and positive attitude.

I intervened in a manner to help the resident relate to me as a positive introject.

I specifically geared my comments in order to "share the badness" in the room and reduce superego resistance.

I helped Horace identify faulty beliefs creating negative feelings.

I helped the patient identify the firing pattern in the BASIC I.D.

We worked to identify how these affects (sensations, images, cognitions, interpersonal patterns) were subtly supporting the present behavior patterns we are working on.

We practiced antidepressive skills during 5-minute+ intervals.

We rehearsed assertive skills in the presence of therapist-induced mild stressors for 10 minutes+/session.

We role-played situations that evoke combative behaviors and focused on socially acceptable alternatives during 15-minute+ intervals.

I interrupted the pattern of negative self-arousal to reduce its potency.

I helped the patient practice these techniques with me for 20 minutes+.

I reacted within the bounds expected in peer relations during this interval of interactive practice, to facilitate generalization.

I helped the patient practice self-affirmation skills for 10 minutes+ during the session.

I mildly cued three self-esteem expressions during the sessions and followed with evaluative feedback.

I employed Socratic questioning to help the patient develop a more functional belief about this kind of situation.

I confronted Jack with the underlying meaning of his requests (talk, actions, proclivities) and helped him to have all his thoughts and feelings in response.

I clarified with Jack what important issues (facets of behavior, thought processes) we ought to examine.

I interpreted to Jack how I understood his unconscious motives, in experience-near language, and helped him react.

I engaged Jack in a process of working through the interpretation that his concern over the effectiveness of the caregivers was a hidden way to let out his anger toward his own children.

We focused on those elements of adaptive behavior that could support Jack in his efforts to self-control lability (aggressiveness, acting out, agitations, episodes of verbal abuse).

I studied with Ann what prevented her from interacting with peers (cooperating with the treatment regimen, practicing adaptive behaviors, asserting herself to the family).

I silently analyzed what blocked Bradley in his effort to function more adaptively in this area.

I explored with Carl what counterforces acted to prevent his cooperation with staff.

I asked Elvira to report on her efforts to take this newly learned pattern outside the treatment relationship.

I asked Frank to detail all the problems he experienced in attempting to generalize this behavior, in order to reduce his resistances.

I discussed with George his efforts to generalize assertive behavior in the presence of milieu-supplied cues.

I provided the proper emotional communication to help Gerry reduce her self-attacks (experience the support she needed to talk freely, to feel understood, to attenuate the resistance to cooperating).

In accordance with clinical practice for severely regressed patients, I observed and respected Jenny's contact function as a measure of what she was able to tolerate today.

In accordance with clinical practice in the case of significant regression, I respected Jenny's need for silence, asking three factual and emotionally cool questions to establish my presence and to prevent pathological regression.

I was careful to let Peggy structure the session and speak freely, to air her thoughts and feelings in a way she needed to.

I turned the exploration to myself, in order to protect Peggy's fragile defenses and to give her a chance to build her skills of rationalization.

I reinforced the coping dimensions of Peggy's neurotic defenses.

I accepted Peggy's idealization of me and encouraged her to more comprehensively articulate her thoughts and feelings.

I explored how I might be represented in that dream (story, fantasy) as a way of making her emotional themes more immediate and accessible in the treatment.

I drew Marjorie's angry behavior into the treatment to better establish stimulus control over its expression.

I silently analyzed the organizing principle that is distorting Marjorie's view of social interactions (causing her to function maladaptively, compelling arguments and victimization, encouraging exposure that results in hurt).

I studied with Margaret how she conceptualized the family's behavior, going with her present need to protect her self-esteem.

I modeled healthful constructive aggression paradigmatically and sought Margaret's reaction.

I explored with Robert what he had against doing that (feeling that), to get at the underlying and unexpressed wish.

I found yet another way to interpret the pattern and give examples, in accordance with the clinical reality of finding many ways to help the patient discover organizing principles.

I helped Moira express herself in a way that she could stabilize and regain emotional equipoise.

I helped Stan articulate the experience of minor empathic failure, to increase ego controls and functioning.

I facilitated between-session risk-taking.

I encouraged Yetta to carry out her homework assignment.

I worked to increase my positive reinforcement value in the treatment.

I facilitated imitation of my behavior, followed by a subsequent
articulation to strengthen antecedents to future expression.

I intervened to maintain the patient's hope (positive expectan-
cies) during this difficult time.

I demonstrated empathy (positive regard, congruent behavior)
toward the end of promoting progressive communications.

I provided for the internalization of the therapist's good-
enough aspects.

I studied with Howard his distorted views on this matter, in a
way to relax his defenses and to allow for a more rational
approach.

I dimensionalized the problem into graded tasks with the
patient.

Therapeutic interventions are intriguing to doctors, nurses,
and specialists from a variety of other fields. Their basic repertoire
consists of exhorting the resident to cooperate and relying on the
power of authority to make a recommendation stick. They will
carefully follow our approaches with the resident and glean what
they can. Thus, in-services are generally well-attended, if they are
aimed at a transdisciplinary sharing of technique. Because the
labors of Echo are sensitive to iatrogenic effects, many psychological
interventions are ethically acceptable for adoption by the nursing
home staff.

At first others are a little suprised by our interventions. It takes
discussion to bring them more squarely into our world. But after a
bit, what seemed sleight-of-hand, paradoxical, negative psychology
tactics become a way of being with the frail and ill when they are in
emotional pain, or causing pain for others. Trying to be as articulate
as possible about our work gains us adherents and helpers.

EMBRACE RESISTANCE

Enjoy the patient. Resonate to him as you would to your infant child
taking his first steps in your living room. Acknowledge the treat of

having an elder share with you the story of his emotional life. Lean forward toward the anaclitic, or early dependency needs, of the patient. He responds well to gratifications that are part of your ongoing emotional communication. Let the interaction reflect that you are willing to listen to requests and honor those that have a therapeutic impact on the patient's life.

Echo knows how to laugh with the patient. Her explorations continue to reveal the absurdity of life. With her a chronic moan can turn into a laugh. People are so sure of the immanence of feeling, sure of its depth, committed to it. They are not going to get any supplies so they might as well moan and declare their entropic need. They are patently amazed when a simple turn of a phrase makes them discard one feeling and flip over to its opposite.

P: I'm dying.
T: Me, too.

The image of the worst possible future loses its horrific edge in that moment. There is at least surprise and usually laughter.

P: I can't remember a thing.
T: Why do you think I carry this leather book around? I can't remember a thing either.

This intervention has literally aroused people to reach forward and hug me tightly. They are so filled with joy they don't know what to do. They have to touch in order to express the love they feel at that moment.

P: My arthritis is horrible. Even the slightest move causes me pain.
T: After years of working in the freezing weather, I have a bad case of arthritis. The doctors say it is just going to get worse and worse.

The patient becomes assured that we are prepared to deliver the narcissistic supplies he needs in order to go on. We take care of him as no one else dares to, by embracing objectionables and by echoing.

P: I'm so depressed I can't talk or move. I'm almost frozen.
T: What do you have against being frozen?
P: I can't imagine anything worthwhile about it. Would you like to be frozen?
T: What would I have against it?
P: That's a wise-guy answer, you know that?

The patient can preserve the defense against overstimulation that depression affords, while at the same time investigating anti-depressive attitudes. He is willing to turn the anger against the therapist in a way that the self-attacks can be worked on and controlled.

P: I don't do a thing all day. I just sit in this one spot. I'm bored to tears.
T: What's the matter with being bored?
P: *You* don't mind if I'm bored! I bet your life isn't boring.
T: Why isn't it boring?

The patient has been prepared to dig his heels deeply into the carpet and prevent anyone from influencing him of his perfect right to vegetate. A simple embracing arouses an interest in the therapist's life. Through this vehicle, motivation is going to build.

P: They piss themselves, they shit themselves, they drool. The pig at the table stuffs her face like she never saw food before. They act like animals!
T: Why do you suppose?
P: Why are you asking me? They've been that way all their lives! Disgusting animals. Used to doing whatever they want.
T: How come they do whatever they want?
P: Nobody taught them any better. They are selfish and hateful

old people. But I think you don't mind them. You condone
them, don't you.

T: Should I do that?

P: Should you condone hateful old people? I don't think so.

T: Why not?

The patient is describing all the warded off delights that he
would never allow himself. He is really talking about his shadow side
when he describes his peers. His own hatefulness and contempt
relax as he feels understood in the therapy. Echo has found a way to
join his hidden resistance; he feels a greater kinship to his regressed
peers than he dare say.

P: You know, I have a special feeling for you. You could be my
      son, or my brother. Yes, it is a very special feeling I have for
      you.

T: And I for you.

What might be overstimulating to a younger patient is generally
safer with the elderly one. Methuselah is in no condition to go into
action, and frank gratification produces strength and trust.

P: You know I find you utterly stupid and I wonder how a man
      like you could be so stupid.

T: It's a real mystery to me, too. Any ideas?

Hateful projections are accepted in a way to reduce the need
for that defense. If we can accept such pejoratives, then so can
Methuselah learn to listen to his self-hate and handle it with some
aplomb.

P: I hate your guts! When I see you I want to spit!

T: And what is wrong with that?

We have all our thoughts and feelings, resonating with Methuselah. At the same time, we show him how to become free from his

entropic acting out. Dementia does not stop us from embracing the patient. We show the staff how validating Methuselah is more likely to arouse enough ego integration to permit the very reality testing they are desperately trying to evoke with direct measures.

P: It's going to be Tuesday all week.
T: This is what my calendar shows.

P: Pull yourself together. You look like hell. You're a sloppy mess.
T: Sorry. I'll get on it right away.

P: Where are my dentures? You promised them weeks ago. Medicaid quack!
T: What's wrong with me? I'll get on it right away!

P: The clock has two second hands on it.
T: Since the Swiss lost control of the clock market, clocks have never been the same.

P: You scared the crap out of me last night, sneaking into my room with a mask on!
T: Where did I get the nerve?

Embracing is not equivalent to kindliness. Echo's resonatings take on different forms for onlookers, and can sound paradoxical or off the track.

P: I want to be like you. You know, easygoing. Likable. So I stole some of your lines. I hope you don't mind. I even put on a tie and suit today.
T: I confess this is driving me to distraction. But it's important I ignore my feelings, and you do what works for you.

P: I was a fool. I cried and told my daughter how much I needed her. She has never seen me cry before. I felt like such a fool.

T: This was the right feeling. Your daughter is not supposed to know you are able to cry. Your job is to hide that from her. It was foolish to reveal your humanity.

P: I accepted the amputation. I let the doctors convince me. Believe me I'd rather be dead. If I suffer it will be all your fault. I will hold you personally responsible.

T: As well you should. This is all my fault.

P: Look how you made me love you. How can I die in peace now? You have taken away my peace. I feel terrible.

T: You are in love and you feel terrible. Congratulations. You have been reborn, and now you are alive.

Anger needs to be accepted in a way that the entropy can be consciously examined and owned. This is the best way for acting out to come under control. This calls for a kind of embracing that the average person may not be used to hearing.

P: I smacked both my wives. I sent the first one to the hospital. I hate this.

T: Why? Are you the only angry, out-of-control man in the world?

P: It has always seemed to me that people were always picking on me. I think it's all right to tell you I have a deep disaffection for others. It starts there. That's where my problems start.

T: It's hate. It's the natural hate for the Other.

P: I killed a man when I was 18. I punched him until he stopped moving. I killed him.

T: You're a murderer.

P: All those months I thought about suicide. I need to confess this. I kept thinking about you. I kept seeing you there. You know what I mean?

T: You were thinking maybe you'd push me off the ledge first and see what kind of a splat I made. Homicide is equally attractive to you, then.

P: Thanks to you I made friends with the snooty old fart next door. The whole time I hated you.

T: You did the right thing. You felt all your feelings, but you acted on your goals.

P: I have been willing to change. You haven't tried to give me any direction. It's your fault.

T: I take all the blame.

P: I'd hate to think I'm this miserable bastard that my kids hate.

T: What do you have against being a miserable bastard?

P: I'm a rotten bastard. A really hateful bastard. No one can stand me. I'm the worst.

T: You are one rotten bastard.

P: I'm so tired. So weak. So unmotivated. I lie here like a lox. I am exhausted.

T: You are bent over like a limp boot.

P: It's me, doctor. You have tried your best to cure me. I am beyond your help.

T: I did my best. You are a hopeless case.

Embracing resistance creates the potential for change. The structuralized entropy of the Freudian colander softens, releasing the energies of being for expression and for capturing in consciousness. We must not be afraid to embrace anything and everything that we are offered.

P: My feet stink.

T: Stink? Why not aromatic?

P: I hate my son, and I would love to kill him for placing me here.

T: Why does that upset you? Why aren't you excited with the possibility?

P: My son's marrying for the fourth time. I'm sure she's another bimbo.

T: You could save his life by marrying him yourself. What's stopping you from proposing?

BE INTEGRATIVE IN APPROACH

Harriet had resided comfortably in the new nursing home for half a year. Her daughter lived close by and promised to take her home should she wish. The care was good and plentiful. The food was of very acceptable quality. At 86, Harriet enjoyed the company of alert peers and attended recreation regularly. She reported general contentment with the placement. She had seen the building go up and had negotiated long and hard for the best room. She felt she exercised a good degree of autonomy.

Although things seemed to be going well during this time, the diabetic disease process that prompted the placement was active, and by the end of the year she required an amputation. She returned from the operation in a severe depression. During this time her three close friends became ill and room-bound. In the next year all three died.

Harriet began to call out repetitively to staff. During the day shift she asked to toilet an average of three times per hour, feeling a continued urgency of the bowels. She asked for water an average of ten times per hour. She called out to people to be with her, stopping each and every passerby from her strategic spot in front of the nurse's station. When the home first opened, she experienced a quicker reaction to her needs, and she felt no panic. During this second year, the home reduced its staffing, and responses were not as quick or as frequent. She was seized with panic attacks.

She sought out visitors and screamed, "Don't put a loved one in this home! It is a damn hellhole. She'll rot and die here!" In the evenings she stepped up her yelling and refused to remain alone, up until the time she was put in bed. The nurses tried sympathizing, encouraging proper behavior, remonstrating with her, telling her how they felt, and ignoring, but to no avail.

The psychiatrist evaluated Harriet and recommended antidepressives, which she refused to take. The daughter, who used to visit daily, told the social worker she could not handle the pressure and visited only weekly. She withdrew her offer to let Harriet come to her home. Frightened, in despair, and feeling she had lost her support network, Harriet asked for psychotherapy.

In the sessions she talked freely for an hour and shared her mortal fears until they came under control. After a few sessions, her need to express her innermost feelings abated, and the focus shifted to getting me to go into action on her behalf. I explored all her different scenarios for action, in turn, getting her to achieve some partial gratification in the playing out of what she wanted. Together we found all the ways she would like to express autonomy.

This process strengthened Harriet and released anger. She spent much of the time berating me for my incompetence, disinterest, lack of compassion, and "laissez-faire attitude about people who are *drowning!*" The daughter was able to explain that this was precisely how her mother had dealt with her father in their stormy forty-year marriage. She felt her mother had killed her father with her constant attacks.

Harriet was at the precipice of death, clinging tightly to me. She could not face the Grim Reaper alone. She had horrible ideas about the end of her life and related sympathetic reactions to the dying processes of her friends. I accepted her attacks and encouraged her to enlarge upon them, to show her how one could turn humiliation into humility. She watched closely and learned.

There was tremendous pressure from the facility that Harriet cease her disruptiveness. I let her know what the staff wanted. She showed no interest in their problems, and at one point asserted, "Let 'em suffer like they make me suffer!" She needed them to understand the unspeakable fears she had faced without their help. She wanted them to walk a mile in her shoes. At this point the disruptions lost their affective intensity and seemed more a way to torture the staff members for continuing to show major empathic failure to her plight. Sympathizing with them was out of the question.

I trained the staff in the principles of behavioral contracting. Because getting Harriet to agree would be a major undertaking, we rehearsed the contract meeting. We did it a few times until the nurses understood everything about it. We role-played all the worst things the staff feared would happen. The daughter was called in to help out and to give us some idea of how well we would do.

During the meeting, the head nurse outlined the problems as she saw them and brought Harriet along every step of the way. She checked things out with Harriet and clarified any misunderstandings before proceeding. She then discussed with Harriet three basic target goals: toileting, disrupting, and repeating. In the hour-long session, it was agreed that toileting would be adhered to every two hours. Disrupting behaviors were identified and examples given. These would be purposely ignored. Socially appropriate behaviors would be acknowledged. Repeating would not bring the staff to her any sooner than once per hour for a two- to three-minute period.

Harriet listened carefully and accepted the contract, reminding staff she expected to be toileted every two hours, to have others respond to her consistently as long as she was civil, and to have exclusive time with a caregiver every hour on the hour. The staff trumpeted the meeting as a complete success, describing the resident's docility. Harriet described it as her own success, telling me her disrupting and yelling had finally gotten her the recognition she wanted. Her behavior came under control.

The staff's subsequent worry was about blinking during this showdown. I understood this as an unconscious interest in continuing to fight with this combative resident. In follow-up meetings I helped the staff explain what fears were aroused about someone breaking the contract. During these in-services I brought up the concept of countertransference. I told the staff the feelings came from Harriet. They were natural and were evoked by her. The negativity that was aroused by this resident's aggressiveness and destructiveness was explored and legitimized in an accepting manner.

There were subsequent outbursts from Harriet, but the staff was encouraged to keep with the program and to ignore such episodes as momentary downturns. Harriet remained calm and cooperative for the next year. Her daughter became more interested in our approach and was helped to understand how Harriet played on her guilt. She understood the concept of entropy and the need to be conscious of it in order to deal with her mother. Her increasing separation from the mother, although it frightened them both somewhat, also allowed both women to be more direct and honest with each other.

Harriet reacted to the therapy and the milieu interventions by channeling her destructiveness into angry talk with me. She used our help to reinstate the denial of death. She needed a multifaceted approach in order to respond to her situation with some degree of adaptation.

These are Echo's labors. They incorporate psychoanalytic technique, existential thought, Buddhist philosophy, and behavioral principles.

12

Echo and the Garden: Arousing the Healing Aspects of the Milieu

Our treatment comes in two forms in the nursing home: contact with the therapist and programming in a therapeutic milieu. Each provides an opportunity for a holding environment that will bring out the best in Methuselah. Yet each vehicle of treatment poses special problems, too. Echo is going to find it hard to be a healing presence. Counterforces will be aroused in her by Methuselah's insistent regressions and defenses. The nursing home environment also confronts blocks of different kinds in attempting to offer Methuselah some quality of life. The consulting role affords us the possibility of facilitating change in the milieu, and our acceptance of responsibility for Methuselah's welfare presses us to look more closely at ourselves.

DANTE'S *INFERNO*

The resident enters the milieu with grave prejudices. He has heard terrible things about it (Butler 1975). He remembers it as the poorhouse of his earlier years, and the stigma remains through much of his stay. Placement in such a facility is tantamount to abandonment by the family. The patient took care of his own ailing mother. No one he knew ever sent a family member to live in a foreign environment. The elderly stayed with their adult children until they became so sick they required hospitalization. This is not just a matter of breaking with tradition. It is experienced as the worst culture shock.

Methuselah knows he is not going to like anything about the nursing home. He had planned to live out his last days among his possessions and close by his family. As we interview him, we get a sense of how strongly he invested his emotions in his home, surroundings, material possessions, and schedules. The family will tell us that the Persian rugs were ratty, the furniture was beyond repair, and the refrigerator was full of food that had ripened past the edible stage weeks before.

The elderly person proudly recounts the day he bought his rugs and how he has carefully washed and mended them over the last thirty-five years. He thinks of all his furniture pieces as valuable antiques and has every intention of using up everything in the refrigerator. He explains that he can do fine in his own home, as long as the aide keeps showing up and helping out. If pressed to explain how it was he fired twelve aides in a row, he will have a perfectly good answer. He has always been particular about people in the house and has always held them to high standards. In fact, if we arrange an aide for him right now, he will even bend his strict standards and overlook the person's failings. He will say anything to get back into the house, but as soon as he is there, he will return to his old patterns. He will not see any inconsistencies in this and will challenge the children for questioning the validity of his entitlement.

The family members recount how they pleaded with their parent to be kinder to the home health aides, and they remember the imperious answers. To the very end, their parents did their best to retain maximum control. None of the patients referred to me had been in therapy just prior to nursing home placement. Family therapy would have been the proper place to resolve some of these problems, but it was not considered an option. Methuselah acted with sureness of hand and rarely doubted his decisions. He did not need to talk things out with anybody. There was a time that rational challenge might have helped Methuselah work out better methods to accommodating to his circumstances in the community, but he and the family avoided it.

Methuselah's sense of strength came from his being able to maintain an ego-syntonic environment. He was not about to engage in any foreplanning that would have raised his consciousness about his growing vulnerability. He made sure that he had things the way he wanted them, and he got people to react to him in a manner consonant with his defenses. But his very success in creating the *just right* environment at home proved his undoing in a new community. The nursing home has revealed the highly canalized nature of his life. He did not accommodate to life's stresses and strains with new learning and development of resilience. He just got his environment to fit him.

This new environment does not fit. As soon as Methuselah comes through the front doors he is assailed by sights, noises, and smells that he rejects. The nursing home may have an atrium, with high ceilings and lots of natural lighting. It does not matter that it is esthetically pleasing. It clashes with his internalized view of the smaller and smaller warren that satisfied him, where everything was within reach and comfortable, including the seat by the window that caught the afternoon light. The circulating air is annoying to him, for he preferred the quiet and still of the last few years.

There are people all over the place, and he is to have a roommate. He could hardly tolerate his spouse's habits and only put up with her out of love and habit. Here he has to get used to people whom he has no intention of liking. The roommate burps in a way as to give new meaning to the word *eructations*. He watches all the TV shows Methuselah hates. He waits until 11:30 to put out the lights. He cannot sleep unless the window is open. Because he was there first he got the bed by the window, and he will enjoy fixing

Methuselah by drawing his modesty curtains across eighty percent of the length of the room, effectively cutting off any direct sunlight.

Methuselah is going to repeatedly react to the dining area as to the set of a Fellini movie. He is shocked and dismayed by the distorted bodies, the post-stroke grimaces, the feeding appliances, the unimaginably bad table manners. Like any driver on the expressway, he cannot forgive the Other for the same excesses he allows himself. If he is ambulatory, those in wheelchairs depress him. If he is in a wheelchair, those in gerichairs depress him. If he is in a gerichair, the bedbound depress him and ought to go to a hospital, where they belong.

He regards disability and impairment as a good idea of where he is going to be soon, and he is petrified. He is angry at regression. It is bad enough to fall prey to inevitable crepitation without helping things along. He steams over people who wet themselves, who drool as they talk, who scream "nurse! nurse! nurse!" with numbing regularity. Really, his own disruptive behaviors seem redemptory in the face of this kind of regression. His soup slurping is merely an indication that he has managed to wrest some small degree of pleasure out of his otherwise arid life. The slurping of his dining mates is part of a plot to turn him into a serial killer, so he will have to spend his last days in maximum security at a federal prison. In fact, he considers his own efforts at self-control saintly, because he knows in his heart he could out-regress everybody in the place.

He sought to nestle himself within the confines of a certain socioeconomic level and now finds his efforts were for nought. The people he has studiously avoided all his life are now fellow residents and will be until the day he dies. The egalitarian nature of placements in nursing homes has been the great social leveler. The housewife, doyen, educator, sales executive, doctor, and small business owner have the challenge of trying to make peace with one another. To a large extent this is going to be a failed enterprise. Cliques will arise around like interests here and there, but mostly the residents will choose isolation. They do not have to read Sartre to be convinced hell is other people.

Methuselah tearfully describes his home. He got up at 11:00

AM, called the daughter, made himself tea and cookies, watched the news, and read a bit. He sat by the window to catch some sun, called the daughter, and made himself some tea and cookies for lunch. He walked around the house to limber up, did his duty, and called the daughter. He can lovingly describe every article he collected over his eighty or ninety years. He made sure his home was in order, handled some of his favorite belongings, made some tea and cookies and called the daughter.

By 5:30 the daughter comes, cleans up, cooks a meal, keeps him company, and gets him into bed. She bathes him every other day, either after work or during her lunch break. She shops twice weekly and cleans out the refrigerator regularly. She finds the parent has rummaged through the garbage to save the old cheese and moldy tomatoes, so she takes the garbage with her. The parent presents her with his work so far on the bills and the reports he got in the mail. He knows she spends an hour or two on the phone to complete such business but thinks little of it. It has not crossed his mind the daughter might say no, even though he has disaffected all his other children. They all said no.

The daughter describes her parent as unkempt and irresponsible. Things are left on the stove, the place is getting dirtier and dirtier, there are cigarette burns everywhere. The parent is trying to survive on a diet of tea and cookies. The daughter has to run over to the house and complete five hours of work in two, because she has to run back to her own home and do it all over again. The parent is uncooperative and tries to retain control in a way that only stretches the process out. If she stops to contemplate, it may seem to her that her husband and parent are conspiring to destroy her.

The bills, explanation of medical benefits, dunning notices, and junk mail pile up quickly. Just a call to the Medigap insurance carrier can last forty minutes. First, there is a menu to get through, then waiting time, and then a busy signal. The insurance carrier must have problems with the telephone lines, because the daughter gets cut off a lot. She has to leave messages on voice mail, only to be bothered at work the next morning for significant periods of time. When it comes to getting paid, the company runs just short of threats. When it comes to paying, the company has developed a tin ear. The hospital the parent spent a week in doesn't want to hear that the problem is with the insurance carrier. It sends a flurry of bills that drives the parent to new levels of anxiety. Much of the parent's day is spent worrying whether the hospital is going to send armed troops over to toss the place for any loose cash.

The daughter is running out of energy. She cannot be everything to the parent. The shingles need repainting, the bath has sprung a leak, the driveway has to be ripped up, and the boiler stopped working at least three times during what had to be the worst winter in memory. She is going to greater and greater lengths to make her parent comfortable, at a time when two kids still need her financial help, her husband has been complaining of chest pains, Northrup is announcing a new round of firings, and the grandson has banged up the second car so badly she probably has to replace it.

Methuselah has found a way to float grandly above the specifics. Things have been running well enough, and they are going to be fine in the future. He shows little empathy for the daughter. Although she tries to make him understand all this is going to be the death of her, he seems curiously unperturbed. The daughter understands this as selfishness and flagrant abuse. The parent diminishes the travails of the daughter, and it is true that he would not mind so much if she sacrificed her life for him. The parent cannot say this aloud, because it would be ruinous to the status quo. The daughter says it but doesn't believe it. She is the one who stayed behind to finally get the special and unique love she has sought all her life. She is risking a lot for the words and feelings she will never get.

The parent pursues his course with a doesn'tmatterness. He has become used to manipulating the environment to get his needs met, and at least one child is left to make the empathic sacrifice. He does not notice her getting older. He does not realize that she actually might die in service of the parent, but when he is in this narcissistic state, he would also let her go. He would have a good cry, he would be moved, he would get to face death at a comfortable distance, and he would learn a lot about the cycle of life. He would be enhanced by the process, rather than ravaged. Unfortunately, it would wreak havoc on the daughter's family, to have her die years before her time, and so it is a failed therapeutic exercise.

The nursing home is a godsend. It is safe and well-supervised. It is cleaner than at any time in its short history. With the advent of disposable briefs it smells fine. The food is healthy and fresh. The staff has more training than ever before, in every kind of caregiving activity. In a number of states even the nurses' aides are certified. The federal government has issued very strict guidelines in every area of long-term care, with a focus on quality of life. Its surveys carry strong punitive potential. The government means to see that the frail and elderly get the best service possible within budgetary constraints.

The hate the resident has for the nursing home is founded on his over-cathection to his former surroundings. It reflects his canalized response to life. It is not that the nursing home is awful. It is that the resident "awful-izes" his perceptions. He despises the walls he could just as well love. He rejects the bed that he could really make his own. He shrinks from food that is nutritious because it is not prepared to the consistency he likes, or with the condiments he is used to. He is sure he has fallen through a hole into the inferno, when in reality he is in a new environment he could cathect to if he willed himself to.

"How could the sleep of a rich man on a bed of feathers be better than that of a poor man on a straw mat, if the poor man's dreams are no less beautiful?" Kahlil Gibran (1989) knew all was perception and attitude. Material things do not inherently possess value. They only gain the power we accord them. Material things do create danger, because when we lose them we fall into an obstructive mourning that keeps us from loving anything new. The love and esteem we bestow upon them betoken hate for everything else. Only a small minority of residents has any epiphanies about this. The ones who suffer losses the most are referred for psychotherapy. They see themselves as cast off the bed of feathers onto the straw mat, and they believe they will never dream beautifully again.

THE MILIEU REACTS

I have had the opportunity to train over 2,000 individuals in health care over the last twenty years. Some came to a one-day seminar, some worked with me for two or more meetings, and the large majority met on a weekly or biweekly basis for two months to two years. A strong optimism persisted in most of these people. They came into the field to take care of the kindly, loving, and thankful grandparent of their dreams, and they still hope to come upon this person. As much as the lone daughter who cares for Methuselah when everyone else has bailed out, they want to get a certain feeling and acknowledgment for their caregiving efforts.

The high point in any caregiver's day is when a resident caresses her face, smiles, looks deeply into her eyes, and says, "You are an angel, dear. I know you have a place reserved for you at the right hand of God!" I have polled staff to see how often this happens. The answer is so surprisingly low that it starts to get at the problem in this environment. Of the 2,000 people who worked in the twenty or so homes where I consulted, fewer than 200 reported ever having such an interaction. And the great majority of this occurred in the 1970s, when there were more psychologically intact people living in nursing homes. The frequency has dropped closer and closer to zero. At this time I rarely get such reports.

The milieu is being controlled by the psychologies of its residents. Negative interactions tend to be more compelling than positive interactions, and primitive feelings tend to be more captivating than refined and progressive ones. As in a treatment group, where the person with the most negative resistance sets the tone for the proceedings, so do the most problematic residents enthrall others who might have acted in more constructive ways. As in a family, where the person identified as the one with the problem is an expresser for everyone, so do the most regressed residents suggest what is going on with everyone else.

The residents turn the home into one large, dysfunctional family. Entropic forces intoxicate the residents until they are unhappy with themselves, one another, the staff, the family, and the government. Depression is epidemic and becomes worse with time. This is not the depression that remits after thirteen weeks of Socratic explorations, in-session rehearsals, and between-session homework. It is one that has defensive proportions. The person is caught up in the depression as a way of avoiding overstimulation. He refuses to cooperate in directive activity. There is a will to defeat the therapist. He will only experience interest in a treatment relationship if the therapist can communicate that he feels defeated, that he is out of techniques, and that this is a hopeless case with no chance of redemption.

The average staff member is going to have a hard time with this. It is not that he cannot reason it out. It is the suffocating gravity of the feeling that threatens him. He came into the field to treat the idealized grandmother; instead, he faces the darkest side of himself. This is a cruel trick. In the induction, he is forced to consider a self that he has fought to repress. He enters the facility whistling. A sense of defeat comes quickly, and because it is carried by unseen vectors past every defense he has mounted, he feels vulnerable. He is resonating without will, caught in the maelstrom of the resident's regressions. It is not too long before he loses his whistle and his joie de vivre.

The government instituted a Resident Bill of Rights, which is strictly adhered to in any nursing home that wants to avoid punitive administrative action. Although the pendulum swing is in the right direction, it has left unclear for legions of well-meaning caregivers what kind of responses they can give in difficult situations. Unsure of the spectrum of assertive actions that are proper, staff members tend to err on the side of compliance. Caregivers are scratched, slapped, and spit on. They weather racial slurs and verbal attacks. The residents bear false witness against them, and this has had a destructive effect on the milieu.

The general reaction is for staff members to be very hard on one another and on themselves. They are likely to be guarded and careful and to pursue their responsibilities diligently. In the process, the resident loses out on the kind of contact that would fortify him the most. The staff members cannot be blamed. They are sandwiched in. Tough rules are emanating from the top, arousing a superego reaction. Inductions are issuing from below, and staff members are catching the patient's ague without much understanding of what is going on. They rigidify with reaction formation.

The nursing home can suffer these circumstances only so long. People leave for greener pastures. An adversarial relationship intensifies between staff and management. The union threatens to enforce a work slowdown just as the surveyors come in to judge the program and potentially levy fines. There is an experience of ever-increasing pressure that has important consequences on esprit de corps. People take mental health days with less worry about the position in which they leave their harried fellow workers. The staff members resist supervision, and the supervisors resist hearing their personnel.

Some nursing homes react with enlightened management. A corporate mission is determined that centers on the quality of life of the residents. One home that I consulted for promised, "To care for those who cared for us" and arranged its resources around that goal. Another home made sure that the nursing home was a home first and enacted all kinds of practices to make this a reality. A third home stressed quick reaction times for service as the most important feature of care. A fourth focused on regular meetings with residents, to understand their felt needs. This home had some younger residents with multiple sclerosis, cerebral palsy, and other physical problems. As a result of the meetings, the owner built a laundry room and a cooking room for resident use and tailored services to reflect a commitment to responsiveness.

Some homes go further and treat the staff with the same high degree of respect and care that they expect the staff to employ with the residents. This is the most enlightened decision any business can make. It humanifies the workplace and reveals a psychological sophistication about how management can influence contacts with consumers. Set the mood and persist, valuing each person in the organization. Aim for a well-functioning family. As part of the decision to take this route, homes have extended privileges to consultant psychologists. Our training seminars in this field stress the equal therapeutic responsibility the owners and managers have to the residents, families, staff, and even themselves.

AROUSING THE THERAPEUTIC DIMENSIONS OF THE MILIEU

From the very first contact, we model the attitudes and behaviors that we also espouse. We observe in a way to better understand the facility. We identify the open and hidden agendas of this corporate culture and embrace their value and necessity. We direct ourselves to the felt needs of the staff. We capture in evocative terms the strengths and positive attributes of the home. We remain accessible to all levels of the organization. Yet we are careful to intervene only where we are invited to.

We determine the themes and subthemes of the facility, many of which center on the stronger personalities in the organization. We understand how the facility likes to talk about itself and its residents. We seek out areas of concern where we can be of the greatest help right away. We do not shirk from residents who are problematic. We treat patients even where a fee is not possible due to their advanced organic impairment, or the family's inability to pay. The facility's challenges become our own. They cannot duck the difficult patient. We ought not. We show proper guest behavior, paying respect to the customs and rituals that guide the staff. We work within the role we have been relegated and gauge our success on our effect rather than on our intent.

We model integrated functioning by displaying great-grandparently precocity. Prior to our receiving privileges, there were others in the organization who were the keepers of the organization's soul. We do not want to displace them. We show a proper respect for those with a therapeutic bent who are perceived as legitimate authorities by others. We are careful not to outmother the mother. We include these people in our work on tough cases, and we succeed as a team. We encourage and identify the therapeutic actions of staff at all times.

Failure gives us a special opportunity to win the hearts and minds of the caregivers. For they certainly respect us when we succeed with a difficult situation, and they appreciate us when we create an inclusive environment for problem-solving, but they absolutely love us when we fail. Our failures determine our human proportions and increase the possibility for relatedness. Succeeding where everyone else has failed can create a lot of resentment. We know there is a hint of schadenfreude when we goof, and we purposefully take it one step further. We accept our mistake with a humility that the staff enjoys observing and will want to adopt for itself. The staff loves us because we show them how humility is the alternative to humiliation.

Corinne had the reputation as the worst resident the nursing home had served in over thirty years. She constantly complained of stomach symptoms even though every test had been done to rule out a physical problem. She would race down the hall in her wheelchair after the charge nurse, yelling "You're supposed to help me, aren't you? Help me. You're supposed to be taking care of me, aren't you? So do it!" Efforts to respond to her demands ended in frustration. Corinne needed to talk to the staff endlessly, capturing each person's eyes and not allowing any deviation. She would stare them down and repeat requests for help. The only thing that assuaged her was one-to-one contact, usually involving touch, for long periods.

She called her daughter over thirty times a day. She called the nursing station one hundred times a day, from her room. She propelled her wheelchair with her feet, accidentally ramming into the caregivers. The nurse had fallen, had broken her arm, and had gone on disability for six weeks. Two aides had also been tripped up. She cornered people who did not give her satisfactory answers and rolled her chair into them. She invaded the nurse's station and got right on top of everybody. There were heated meetings about other floors in the building shouldering some of the weight. But their head nurses would agree to take many more heavy-care residents just to avoid working with Corinne.

She was my first referral in this facility. I had recently completed my fifteenth year as a successful and sought-after professor of behavior modification at Adelphi University. This was going to be easy. I met with staff and the daughter to identify all the antecedents and consequences supporting Corinne's maladaptive pattern. I met with Corinne and had a chance to observe her. Thereafter I brought everyone into the room and we negotiated a contract. The daughter would take five calls a day. She would install an answering machine to screen further contacts. Corinne would be allowed five-minute sessions with the daughter.

The staff would give Corinne two minutes per hour of direct and uninterrupted contact. During all other times, any and all staff who passed by would contact her and give social reinforcement. Among ourselves we chose a number of adaptive behaviors that we would reinforce. Disruptive or aggressive behavior would be consequated by five minutes of timeout from reinforcement. Doors would be installed in the nurses' station to prevent entry. We would meet once a day among ourselves to maintain consistency of approach.

The staff learned how to give assertive answers and firm redirecting when they were cornered. They were encouraged to support one another in getting Corinne to her room for timeout. The plan was agreed to by all parties, and it became part of the care plan. A clinical rationale was given for all the interventions. I met with the staff to keep them strong and worked with Corinne in individual therapy to let her have her thoughts and feelings about the changes in her life. This seemed to be a well-integrated plan. Except, it did not work.

The daughter found it difficult to install an answering machine. The head nurse repeated all her complaints and said the contract was meaningless. Corinne had to *want* to behave, and she did not *want* to, so why go to all this trouble? Why did the staff have to work so hard to help her get well if *she* did not care? The aides decided timeout from reinforcement was an intervention out of proportion to Corinne's provocations. Putting doors at the nurses' station was a communication that the elderly were not wanted there. Forget that

Corinne was the only resident with the chutzpah to cross the imaginary line and enter the nurses' domain.

The social worker met with me to assess where I had gone wrong. She had been sure I was going to be successful, and things were turning out terribly. The physician second-guessed his referral for psychotherapy. The tall and imposing big shot from the outside world was getting his comeuppance. His training was in Special Education. Little did he know how difficult the elderly were. He was out of his league. This field had a collective wisdom of its own, and he was missing it. He might never get it!

I took my humiliation with grace and enlarged upon it. I met with all the staff members to tell them how this case had sobered me up. "Not all stories have a happy ending, the good guy doesn't always win, and there isn't always an uplifting moral." I was defeated, pure and simple. Corinne's powers were greater than mine. I was out of my league. The staff felt sympathy for me. They said I wasn't *that* bad. In fact, they liked some of the things I had taught them and were using them at home with their children and their own mothers.

That may be true, I countered, but it was only a measure of their ingenuity. They could turn a cow's ear into a silk purse. They could take a failed mission and find some good in it. I just could not hide behind such justifications. This field had a collective wisdom of its own, and it would take me twenty years to learn it. I could not become an elder in geriatrics until I put in my chronological time. I had a lot to learn. I had to start from the bottom up, like a tot learning to walk.

The staff members became congenial and decided to share with me what they knew about the frail and ill elderly. I showed the same deference before their knowledge that I wanted them to show before mine. But I focused on their knowledge more. God gave us twice as many ears as mouths for a reason. I used my ears. The daughter called and told me the answering machine wasn't going to work. Instead, she was just training her mother to call less. After about ten calls she was warning her that she would leave the phone off the hook. I congratulated her for her inventiveness.

New staff came on board and I told them all about my gaffe. My error had achieved mythical proportion. I was Hercules, possessed of too much hubris, and for my sins the gods threw me a pitchfork and pointed in the direction of the Augean stables. The staff loved my analogies and laughed heartily. They had never met a psychologist who had failed so miserably. Our in-services subtly shifted to the gaffes and errors of caregiving. Everybody had a story. But no matter how they tried to make me feel better, I made sure they knew my awful error would never be erased.

Now I started the biweekly in-services with, "My name is George. I am a toxiholic. I began using toxic interventions as a young man. Since I have been working here, I have had thirty-seven sober days." The staff fell in love with me. I might have lectured them on the value of self-examination and taking failure in stride. I might have given pithy lines:

"Sir, did you learn to succeed so well through practice?"

"Yes, I did."

"And what did you practice?"

"Failure."

All of these would have contained more than a hint of emotional dishonesty. When I used myself in a paradigmatic fashion, I got the point across. I am as you. I make mistakes. I am willing to learn. I am willing to open myself to the vulnerabilities implicit in cross-examination. If there is anything going wrong with this therapeutic plan with Corinne, let me be the one to model the learning process.

Without mentioning it to me, the nurses had half-doors erected at their station. Timeout was instituted. Free operant conditioning of proper social behaviors was enacted by staff at large, at the behest of the social worker. The daughter installed an answering machine and encouraged her two uncles to do the same. Corinne's furious acting out came under control. No one sought me out to tell me the news.

For years I told the story of my miserable failure with Corinne. It became part of this nursing home's hagiography. It was appreciated by all, and some people just could not get enough of it. Almost all the staff members who were involved subsequently sought me out to discuss private issues. Many referrals came from this original group, and still do. Something was touched in my colleagues, and something was touched in me.

Corinne brought the staff members into an uneasy confrontation with their own entropy. They wanted to be loving and kind, but this resident aroused the opposite: a wish to withdraw, to mentally obliterate her, to reduce the tensions she aroused. They could not handle my direct addressing of entropy. My approach was to be properly aggressive with Corinne, and in this I took their unspoken entropic demand, accepted it as my own, brought it to the surface, and turned it into a therapeutic contact. A behavioral structure is a dystonic communication to someone who is acting out. It helps, but at the same time it communicates proper aggression.

The group could have gone two ways. It could have relished the conscious experience of dying as represented in the Procrustean actions toward Corinne. It could have shied away from this invitation to precociously apprehend the dynamics involved. The second path was chosen. The aggression was left to me to own. The economic solution was to own it, yet find a way to make it palatable to the staff. This was crystallized in the concept of *failure*. The ostensible failure was that I did not influence Corinne's adaptation, but this was because no one went along with the plan.

The real failure was one of constitution. I was found to be built of entropy, as well as eros. My failure was that my entropy was showing. I was portraying in more extreme form what the staff members felt about themselves. Thou shalt not let thine entropy show! Rather than run and hide, I elaborated on the theme and fully accepted this Achilles heel. Yes, I did have the capacity to use my aggressive instincts to deal with this difficult patient. I was on safe ground because the interventions were based on solid principles of learning and also were not iatrogenic.

When I showed the way, all the players in this drama slowly gave up their reluctance and joined in, to provide a therapeutic milieu for this most difficult of residents. My constant reminders about this case were purposeful. The entropy of every person seeks to fall back out of conscious ken again, and to find expression in all the culturally accepted forms of acting out. It needs continued legitimizing to find a place in people's conscious repertoires.

WORKING ON A CASE TOGETHER

The attending physician judges medical necessity and orders psychotherapy. He has reviewed the resident's situation and sees a clear need. Different staff members have played an important part in bringing the resident's problems to the physician's attention. Thus implicit in the referral is how the staff operates as a community to the resident. The resident's problems may have merit unto themselves but also achieve sharper relief in the community. Staff perceptions are crucial.

The staff either meets formally or gathers for quick, impromptu sessions to discuss the resident's progress. During that time, there is an investigation of what works and what does not work. Even though the staff may feel the resident is beyond help, there is at least one person who is making headway with the resident. The success is examined for any help it can give the rest of the staff. There is a backdoor provision to this exercise. The staff is helped to understand that one person's success may be idiosyncratic and not at all generalizable. The success of one person is not meant to arouse self-attack among the rest of the staff. Sometimes there are ineffable forces at work, beyond anyone's control. We call it chemistry.

Protected from self-attack, the staff studies the resident and is helped to say everything about him. During the meetings, the staff members find a way of repeating what they are experiencing with the resident. For example, the resident is not cooperative with washing and toothbrushing. He avoids the caregivers at the appointed time for what we call *activities of daily living.* Some of the caregivers are missing my meeting. They are avoiding being with me at the appointed time.

Why be didactic when I can go all the way? I can demonstrate the vectors for getting along with the resident, by modeling them with the staff. I ask the staff members how I might be implicated in their missing the meeting. Much good information is gained about a better time for the meeting, how the content is frustrating, how the aides have better things to do. What would prevent them from coming next time? What can I do to make things more comfortable, more stimulating, more relevant?

The staff members repeat these interventions with the resident: "What am I doing, that you don't want me to wash you?" The aides receive valuable information about what the resident needs. "How can we prevent these problems in the future?" The resident gets to explore this question and preserve his own self-esteem. It is no longer put on him as his problem. "So we have arranged for me to come in at 7:30 tomorrow, instead of 7:00?" The resident agrees he is going to try it. "And we agree that I will make sure the water is warm enough?" The aide is responding to the resident's concerns.

My meetings with staff continue in this fashion. I must replenish the desire to turn around and do this sort of thing with the resident. For entropy is at work. Without this kind of caring stimulation, entropy drives the aides back to responding defensively and losing touch with key interventions. By taking the aides' criticisms, and holding them above blame, I am maintaining a conduit for the entropy. It is brought into the supervisory relationship and I take it. This frees the aides to establish the same kind of relationship with the resident and to encourage him to voice his entropic press, instead of acting it out.

The aides do not fail. We fail together, but I mostly take responsibility. This may sound too psychoanalytic for some practitioners, but consider the following story. After World War II, management theorists in America were investigating participatory techniques to alter the demeanor of the workplace. But American companies were doing such good business the old way that they were not motivated to adopt any of the principles. America dominated the world, and its spheres of influence resulted in the import of cheap raw materials and ready markets for the export of expensive items.

Business was so easy that participative management as an intervention would not have merited even a small blip on the screen. The Japanese took these theorists in and used them to rebuild their industries. They were desperate. They heeded the consultants' advice, and the Japanese juggernaut was born. One example captures the wisdom of their management ethos, a blend of Western ingenuity and Eastern manners. It says everything about the success of the *kaisha*, the modern Japanese corporation, and why it outflanks us.

A worker makes a mistake on the floor of the assembly plant. It is a serious one and causes the machinery of the plant to grind to a halt. The supervisor, who has been viewing events from his perch a few stories up, comes down to the factory floor. He assembles the crew, and when he has their attention, he bows deeply and asks forgiveness for his error. He puts no onus on the factory worker. This gesture is accepted by everyone, and the staff returns to its labors (Takeuchi 1985).

By way of contrast, Lee Iacocca (Gordon 1985) described the misery of approaching the U.S. Congress to bail Chrysler out in the early 1980s. He wrote that he would leave the hearings feeling like he had rocks in his head. Yet his method of keeping his own organization in tiptop shape was to put a manager a month "into the shooting barrel." A manager was chosen and his colleagues were encouraged to savage him. Of course, it was only constructive criticism, we are told. But let us know from this point on that *constructive criticism* is the leading oxymoron of our culture, a way to act out on entropic press and not be conscious of where the murder is in the room.

Iacocca was subjected to horrible pressure, and he turned around and repeated it with his managers. Within the construction of his biography, this all makes sense. He is a fellow who can take it, and who can then dish it out. He can survive in a world that the rest of us would find daunting. The amazing thing is that no one took issue with his practices. It is still perfectly honorable to act out on entropic press in the American company. Imagine how the frequency-of-repair of the Jeep would drop if management were steeped in an ethos that motivated a supervisor to bow before his workers and take responsibility. The manager kicks the supervisor who kicks the employees who kick the car.

The practice of demonstrating grace and self-effacement not only is psychoanalytic but is reflected in the best practices of Japanese management. The therapist is a transference figure, from the first time he enters the organization. Everything he says and does will be remembered. The nursing home is a fishbowl. Nothing can be hidden. No conversation can go unrecorded. No actions are meaningless. Everything is a communication. Each and every day, the therapist gets a chance to experience this environment, to resonate to it, and to offer transcendent resonations of his own. Echo knows the power of staying with the Other in a way to integrate him. Our taking responsibility is a clear example of our forthrightness in maintaining a holding environment for those we encounter.

We are playing to a packed audience. Today's world is a psychological world. Five minutes in the staff dining room will prove that. Everyone is dispensing psychological wisdom. Everyone wants to know what makes people tick, how one transcends his own mean beginnings, and what is the best way to approach residents, supervisors, spouses, and children? Our efforts are made easier as we choose understandable idioms to capture and reflect the dynamics the staff likes to talk about on its time off.

For example, the east wing has been buzzing about the concept of *enabling*. An influential nurse has been in therapy and the word came up. The joke in the facility is that nurses are born enablers. They have to work extra hard to control the urge to nurture their lovers, spouses, children, and parents. This is a powerful idiom that captures the imagination of the staff. Echo has a chance to communicate more effectively by weaving this into her patient progress notes.

Corinne has been trying to get the nurses and other staff to enable her dependent pattern. She has presented herself in a way to evoke this reaction in the caregivers. But we have talked at length about this, and they have been able to supplant enabling with empowering interventions. Today Corinne told me how frustrated she was that the staff kept "throwing things back in my lap." I helped her have her thoughts and feelings about this, to reduce the press she usually feels to act out. I reinforced self-control over labile behaviors 15 minutes+.

The staff may have some difficulty discriminating between assertive and aggressive responses to confrontation and may resort to avoiding problematic residents rather than being put in an uncomfortable position. Information is put in the notes to highlight this issue and give it some exposure.

Corinne proudly described how she cursed a fellow resident for her lack of manners. "She spit on the floor when my daughter was here, and I told her she was a lousy pig and a sonuvabitch!" I explored with Corinne how embarrassed she was by the resident's behavior, and we rehearsed an assertive alternative: "I take no pride in seeing you behave like this! I want you to show some self-control!" I differentially reinforced the assertive dimensions of her aggressive talk 10 minutes+ as we practiced the alternative declaration.

A caregiver who has lost a loved one may feel cold, isolated, and dead. She refuses to speak to anyone about her situation. The note can help provide an invitation to share.

Corinne cried bitterly over the death of her granddaughter. "God should have taken me instead. I'm an old woman!" She beseeched me, "Why? Why?" but did not want a response as much as an emotional communication. She wrapped her arms around me and cried. I held her, in my wish to let her know I had every intention of being available to her. She asked me where to go from here, and I suggested she talk about the granddaughter. She reminisced, and I helped her properly mourn her loss.

My experiences with staff members have generally gone like this. First, they do not think that talk therapy is going to have any effect on the elderly. They watch closely and see some success and some failure, too. They are helped to realize that the nursing home resident is going to do a lot better when the milieu responds to his needs and accentuates its ego-syntonic dimensions. So they get involved. They are empowered by their positive effects on the residents. Lo and behold, all their progress is mediated through listening and talk. They find that the elderly residents are just like them. They want to be understood and they want to experience resonation.

Next the staff members get a bit jealous. The residents are getting all this attention and are doing better. But what about them? Where is the chance to talk out some of their own concerns? They are afforded the opportunity. They become devotees of talk therapy and its uses in all areas of their personal lives. There are some holdouts, but that is all right. These Doubting Thomases will join the rest of the staff in the years to come. And when they do, their commitment may be even stronger than that of the people who came over to the side of psychotherapy right away.

SEMINARS IN LEADERSHIP

It is gratifying to treat fifteen or twenty percent of the residents, and to work with the staff in order to provide a therapeutic environment, but it soon becomes clear that access to management offers a chance to do the greatest amount for the greatest number of people. In terms of expenditure of energy, it is the most promising way to spend what extra time we have available. The business rule of LIMO holds well here: Limited Input, Maximum Output.

The seminars offer a place for managers to learn approaches that would humanify the workplace, increase the mutual respect within the organization, and create a mood of interdependence. Each resident has his own Integrated Care Plan that requires staff members of various departments to work closely together. Interdependence among staff goes a long way in heightening the professionalism of this activity and in increasing the quality of life of the patients.

Unfortunately, this is the type of advice managers read in their professional journals:

IN A RESISTIVE ENVIRONMENT. If the majority of employees resist cultural change, one option is to consciously alter the composition of the workforce—perhaps by encouraging employee turnover. Employee turnover can have negative consequences in terms of continuity of care and increased training costs. But in the long run, the costs may be worth it. [Riter 1994, p. 12]

This quotation appeared in the *Journal of Long-Term Care Administration.* The managers need viable alternatives to such a widely accepted approach. Anyone who has witnessed an administrator "encouraging employee turnover" knows that the bloodletting and hurt feelings leave the organization with the most hollow of victories. If you want people's loyalty, you need to show them that you are willing to work with them.

But the administrators are not at fault. They are confronting the same frustrations that Freud did. They react to the evoked impulse to smash the stone wall of resistance. When nothing works, they end up firing the person. Freud described psychoanalysis, governance, and education as the three impossible professions. The reason for this is clear. Presented with the entropic dynamics of the other person, we are hard-pressed to come up with solutions. Most of our directive techniques only seem to mobilize the stone wall we are seeking to negotiate, in reaching the other person.

I have had close to one hundred managers in the Leadership Seminar. I present them with material such as the quotation from the *Journal of Long-Term Care Administration,* and I tell them that such feelings have been historically evoked in professionals attempting to work with difficult populations. Psychotherapists also were overwhelmed by such feelings from time to time in the early history of our field, until we learned we were disaffecting the very people we wanted to work with. This is how management psychology might rewrite that paragraph:

IN A RESISTIVE ENVIRONMENT. Resistance is the natural consequence of a mismatch between people's repertoires and the demands of the workplace. Freud originally considered resistance a pathology, but in his later years he concluded it was only the character of the human being, brought into defensive relief by the environment. We welcome the resistance of the staff, we study it, and we learn to embrace it. When the employee is able to put his resistance into words, within the helpful relationship established by the manager, its counterproductive qualities will reduce. In the process, the manager has evoked the trust and loyalty of the employee, who finds that in this job, people finally understand him. He can get his basic needs met, and so he can be an effective contributor to the group mission.

During our meetings we learn to help employees come to work on time and keep their jobs. We find ways to understand the interdependent nature of human services and better intervene to support cooperativeness. We learn how to avoid mobilizing resistance. This occurs directly through the seminars as a laboratory experience. The managers find various ways to bring their difficult situations into the seminars for study.

Once we find a time to meet, one or more people in the group make a special sort of sacrifice. They typify the problems they have to face daily, by coming late or by being unable to come at all. They are usually unaware of the sacrifice they have made, which only increases the value of the learning experience. Rather than being didactic, I get to deal with them in the precise way I am suggesting they deal with their charges. We investigate whether I offered good times for us to meet. We show an interest as a group about what is going on in the person's life. We take a problem-solving approach to the issue of arriving late or missing meetings. I place the responsibility on myself for making the meetings accessible. If we get this far, I study what I might be doing to keep the person from getting to the meetings.

As these issues are examined, the person finds he can make it to the meetings. He also reports that he is adopting aspects of what he has experienced in the group. He is finding the time to reach out to his latecomers at work and to investigate what is happening. He takes a problem-solving approach. He accepts responsibility for maintaining the kind of milieu that would motivate the worker to be loyal and caring. This happens without epiphany. Rarely does the person call out, "Aha! I see what you did! I'm going to try the same thing at work!"

This is assimilative learning, but of a developmental sort. The capacity to do this is discovered in the self. It was always there. It is not a matter of the manager practicing a thoroughly foreign behavior. He was always able to do this. His own resistances have been quelled to the point where he could find this capacity and put it into action. His life gets better only because he gets in touch with his own resources. Because the interventions I used are not particularly directive or challenging, they do not stick out in any memorable way. I function as the facilitator.

The seminars become a safe place to discuss the recurring problems of management. It is progressive to help the participants talk freely and exhaustively on any topic they feel needs immediate attention. They are guided in studying the situation and in getting reactions from one another. Just as their frustration peaks and they demand to know, "But what do we *do*," I suggest they need to repeat our exercise with their own staff. That is, rather than acting on the staff in some particular way, they might encourage people to talk up and express their understanding of the situation.

Along the way, relationships are forged, people learn to talk and to listen, communication is enhanced, and the affective climate changes for the better. Without telling the participants directly, I have helped them exhaust the energy behind any potential attack, so that a more sober and transcendent dimension of their repertoire can be manifested and used. Having modeled a way to approach a problem, I find that people gravitate to it and adopt it in their own work.

The undergirding reality to the management training is that employees bring a group entropic press to the next level of the organization. The manager, department head, or supervisor needs to learn what to do with the resistances: treatment-destructive resistance, status quo resistance, and resistance to progress. To push for any goal in the facility further mobilizes these resistances. The manager learns to understand the resistance, embrace it, and love it in the same way Echo deals with Methuselah. In this way the manager controls the affective climate and even the activities of his milieu.

The staff has to believe that the nursing home is a garden, in order to help Methuselah give up the notion of hell. For the perception of Dante's *Inferno* is only the entropy of the elderly gone out of control. The aggression has nowhere to go, and it inflames the perceptual processes. Two hundred elderly people acting out entropy command the affective climate. They infect everyone around them. They create an emotional contagion. A three-pronged intervention turns things around.

Echo meets with Methuselah and resolves his resistance to contemplating the experience of dying. She meets with about fifteen to twenty percent of the residents. This reduces some of the entropic press in the facility. Next, she meets with caregiving staff to neutralize some of the resistance aroused in them by the residents. The resonations have been upsetting, and even corrosive. She serves to strengthen defenses and to protect the staff against unwanted resonations. At the same time she resolves the staff's resistance to contemplating the experience of entropic press in the conscious mind. Last, Echo meets with management to accomplish the same goals she set for herself with the residents and staff.

13

Personal Transformations
in the Therapist

As long as I saw only a few patients a day, I was able to get along with a lower state of consciousness. Whatever was being aroused in me could be put to rest by hidden palliative processes, as I kept a lot of space between sessions. There was work, some uncomfortable arousal, rest, and a resumed quiescence. I kept this up until I eventually grew tired of it. I remember a conversation in a psychoanalytic training group. A learner asked how it was that the patient gave up his narcissistic position and moved to an oedipal one. There was a lot of technical talk about this, but then a brilliant colleague gave us the answer in one short sentence. "After a while he just gets tired of narcissism."

Not much of this was evident to anybody. My work had a strong behavioral element. The clinic I worked for sent me to difficult placements and I did well. My colleagues steered the most problematic cases in my direction. I was seen as someone who knew how to handle high-pressure circumstances and work things out so everyone looked good. The residents made their functional adaptations, and the staff took part in the glory.

But I was getting tired of functioning at my level of consciousness. To press myself, I increased the number of hours with the residents. This shook things up a bit. The differing needs of such numbers of people were challenging my status quo. I was not so sure of what I knew and what I did not know. I confronted contradictions that seemed to have no resolution. Why was there no integration? Was it the failure of language? Was I heading toward paradigmatic seasickness? I would write pages and pages of ideas. My feelings raged.

> I am dying. I am part dead so another part of me can be alive.
> I am alive.

> You cannot trust anyone; people will hurt you whether they
> mean to or not.
> You take a chance, you trust, try to alter the odds in your favor.
> You can trust everyone.

> Man is a smokepot of instincts.
> Man has a mind that functions independent of his baser nature.
> Man is a potential angel, seeking actualization.

> Resistance is pathology.
> Resistance is only childhood character, expressed in adult life.
> Resistance is what the child had to do to stay alive in his family.
> Resistance is the biological penetrance of our essential constitutions in our ecology.
> Resistance is an artifact of mediocre therapy, where a proper
> task analysis has not been conducted.

> The patient is out to defeat the therapist.
> The patient communicates how poorly he does when we make
> empathic errors.
> There is no untreatable patient; he just hasn't found the right
> therapist.

There is a cure.

There is no cure.

The concept of cure misses the point of therapeutic process.

Sometimes you have to go backward to go forward.

The patient said everything, had all his thoughts and feelings, finished the analysis, went home and shot himself in the head.

The homicide is better off than the suicide.

The pedophiliac is better off than the autiste.

Cure the patient by making those tough and stringy fibers soft. That's the meaning of cure.

There is cure, only if you take care not to want it; beware therapeutic ambition.

It is acting out. It has to stop.

It is acting in.

It is reenactment. It will have to continue until the patient is ready to give it up.

Action is giddy, gratifying, a panegyric. The alternative it avoids is depression.

Put the acting out into words, to increase consciousness.

Take your static words and put them into actions, to increase your consciousness.

People get better when they feel understood.

People need to feel misunderstood. That really makes them feel understood.

Understanding is not enough.

Nobody gets better. Character will out.

I want to help you get what you want.

Help only renders the patient more helpless.

There are only two kinds of people in the world: the helper and the helped.

Help is a mean trick; it is a plastic arm in the sleeve of a jacket that we proffer to the man in the quicksand.

There is one sure way to make a friend into an enemy: help him.
To get in the graces of another, ask for his help.

Analysis is precious and valuable.
Analysis is an impossible profession.
Anal-ysis is the breaking down of shit.
The good analyst is a voyeur.
Clinical psychologists score high on Machiavellianism.

From misery to joie de vivre.
From neurotic misery to normal misery.
To feel alive.
To actualize.
To feel all our feelings.
To act on our goals rather than our feelings.
To integrate thought, act, and feeling.
To integrate mind, body, and soul.
To elongate the meandering path toward death that is called life.

I hate you!
I am having the feeling that I hate you.
I am willing to hate you, he thought privately.

Some frustration in the relationship.
No frustration.
Frustrate.
Take them out dancing.
Go to dinner with them.
Offer them your pinky finger.

Say anything you want to say.
Say everything.

Talk.
You just have to come here and be with me.

Come on time, take the couch, speak freely, and pay on time.
I want to hear everything about your emotional life.

The analyst must be able to feel his psychotic feelings.
Psychosis in the analyst is a sign he is in the wrong profession.
We are all psychotic.
Psychosis is okay if the patient has induced it in us as part of his
  own story.

There is one intervention that most economically deals with the
  patient's need.
Once you have made an interpretation, you have to find seven
  hundred new ways to repeat it.
You don't have to say much; it's a matter of having the right
  feelings for the patient.
From the analyzed countertransference resistance comes the
  right emotional communication.

Ego is reclaimed from the id.
Creative evolution.
Corrective emotional experience.
Minor empathic failures cause the ego to expand in order to
  take care of itself.
The analyst is absorbed as a positive introject. His presence
  creates choice.
The working through of an interpretation creates new behav-
  ioral options.

Transference is necessary for cure to take place.
Transference is an addiction that is pandered to by the analyst.
Transference is not required at all to treat a patient.
Participant–observer.
Authenticity of the analyst.

This was a small taste of the paradigmatic vertigo that gripped
me. Training in behavior modification, Gestalt therapy, reality

therapy, family therapy, psychoanalysis, and psychodynamic therapies jumbled together. The neat compartmentalizations fell away. Skinner assailed Freud kicked Ellis in the pants savaged Spotnitz. Round and round it went. I was becoming successful. The old organizations were beginning to weaken. There was a smell of higher consciousness.

I increased my hours. The referrals came. I was willing to put in the time to meet with the residents, contact their families, do staff in-services, and conduct meetings with managers. My skill with the elderly was developing. The private ponderings were not adversely affecting my work, as things moved toward some critical mass. The alteration of consciousness arrived after a year of pursuing a very busy schedule. Things were never the same after that. I wrote a poem to commemorate the disorganization of my lifelong grasp of self.

VICTUS

Insides   trashed   beyond recognition
Center gone   pieces flying
Rutting   banshee   fearing   light
Howling   sounds   no one hears
All   alone   with   measured   increments
Of an unstoppable insanity   I am
Slipping more each day   Dying
No   more   taste   for   the   fight
Then gone   Pointless   Dark

Is it death I seek?   Or some
Quiet   warren   where   I   can
Salve my   wounds?   Will talking
Help?   It doesn't seem to

Ad-just   Get in line   Sounds
So simple but it means a force
Scatters   the   remains   of   my   conquered

Self   I relinquish all protection
Give up the boundaries and
Show   that   inside   nothing
Has been left   It

Is poison to pretend
All   is   well   Forcing a unity where
None exists   Limbo   Let
Me die   But I don't   I
Persist   Damaged   Hollow
Going neither forward nor
Backward   Neither   succeeding
Nor failing   Marathon   Thermopylae   Alexander   clear   direct
Uninhibited   Succeed or die trying   Limbo is no place for
A Greek

I had no idea of the meaning of what I had written. I was suddenly gripped with a desire to express what was happening to me. The simple words belie the great amount of emotion that was released. I got it all out and saw this catastrophic phase of my life as an unredemptive breaking apart. My unconscious spoke here and revealed things I would only be able to interpret later.

The texts that guided my life imploded. They rattled around in such a mess that I could see my experience of the world was in fact textualized. I was never going to be able to be a Greek anymore. The Western cultural tradition was shaken at its roots. I was found to be some thing more akin to Grendel nursing his armless and bloodied side deep in the awful mere where his mother gave birth to him.

I was some thing between man and pure Being, and my reaction was to rut, to sexualize experience so as to set the texts back in place. But the texts lost their clarity and my sounds were no longer communications. We are known through the sounds we make—the persona—and my persona deconstructed to howls. The ego structure was dying, and I lost a taste for the good fight. There seemed little reason to go on feeding the mirage that I had a self and was an ego.

I was shifting to the East, and there was no one in the West who could help me. Talking was not going to help. The answers to the most important koans do not involve talk. There was a pressure to adjust—to move back into the channels of orthodoxy—but now too much was at stake. Such an effort would involve destructive forces leashed upon whatever there was of my false self.

Nothing was ever going to be clear again. My behavior would lose its decisiveness, except where it came to the facts of indecisiveness. I could be decisive about communicating the indecisiveness of things. My overused, childhood character shattered, and over the next few years I molted out of it like a snake out of an old skin. The elderly patients had brought me to the brink of detextualization and then had shoved me into the abyss. They say when you confront the abyss, your character shows itself.

Nothing of the kind happened to me. I fell into the abyss until I found a spot where I floated. Damaged and hollow, I went neither forward nor backward. I was not saved by another false self. The limbo I experience is my hovering state right over the miasma, where text generates to give Being access into being. It is here at the site of textualization that I can know every person as another facet of my possible self. As every person forms out of the miasma, I look to repeat the same dynamic in my resonations. "I am a murderer, an arsonist, a rapist. I have within me the worst of humanity."

P: What's that awful smell in the room?

T: Do I know what it is?

P: I don't know if you know. But it's awful. It . . . smells . . . like . . . shit. Shit is what it is. An awful shit smell.

T: What's awful about shit smell?

P: You like it? You like shit? Maybe it's yours!

T: It might be.

P: It *is* yours, isn't it? What did you do? Shit your pants? Jesus Christ, you shit your pants. You ought to be ashamed of yourself.

T: Why ashamed?

P: You worthless person. Shitting yourself. *I'd* be embarrassed.

T: Why would you be embarrassed?

P: It's not ladylike to shit your pants.

T: So what?

P: What do you mean, so what? Are you telling me ladies should shit their pants?

T: Let's say I was?

P: It would be a smelly, smelly world, a dirty world, a filthy dirty world full of shitters. So tell me. Are you confessing to this crime?

T: Why not?

P   (filled with love, and connected): Maybe you need to step out and get cleaned up.

This patient had ignored the imploring of staff and family. She sent the psychiatrist out of the room. She told the rabbi where to get off. She had no interest in talking to people who criticized stink. Me, a fellow shitter, she adopted. The offer for some time to clean up was such a therapeutic one, she decided to do the same for herself. She became a nice, clean old lady for the facility, as long as the two of us with our shitty personalities could revel in the muck twice a week. I could "unselfconsciously" echo in this fashion. There was no distance or difference between us, and I could invoke an autonomous merger to help with the healing process.

Such conversations with the elderly are a clear indication to many that the patient suffers from dementia. In fact she had mild cognitive impairment, but this was not the source of her problem. I have had similar situations with youngsters and adults who have passed wind, wet themselves, defecated, or thrown up. My conduct during the sessions was the same, and all were able to give up their valuable regressions for another way to bring more of Being into being.

Having relented in the energy-sapping exercise of shoring up a false self, I can befriend the instincts of the patients. This is what they were trying to communicate to me. My poem "Victus" is as much a revelation of the induced feelings from the elderly as it is a personal statement. They are persisting with overworked defenses that never protected them satisfactorily from the beginning and are ready to be resonated with. They do not need my defensiveness and reaction formation. They need to be embraced, so that they can reduce the frenetic use of text.

The suffering of the residents is replete. Their feeling creates a dangerous whirlpool most people want to steer clear of. Professionals in long-term care are exposed to more suffering in a week than most people are all their lives:

"After I die, I go into the ground. There is nothing more to it."

"Nothing matters. I die soon. As for me, it all ends."

"There is no God. God is a child's fairy tale."

"Four years I spent in the forests, eating roots and bugs, living on handouts, freezing, avoiding the dogs and the troops. Four years, until the liberation army saved us. I thought I was forever free. But fifty years later, I am back in the forest."

"I know of a woman who went into the hospital one night, and the next night she was gone. What a blessing. Why can't this happen to me? I can't take it anymore. Not this suffering, day after day."

"Help me help me help me Help! me. You sonuvabitch. Help me help me HELP! me. Help, help, help, help, help me help me help me."

"I could quote Shelley, Keats, Byron. I read every book in our public library. My grandchildren question me about my background, and I forget. I feel horrible."

"With this hand I could rip a wall down. With this hand, I'm weak as a baby. Half of me is gone. I've never not worked. I'm half dead."

"I don't feel that I can go on. I'm suffering so badly. My living is suffering. When I was 60 I spent my days enjoying my memories. When I was 80 so many of the memories had gone. Now I lie still, with no memories at all. I have nothing to do, nothing to think about. I just suffer."

The suffering is the acting out of entropy. Even though talk of death is scattered throughout their ruminations, the elderly are not contemplating the cycle of life and approaching the end with a sense of equanimity. Dying does not seem right. It has no place in their worldview. It does reserve a faux place, though. It seems to the elderly that they have never truly been alive. They have been cheated from the earliest time they can remember. They have always wanted just to feel truly alive. So death has seemed to have them in its grip. But this does not mean there has been a conscious awareness of the experience of dying. The constricting malaise that has surrounded them like a heavy garment has never clarified into the clash and subsequent neutralization of the two foundational forces, eros and entropy.

A like suffering is aroused in Echo. She is willing to mirror Methuselah, so that he can return to his maturational path. But Methuselah's depression will arouse a depression in her, as his regression will arouse a regression, and his somatizations will arouse somatizations. If she cannot clearly identify the source of her own being through contemplation, then Methuselah is going to blindside her with an intimate understanding she is not ready for.

This happened to me in subtle ways, as soon as I started treating the elderly. I remember attempting to pull myself out of a deep, low chair that was stationed by a resident's bed. Our time was up, and I was bound for the next patient down the hall. What used to be the smooth and graceful action of standing up was marred by some competing process. I intended to rise, yet there was no movement, not until the point that I accentuated my effort. Then there was a ragged motor pattern. I lurched up, releasing the energy that had accumulated during my movement latency. Now there was a quantum, where continuity used to be.

Why were my muscles reacting this way? It reminded me of the effort it would take to get up some mornings. I would decide to get up. I had every intent of getting up, but it did not translate into action. Now it was happening to me during the day. This was entirely new. I finally realized it was not happening anywhere but in the nursing home. Later in the afternoon when I left the home and walked out into the rough, neighboring community, I noticed youngsters rolling old tires at an elderly couple crossing the street. I boomed out a warning to the boys in my old principal's voice. I was immediately cured. Smiling, I got in my car. I recognized what was happening. I was somatizing the same entropic energy I had used for years to keep order in the high schools I ran. I had caught the patient's ague and was resonating with it.

The elderly arouse a mortifying countertransference. They get us to act out deadness the way they act it out. We resonate with their entropy but encode it as a denial of death, just as they do.

Echo has at least three choices. She can remain evenly sympathetic and positive to everyone. Here she protects herself from disturbance by taking a stock approach and by avoiding a more distinctive reaction to each individual resident. Second, she can be more directive, offer behavioral guidance, and encourage the repression of transference. Both these approaches have their value. Echo still has to live her life. She should not have to give up her joie de vivre in order to treat Methuselah.

The only problem with these two choices is that Echo has set herself up for a big surprise. Her attempts to block the hurtful feeling states fail in more subtle ways. She may decide she is not going to let depression touch her, and so she deflects that experience in the treatment. Later in the evening, she finds that she cannot sleep, that she is developing pains in her abdomen, that she is experiencing a flareup all over her face akin to the lupus that her sister has lived with for years, and that her husband is increasingly avoiding her. Her mother died of breast cancer and now the doctor is noting a profusion of calcifications.

Hyman Spotnitz told a group that the conversion hysterias worked in the late 1800s because no one had neutralized them by intuiting their meaning. The hysterias were a safe way of expressing taboo feelings. A glove anesthesia sufficiently expressed in a symbolic and hidden manner the wish to use the unfeeling hand to commit murder. When the hysterias were interpreted, they were no longer a safe haven. Bit by bit, the analysis of the neuroses destroyed their integrity, creating further opportunity for the psychoses. They became more utilitarian, in all their forms and levels of intensity. But as the psychotic defense yields its secrets and narcissism no longer affords us protection, there must be a further retreat. That will be to the body. Spotnitz predicted the analyst of the twenty-first century would focus on psychosomatics. This is a good analogy about what happens to therapists who know about hysteria, neuroses, and psychoses as defenses. The hungry press for being to express itself shifts to body language. The corrosive effects of countertransference in sophisticated and well-trained therapists are to be found in the soma, because it is too easy to locate and interpret in the areas of thoughts, feelings, and behaviors.

One of the things I have done to preserve myself in this work is to organize peer supervision. Five of us meet every other week to discuss our thoughts and feelings about our cases. We try to talk freely and hold nothing back. Anything goes. It is a wonderful session, filled with deep feeling and with joy. We support each other. We give one another the courage to face ourselves. We mirror each other in a way that will allow self-acceptance and -love. We are a forgiving bunch, because we know the fragility of the sublime organization of Echo. Entropy could easily turn to hate and obliteration, and it does so with cruel regularity in our culture. But we take care of one another, trying to be conscious of the experience of dying and living too, so we move toward integration.

PROTESTS AGAINST THE EXPERIENCE OF DYING

As the years pass, changes occur within us that signal the necessity to slow down our pace. At every level of the soma, forces are operating against the peak performance we demonstrated in our earlier years.

Bodily systems, organs, cells, and even the mitochondria that supply each cell with energy find increasing blockages to fuller expression. We took the first forty years to achieve as much as we could. Now the body is telling us to make adjustments. If we are careful, we can stretch things out another forty years. This reality would seem incontrovertible, but the culture has been steering us in another direction.

One of the heroes of the culture is an elderly executive who is outperforming juniors in speed, motivational desire, and sheer amount of accomplishment. He is only a screen for the youth of our culture, who we idolize and attempt to emulate. The vast and pervasive commercialization of youthfulness can only find acceptance because it mirrors our denial of death. It is the youthful dimensions of the elderly person that count. But our fantasy model gives us away. Gray, yet still exuberant and given heroic substantiation in his square-shouldered suit and radiant shirt, the powerful figure does one thing best: he creates monetary wealth.

Money is played against death. The accumulation of wealth empowers the hero and he is never going to have to face his end. It would seem he is going to go on forever. Collecting the dead matter and piling it high shows a splendid economy to it. Death has been concretized and captured. It has been put in its place. Man has dominion over it. It has been manipulated in a way that we do not have to see it as dead matter. We rename it live matter. Accruing it lends us immortality. Its worship is a hidden effort to revitalize what has no life to it in the first place. For the equation between "filthy lucre" and shit is obvious. Turning shit into gold is central to our denials about death. The choice, God or mammon, is put to us in a way to reveal that they are both an attempt to do the same thing—find a sense of immortality (Brown 1959).

The elderly who feel worthless are the ones who have bought into this point of view, and who have lost their power and their money. We quake with their fears when they articulate the void they are falling into. I met with a number of aging therapists to get their ideas about Methuselah as a patient, and I found they needed to talk out some of these issues. When there was mention of an older colleague who was forgetting more and more, or who fell seriously ill, or who had to severely limit his practice due to his frailty, there was a discernible anxiety or fear.

This has been very helpful. I find it is paramount to contemplate my own cycle of life and to find acceptance for it. The therapist is not automatically protected by his compassion and his understanding of others. I think part of the problem is that the people I interviewed do not treat the elderly to any significant degree. If they did, their own problem-solving would be going well because Methuselah returns to the same terrain over and over, demonstrating how his protest against the facts of dying have thrown him out of balance and have created his horror and suffering. If Methuselah had contemplated the meaning of the changes occurring within him from middle adulthood, he would have a better chance of remaining on the path near the end of his life.

There is a progressive and worthwhile decline in our activity level, usually without serious loss in effectiveness for a time to come. This occurs because we become proficient, we restrict ourselves to our areas of expertise, and we give more thought to the future. We learn to say no to advantage, opportunity, and extra work. Our physical selves become increasingly accurate in ferreting out the hidden costs of expansiveness. No opportunity comes without sacrifice, and the economy of the self discovers the debit side of the adventure.

The forties and fifties are a good time to learn this. If we want to survive, we turn into relentless conservators of libido. This is the age at which Ulysses headed for home. He had fought his war, had done his damage, and had sowed his wild oats. Home was waiting. This is acceptance. It is a signal of the continuing erosion of the denials and intellectualizations that we employed in pushing to the limits of our endurance.

It is our clear-eyed assessment that the 75-year-old captains of industry, marathon contenders, and jet setters are anomalies fueling one of our favorite myths. They are not us. We accept aging tissue.

We react to the obvious facts. A skin-tuck accomplishes only what the words suggest. It offers a cosmetic answer to a fiercely dedicated teleological process. Inside, we know the transformation is underway. If we are to be counted among the living, we do best to heed the signals and amplify their message.

Death is not such a horror if we are aware of the experience of dying that is occurring in us at this very moment. If we learn to tag the experience of dying and be one with it, we are less likely to act it out and hurt or kill ourselves. There is a minority among our friends, relatives, and associates that tries to ignore the imperatives of aging, and as a result we all have our stories about people dying in the prime of life, burning themselves out, destroying themselves, and leaving grieving families behind.

As I turned 40, six of my fellow professors who were a decade or more older faced terminus. One died in a bicycle accident, one died on the tennis court, one died of a heart attack. Three more hurt themselves seriously. The median age of these people was 52. The professor is supposed to have the least stressful job of all, but lack of stress does not seem to be protection against the unguarded and unaware expression of entropy.

In my wife's school, over two dozen from her fifty colleagues and their families met untimely deaths. There were heart attacks, sudden grave illnesses, terrible accidents, and chance-taking behavior. The median age of these victims was in the early forties. My wife's experience is more understandable. The urban public school she worked in was a hotbed of tension. The pressure was unremitting. A good friend, a retired police officer, brought me statistics on his field. Half of former law enforcement professionals die within four years of retirement, and their retirement age is younger because many are allowed to leave and collect a pension after twenty years on the job.

The danger in wholesale denial of one half of our being is that it secretes entropy in our farthest recesses, increasing the potential of somatizing or destructive acting out. We enter the garden to echo Methuselah, but we remain fully aware of the living and the dying we will be confronting in ourselves, in order to treat the old man. We are the keepers of the soul. If anyone is to know this, it ought to be us. We learn to understand our basic nature and to engage others in a non-iatrogenic contemplation that will resolve their resistance to understanding too.

14

Modeling Advanced Patterns for Others

The colleagues we work with in the nursing home are at different milestones along the path to self-understanding. We offer them a full menu of ethical and safe interventions with the elderly so they can choose those that insulate them and that reveal to them at a level they can tolerate. This involves mixing behavioral and psychodynamic approaches, so that everyone can participate. We model these interventions at every turn, with patients referred to us for individual or group therapy, for residents the staff needs help with, and for residents the staff has not targeted.

FREE OPERANT CONDITIONING

This has been one of my favorites since the early 1970s, when as a principal I was responsible for coordinating therapeutic programs throughout the building. It involves targeting a goal behavior for an individual in the milieu. I meet with all the staff to model and rehearse this intervention, and I get everyone to do it with me. I mean everybody. The nurses and aides are joined by the therapists

and physicians, and then we bring in the housekeepers, plant maintenance people, kitchen workers, security personnel, gardeners, and
staff from the business office.

For example, we are looking for Nellie to demonstrate good eye
contact, smile, and make acceptable verbal social responses. We
make sure the whole staff knows what this behavior looks like. Then
everyone practices. The pièce de résistance is to explain that if every
person reinforces Nellie's behavior all during the day and evening,
she will get the experience that we are acting with one hand, and
her behavior will alter dramatically. Then I model. No matter how
many times I pass Nellie by the nurse's station, I congratulate her on
her winning smile, wonderful manners, great eyes, and appetite for
social contact, contingent upon the behaviors we are looking for.

I walk by with the staff. If they are shy I nudge them. I whisper
in their ear. I do not let them off the hook. They just have to do it.
It will be good for their development if they learn this. Most of all,
I model the behavior consistently. If I pass Nellie eighty times during
the day, I make eighty comments. I also make the same comments to
the staff members, although the form of the evaluative feedback
may be more subtle. I let them know I get a lot of gratification when
they look me in the eye, smile, and have something pleasing to say
to me.

Nellie is being bathed in contingent reinforcement. She likes it,
although if we were clear with her about what we were doing, she
might not like it at all. It brings her around in rather quick order. As
her sociability increases, she gains access to naturalistic reinforcers
with staff and peers, and we are in a position to thin the schedule of
contact to variable interval reinforcement. Skinner and his people
were geniuses. I have managed some of the toughest schools in New
York with this simple contact as the backbone of the therapeutic
milieu. The intervention seems to neatly meet the needs of the
helper and the helped.

After we do a few of these cases, it dawns on the staff that they
were inadvertently reinforcing with their contingent attention the
behaviors they found most undesirable and regressive. They learn to
use the precious resources of social reinforcement and evaluative

feedback to more positive ends. They complain less frequently of residents who display negative attention-getting behaviors. They now have a way of approaching them.

The caregiver's entropy is pressed into therapeutic service. Not only is the resident benefiting and growing from the kindly and loving contact. He is also cooperating in the control of entropic expression because conditioning of others' behavior is a properly hostile act. The caregiver has chosen which behaviors are desirable, in keeping with the interdictions of the social contract. He becomes the arm and hand of the culture, shaping and containing the resident's narcissistic expression.

The genius of conditioning is that the therapist is able to bring entropy into the relationship in a sanctioned manner, and without any necessary awareness on his part or the part of the patient. He can properly vent impulses that, untended, could develop into countertransference problems. Psychoanalytic interventions require sensitization about where the murder is in the room. Here the therapist learns to become very aware of his own frustration, hostility, urge to obliterate, and general destructiveness. He works at having all his own thoughts and feelings, so that the patient can learn to tolerate his own.

PROSOCIAL BEHAVIOR

I find it generally helpful for staff to see how therapists handle all kinds of situations. I stop to chat with residents who are not my patients. No matter how busy I am, I try to get to a needy person. Even if I cannot stay, I explain that I will be back in a few minutes. If there is an emergency, I pitch in. During fire alarm practice, I participate within the prescribed limits. I show my availability for difficult situations. If a person is screaming and everyone else has thrown up his hands in despair, I go see what the agitation is all about.

I get down on my haunches to address a resident who is in a wheelchair. I maintain eye contact. I touch and soften my speech because I am up close. I show how to modulate one's voice to preserve the resident's privacy over whatever issue has come up. If I am going to move a recalcitrant resident to an activity, I stop by a minute before and gently remind him. I ask if he has any objections. "Yes, I think you can drop dead right now and leave me alone!" I return one more time, and when I finally move him the resident is merely disgruntled, rather than digging his heels into the carpet and wishing vicious calamities upon my person.

I allow people to observe and criticize. I welcome their comments and show them I am always willing to learn. I weather criticisms properly and show a malleability to supervision. Even though none of this is expected of a psychologist, it is nonetheless important to model the behavior. I show the staff how to take in information without getting stepped on. There is a difference between supervision and sadism, and bosses can be encouraged to stick to the former if the employee participates actively in his own professional growth. Staff members will comment that they would never have been able to react in the same manner, and we can work on their reluctance.

REINFORCING DESIRABLE BEHAVIOR IN A GROUP SETTING

The staff members are shown how to time social reinforcement so that they "catch" one resident "being good" and get the attention of another resident who is demonstrating undesirable behavior. This sets up a modeling procedure between peers. Without knowing why, the resident without adjustive skills starts emulating the resident who is getting reinforced. We use evaluative feedback to let the adjusted resident know what he is doing that is attractive and a pleasure to experience.

If this is executed in a heavy-handed way, it may create disgruntlement against the adjusted resident, or it may arouse the negative suggestibility of the onlookers. If the intervention is subtle and graceful, everybody gets the message in a therapeutic and progressive fashion. Again, this puts the staff in the driver's seat and gives proper vent to their aggressive reactions concerning the untoward behavior of the residents. People need continued support to intervene in this fashion. A common fallacy of American management is that one in-service or one seminar is going to fix a lot. The Japanese opt for continuous training. They are more willing to recognize the need for people to receive a lot of feedback and skills honing in order to pursue progressive policies.

DIFFERENTIAL REINFORCEMENT

The staff needs a lot of direction in developing this skill. It involves choosing from the resident's repertoire aspects of a goal behavior that are infrequent, weak, and buried by other behavior. It takes some viewing to understand how I pick through an aggressive presentation and differentially reinforce assertive dimensions. Although all the resident's thoughts and feelings are acknowledged, the assertive aspects are attended to with more interest. We use our personal power to shift the resident's focus, and we work on this day after day with a dedication that outlasts his.

Usually, none of these residents are patients in individual therapy. In our role as shapers of the milieu, we are functioning adjunctive to the social services department. We are intervening to help things run better in the facility, and to help the residents say what they have to say so they can experience increased adjustment. If our own patients are the subject of staff meetings, we help the caregivers by getting them to discuss the situation freely and to apply some of the techniques we have been practicing in the program at large.

DISCRIMINATED OPERANT CONDITIONING

The staff practices approaching the resident and making it clear what behavior is called for under what particular circumstances. The resident will be encouraged to raise his hand in a group activity and be called on before he speaks, or to wait before getting on the elevator if there are three people before him. He will be asked to interact with peers during a certain time, or to seek out the nurse for medications.

These behaviors are cued and then reinforced. The staff members can be clear about basic expectations and can let the resident know that all these behaviors fall within the categories of prudence, sociability, health care, and quality of life. They like this approach because it is more straightforward, but I find that free operant conditioning yields greater payoffs. By the time the staff members have to be so specific, cooperation has already become a pivotal issue. Basically, the caregivers are not going to get any easy cooperation. Many of these intervention attempts have to further solidify into a behavioral contract.

The staff members set out their expectations and the resident sets forth his. There are some negotiations and an agreement. Reinforcement of various types is used to strengthen the agreed upon behaviors. Central to this is the zeal with which the staff members keep their side of the bargain. We end up helping the staff create a lot of these contracts, because situations arise where it is necessary that everyone have expectations thoroughly spelled out.

DEFLECTING AGGRESSION

The residents can be meanest to those who give direct service. Nursing aides suffer self-esteem problems, because of this and because of their socioeconomic status in the larger society. We have altered our values very much in the last century. Those who are laying on hands now get paid the least and are seen as occupying the lowest rung of health care. It is easy for them to conclude there is something wrong with them, and they reflect this with the amount of teasing, criticism, and attack they take from the elderly before they say something. The resources of the facility are put to use to confront this issue. The managers are encouraged to discuss the great value of washing, dressing, and shaving someone. Personal ministrations are returned to their former value.

The aides are helped to perceive and articulate the gratification they are giving, and to further distrust the aggressive comments of the residents. We trace the antecedents of the residents' anger and program different approaches. But we end up with a core of residents who are going to upset the caregivers. I show them how to take the heat.

R: F— you! F— you, shithead! You're a lousy shithead! You know that? A f— lousy shithead!

D: I want to thank you for speaking freely. But have you said everything that is in your heart?

R: I hate you!

D: It's well you should.

R: What are you doing, making babies when you don't even have a man around?

D: It was good enough for the Vikings.

R: You're a bastard!

D: That's what I understand.

R: You're fat!

D: I must tend to my diet.

R: What are you saying? You don't even know when someone is ridiculing you.

D: What's the matter with me? Why don't I know?

R: Yeh, you're just a pervert, playing with my balls!

D   (Washing the resident): It's something I should take up with Dr. Bouklas.

R:　If you had a brain, you wouldn't be working here.

D:　Then I wouldn't have had the good fortune of meeting you.

Modeling this behavior is the best way to communicate the tone, the acceptance, the full knowledge of the murderous feelings of the elderly person and the feelings that are induced. It is an eye opener, and the staff members report using such comments with increasing effectiveness outside of work, too.

TAPESTRY WEAVING

The staff observes how I create a picture for the resident of how he would appear with the development of certain characteristics that are already in his repertoire. This can be seen as taking the "expectation effect" and making it work for us therapeutically. I treat the resident as if he is already showing the desired and advanced behavior. I talk about the resident as if he demonstrates this behavior all the time. The staff then follows my lead and makes the same comments to the resident with the right emotional state of hope, interest, and a sense the resident is not going to let us down.

What I have done is assess the incipient organizations that have yet to prevail in the person's development and have provided a keystone expectation or support to help him realize this more advanced organization. I am tapping into the person's multimind, alerting the transcendent dimensions. It is an indirect appeal to the persona who possesses the requisite skills to make it in the milieu, and my cues and reinforcement make it competitive with the persona the resident thinks he is stuck with.

The resident savages an aide with a milder degree of acid commentary. He begs off at the end, and goes his way. He has been less hostile than usual, and his behavior has suggested that it was less compulsive. "You let her down easy. You are clearly a man with a heart." The resident may respond with sarcasm, but the seed has been planted. Various opportunities like this are role-played in staff training, with numerous examples of how to weave a tapestry. When he hears it enough, the man tells the nurse, "You know, I get mad when you move my foot that way. Do it carefully and I won't have to show you what a bad temper I have."

The resident yells at the top of her lungs, "That lady is disgusting! How can I eat my food? Get me out of here!" A tablemate has choked on a piece of carrot and has spit it out. The staff member takes her out of the dining room. "Really, I'm sorry," says the resident, "but I cannot take such a sight. I gag right away." The staff member remembers what we practiced. "I call it your sensitivity. You are supersensitive to the plight of others." When enough of us do this, the resident forestalls her critical reaction the next time and alerts us if a tablemate is having a problem. "For God's sake! Go tend to her. She's going to choke on that carrot!"

We take a moment to stop by a resident and exclaim, "You look great! You took a lot of time to get your hair just right, the jogging suit looks super, and I love those earrings! You're perfect!" The resident is not perfect, but she attends more to her appearance and grows to fulfill our expectations. "Look at that tie! That hair is perfect! I'm a hair fan. I have none of my own, so I spend a lot of time admiring everybody else's. Great look. Just a great, great look." This fellow is going to allow himself to be shaved and washed more regularly, but only if I am a good tapestry weaver. I can say all of this in a hollow way, or in confrontation, and exert negative control. I can offer blandishments that will have the opposite effect. That's why it is hard to triangulate just the right words and affect, and that is why I do it first and then share it with staff.

PUTTING MONEY IN THE RESIDENT'S EMOTIONAL BANK

Why would the resident want to cooperate for you if you had no pull with him? And if you were very close, why wouldn't he go along with you all the time? The aides are shown how to anticipate the resident's needs, do the little things that count, respond to dependency hungers, develop a relationship, kid around, and be there for the resident. As with any beleaguered individual, the motivation to build bridges is low. We build ninety-five percent of the bridge and leave only five percent to the resident. It might be said we are developing power as a reinforcer by our actions. We keep putting money in the resident's emotional bank until there is a pressing situation. He refuses to go to the opthalmologist after all the time it took to set up the appointment. He refuses the shower that is necessary. He fights with the floating aide who has been assigned to take care of him this evening. The staff member strides into the room. It is time to make a withdrawal.

"Bruce, I heard what was happening and I cannot believe it. After all that you and I have been through, after all we mean to each other, how can you put me in such a position? Yes, me! Don't you know how this reflects on me? I have done everything I could to make your life easier. This is no way to repay me. Now I'm sending the aide back in, and I want to hear that you two were able to come to a meeting of the minds. Do you understand what I am saying?"

This approach is heavy-handed, and effective. In the early 1980s the New York City Schools gave me its hardest-to-place adolescents. These were kids who had tried everything once, and none of it was pretty. Regular schools and even Special Education programs were no match for what these kids could dish out. I visited each of their homes, I broke bread with their families, I went with them for working papers, I helped them get and keep jobs, I was there for their worst times. When the teacher would march them into my office for failing to get their work done, it was time to make a withdrawal from their emotional bank.

"You're kidding! You're pulling my leg! After all I have done for you? After the sweat and the tears and the grinding of teeth and the long hours and sticking my neck out and going out on a limb and wearing myself down to a nub, this is how you repay me? Am I getting this right? After looking like a jerk to the parole officer and begging to the judge and kissing your boss's butt and running around the whole city to take care of you, this is what I get? After convincing your mother to take you back and convincing your stepfather not to batter you to death in your sleep and getting the gang to leave you alone, the gang that was looking to cut you to shreds just for the fun of it, that's what I get? You don't want to do your math? You don't want to do your math? What does that mean, anyway, you don't want to do your math?"

The funny thing about this was that the hugest, toughest guy would get a hangdog look and would sink lower and lower until I had him folded in half. I got it down to a science. If I went long enough, I'd have the kid on his knees bawling and begging for forgiveness. I knew where the murder was in the room. It was in the form of a club that the kid was wielding, and I was the guy who knew how to take it out of his hands. The teachers would usually snicker in the beginning of this exercise, finding it immensely entertaining. These were the educational holdouts who were torturing them in class, and there was a certain *schadenfreude* in watching them fold. But by the time I finished the teachers were crying, too, because everything I said was true. I was only withdrawing what I originally put in. It may have been a science, but it was no act.

AN M-M A DAY KEEPS THE DOCTOR AWAY

For this kind of work, I stay with one level of the organization. One time it might be aides, another time nurses. It is not good practice to let supervisors and supervisees in on each other's thoughts, when it comes to this topic. We discuss our most difficult residents, what they have done to us, how they make us feel, and what it is like working with them. Gentility reigns, until some point when I ask whether there aren't stronger feelings. I model the appropriate feeling, again and again, on case after case. I explain that therapists need to have all their thoughts and feelings to treat patients. They go into therapy to be able to have all their thoughts and feelings. They receive supervision and spend time with peers.

I tell them health care workers have the same degree and type of exposure to patients, only they are called residents instead, and the health care field does not offer the same supports. I tell them that they are exposed to the same corrosive toxicity as therapists are, but they have no place to get out their thoughts and feelings. So let these meetings be the place. The staff members are supported in getting it all out, the misery, frustration, anger, and hurt. I tell them that what we talk out we are less likely to do, and we get ample feedback that our procedure humanifies the caregivers further. The feelings that are being suppressed are the angry and hostile ones. They are given legitimacy. To protect the staff I stick with induced feelings. Feelings part and parcel of their individual histories are the subject to be taken up with their therapists. This is more a supervisory meeting on the feelings anyone might get with a certain resident. And it is true that a mental murder a day keeps the doctor away.

FINDING SEVEN HUNDRED WAYS

Once an interpretation has been made to a patient, there is rarely an epiphany. It takes working through to help the patient understand how the interpretation applies to his everyday life. Spotnitz said that once you make an interpretation, you have to find seven hundred new ways to say it until the patient accommodates to it. I will not supply a nursing home with an interpretation that I have made to a patient of mine, but I will work with the staff in honing an interpretation they are interested in making with a resident.

The family told the staff at the care plan meeting that mother had been placed in an orphanage when she was 3 years old, and her parents never visited her. She lived there until she was 16, at which time she found a halfway house. Her overwhelming fears about being abandoned by her children and grandchildren are no doubt related to this history. It is put in the care plan to intervene in ways to help the resident deal more adaptively with her separation anxiety.

At a family meeting, the staff has the daughters reiterate they have no intention of abandoning their mother. They tell their mother that she is concerned because of the abandonment she suffered as a child. They wish they could keep her at home, but they are all in their mid to late sixties themselves, with ailing husbands.

Then the staff is prepared with seven hundred ways to remind the resident that her present fears are related to her early experience.

"Hannah, remember. Your children are not going to do what your parents did to you."

"Hannah, your children gave testimony before witnesses of their love for you. You're mixing up two different events: going to the orphanage and coming here."

"Hannah, take a good look. Is this an orphanage? Your daughters are coming today."

"Hannah, why are you saying your children will never come? Haven't they come daily?"

"Hannah, look. Here's the calendar. It's got a smiling face for each day your children came. Did they miss even one day?"

"Hannah, no matter how much you moan, you are not going to chase the children away. They will come today. They are not going to repeat your parents' mistake."

This works quite well and underscores the therapeutic nature of the milieu. Brainstorming interventions with the staff members increases their understanding of psychodynamics and adds several interventions to their armamentarium. They find they can use many of the comments we have devised for one resident in helping another one with similar problems.

RECOGNIZING FLUID RESTABILIZATION

About half the residents in any nursing home display mild to severe dementia. Their cognitive and memory skills worsen over different kinds of gradients. Some residents show vast decrements in just a year, whereas others will function much the same after four years. With some residents the dementia destabilizes their personality right away. With almost all residents who have dementia, the disease process eventually disturbs the integrity of the personality. Whether it happens sooner or later, few people with this diagnosis escape major disturbances to the personality.

This is a terrible ordeal for the families. They mourn the loss of their parent way before he has physically died, because the parent who raised them is gone. The parent is gone, and an apparition is walking the halls, eating, sleeping, nodding at them, forgetting their names, and acting in every way as an individual but seeming to them to be an empty shell. Only the elderly person is not an empty shell. Important contributory centers in the brain have died, but others are still alive. In a way, this is now a different person, who needs our support.

Echoing the resident with dementia restabilizes him at a new, lower level of mental organization. Creating an ego-syntonic environment of helpful, supportive, and resonant interventions brings forth a new person. Designing a wing that has the right lighting, cues, places to rest, and right things to do evokes a repertoire that is not the old, complex repertoire but is still adaptive to this engineered situation. Then there may be new neurological accidents, or the subtle disease process continues, until more of the important centers break down.

We echo the resident at his new level of lower functioning. We keep shadowing him and giving him the cues and reinforcers that will make him look best in his environment. We recognize the phenomenon of fluid restabilization. The nursing home has to do this. It is charged with maintaining the highest quality of life possible for the resident. The person is not valued any less because he can no longer sell insurance or conduct a graduate class or drive a taxi. He is valued as much as another person who came to the home with no such skills. As his repertoire continues to devolve, the nursing home keeps on treating him with the respect it would accord to a new person who entered with a lower level of function.

This is a phenomenon unique to long-term care. In all other

health care settings, the accent is on progress. The fact that a caregiver or professional has to shift from progress in an area to plain maintenance suggests a failure of the intervention. Long-term care starts with maintenance and deals more with devolution. We have to reframe our work so that we can keep a proactive focus on the resident. The concept of fluid restabilization keeps the staff attending to the integrative needs of the resident. It is not that he is disintegrating. He is undergoing another round of fluid restabilization.

Izzie walked by himself into the nursing home. He checked it out thoroughly before deciding to become a resident. He interviewed the staff and asked hard questions about the philosophy of the home. He was having periods of confusion, had left the stove on, had walked out into traffic a few times, and had wandered from home. He understood he needed a placement, but he reserved the right to reject the home if it was not up to his standards. He participated in his care plan meeting and made a special arrangement to get the types of food he liked most.

Six months later Izzie was falling, but he refused a wheelchair. He was given a soccer helmet and he traded his sneakers in for slippers that would not catch on the floor. He used to gather with the men in the solarium and give stock tips, but he rarely went there anymore. He pulled away from his peers and took to wandering the halls. He was very frightened when he became aware of all the skill he had lost. But the staff made no mention of his weaknesses. They had been prepared in in-service to deal with the new Izzie. Because their treatment of him was unremarkable, he calmed down. When he became anomic and started missing nouns in his speech, they subtly and unobtrusively supplied them, in a way to make them his.

Six more months passed and Izzie stopped referring to his wife by name. He took a wheelchair but frequently bounded out of it in a state of akathisia. He was quite disinhibited and could not sit down for long periods. The Alzheimer's disease had released a tremendous appetite. He ate two or three plates of food at every meal but never gained a pound. A new Izzie formed. His pattern consisted of putting on and taking off his clothes until breakfast. Breakfast lasted for two hours. Then he wheeled himself to his room, stopping to bound out of his chair as he had done all morning in the dining room. He put on the radio and repeated his clothing ritual. The same for lunch and dinner. This is how Izzie filled his time. He no longer talked to anyone and registered confusion and frustration when others talked to him.

The staff learned to remain patient, to leave him a corridor where he could get up and down for hours, to communicate nonverbally, and to allow him to do what he liked best. Options were offered, but Izzie became flustered and uncooperative. So he was watched carefully and allowed to express this new level of personality organization. Under these conditions he smiled and he registered contentment. Although his akathisia made him seem frenetic at times, this was a physical discharge of energy without attendant upset. Everyone shifted to new norms and accepted the resident just as he was. The staff modeled the appropriate acceptance for residents, who were puzzled by the vocal and expressive man's newfound withdrawal.

Three months later Izzie took to bed. He spent his time dressing and undressing, fingering his zippers and buttons for hours. He was afforded help but did not want it. The visuospatial damage that is part of the Alzheimer's syndrome seemed to fill up his time as a challenge. He wanted to be fed, stopped giving eye contact, and did not acknowledge his wife or family in any way. As long as proper supports were given in the way of understanding, patience, and accepting him the way he was, Izzie registered little frustration. He died two months later.

MAINTAINING A TRANSDISCIPLINARY FOCUS

We find time over the month to get together and discuss a case from the point of view of all the disciplines. This accomplishes a lot. We get to share interventions that can ethically cross professional boundaries. We each get to hear how another field conceptualizes the resident's needs and strivings, and we each get a better idea how our own work is contributing to the larger goal of providing quality of life for the resident.

Cindy was giving the caregivers of different departments a hard time. She was in her mid-seventies, had had a stroke, and was in physical therapy. The recreation department was working with her to involve her in some activities. Social services was counseling with her because she kept responding to the roommate, "Bullshit!" Whatever the roommate said, she would bark out "Bullshit!" We held a meeting to see how well she was cooperating with her care plan. The staff members of different departments saw how they could help each other with some simple goals and practices.

The physical therapy department was doing some complex exercises with Cindy, but also some range-of-motion exercise with the right hand. This consisted of her reaching her arm straight out and then pointing straight ahead and in a ninety-degree arc to the right. Cindy fought over every exercise. So everyone pitched in with range of motion. The aides had her do it in the lunch room just prior to receiving her tray. They had her do it in the tub during her bath. They put on her clothing in a way that they got her to reach out. Recreation staff encouraged it during one-on-one visits in the room.

The recreation department had socialization goals. Socialization is an antidepressive activity, and there has been an organized push to create environmental interventions for depression. Medications are considered "chemical restraint." But Cindy refused to leave the room. So the therapists who worked with her made sure she was around chatty residents. In the lunch room she was seated where an aide assisted residents in feeding. The aide encouraged and reinforced peer contacts. Reinforcers were given by other departments when Cindy cooperated with the recreation staff and attended at least one activity per day.

Social Services found Cindy frankly resistant over the roommate. "I can say 'Bullshit!' if I want! It's my prerogative!" She happened to yell it out one day as I was on the wing. I dropped in and told her that that word reminded me of a funny joke I had heard recently. Cindy was used to getting a lecture when she cursed. She was willing to hear a joke.

"Two friends each return from their vacations and they are comparing notes. The first one says, 'What did *you* do over the summer?' The second one waxes eloquent. 'I went to Europe, where I saw major works of art in Paris, Venice, London, and Athens.' The first one replies, 'Fantastic!' The second one goes on, 'I polished up my ballet skills so that I can appear in *Swan Lake* this fall.' The first one replies, 'Fantastic!' The second one finishes up, 'I read *Finnegan's Wake* and will be giving my interpretation to the Reader's Club next week.' The first one replies, 'Fantastic!'"

"Now the second one asks, 'So what did *you* do this summer?' The first one says, 'I took a Dale Carnegie course. Remember how I used to say "*Bullshit*"? Now I say, "*Fantastic*"!'"

Cindy loved it. We practiced saying "Fantastic!" with power. We said it with hidden gratification. Everybody encouraged her to say "Fantastic!" It become the favorite word of the wing. All the departments got at least one "Fantastic!" out of her a day. "Bullshit!" dropped to a very low frequency. When we did hear it, we redirected her and practiced "Fantastic!" The staff members got a good feeling backing each other up on aspects of the care plan. They also got to know Cindy better. Compartmentalizing who was responsible for what piece of Cindy's care plan probably doesn't make much sense to begin with. But most people go along with it. The difficult residents force us to rethink our modus operandi and come up with better solutions.

Echo can bring Methuselah into the garden by bringing out the nurturing, blossoming, resonating aspects of the nursing home milieu. In this, she faces herself all over again. She also helps the staff face what they need to in order to play their part because Methuselah's health in his old age requires the health of those who care for him. Every aspect of our developmental life span is reflected in this environment. The hope of the infant is the hope in every heart in the building. The will of the toddler plays itself out as motivation and resistance. The purpose of the preschooler is evident in the way people approach one another. The competitiveness of the preadolescent is played out among the staff, and between staff and resident.

The fidelity of the adolescent determines how people will remain predictable and dependable for the other person. The love of the young adult still burns brightly in the aged, only to capture a deeper and more intense reflection in the caregivers who are now living that stage of their life. The care of middle age is also an issue for the older staff and one the elderly rely on for empathy and relatedness. The wisdom of old age is the one great gap. Methuselah is not showing it, and the staff has to develop a precocious great-grandparentliness to show the way. The oceanic merger of late old age is a hint of the Being that makes us. With the ego mirage melting away, oceanic merger can be seen to be our elemental relation. It requires a cosmology that will form it into regression in the service of transgression, so the elderly do not die in a state of suffocation and painful transfiguration.

THE TRANSCENDENT ELDERLY

> Whence this surge of strength in him
> Now he's no longer young
> With very little of Life's song
> Remaining to be sung?
> Why reach for things beyond the reach
> Of any such as he
> While winds of Fall are blowing chill
> With Winter's prophecy?
>
> Leaves of Autumn often save
> Till last their brightest hue
> Undaunted by the fact they soon
> Must curl and wither too
>
> Are they akin those leaves and he
> Some force in each the same
> That bids them not to shrink from death
> But to meet it in full flame?
>
> [Edward Bjorkman, 1987]

It helps to know healthy older people, to get some idea of how the instincts handle their vicissitudes in a way to bring a maximum of Being into being. John is pleased to hear my voice. He is going to be 103 years old tomorrow and wanted to make sure I could celebrate his birthday with him. He blesses me, "May the Lord watch over thee all the days of thine life."

He wants to describe yet another passage he remembers from a liturgy he learned over ninety years ago. He was a cantor most of his life, continuing even when he became blind and needed a wheelchair. He sings the passage and this reminds him of the European village of his father, the green fields, the friendships, the early loves. He lapses into his first tongue, but in a departure from our early meetings, he recognizes the need to have me understand and switches back to English.

He invites me to lunch. John is no longer a patient. He suffered a short-term adjustment reaction upon coming to the nursing home at the age of 100, and we spent several months together. He sought out my friendship after that and enjoys breaking bread with me. He does it literally, feeling the plastic wrapper for its seam, pulling it open, gently taking out the slice of wheatbread, holding it reverently in his hands, praying to God to bless it, separating it in half, and handing me a piece.

He listens to every word of mine as if it is a gift, and in turn I find that my words each ring softly and clearly, shaping themselves to be worthy of his reverence. I love this old man dearly. He is the best I am yet to be. He shows one possible way to the gateless gate. For he is already in the arms of the universe, connected in a fashion that the mere facts of his physical existence mean little to him. It does not matter to him that he is alive versus dead. He has reached that position of doesn'tmatterness through his years of contemplation.

It does not matter if we are sitting in the bustling dining room, in the quieter atrium, or outside under the 200-year-old maples and the younger evergreens, where all is a hush. We are in omniconnection. He brings me there right away. He possesses Echo's sublime organization. He has resolved the puzzle of transcendence. You get to it by regressing. You give in to the humus. You go forward by easing backward without a fight, without a frenzy, without anxiety. You ease backward with the total trust of the infant whose mother must surely swathe him in her arms and would never drop him. Primary process was never subjugated by secondary process. They rule side by side throughout our lives (Noy 1979).

He knows I listen to every one of his words, and he does all in his power to make them worthy of my reverence. He speaks in a whisper, but each word peals with meaning, one paragraph meant to carry the whole of his history into the present, because he has that grasp of his life. It is all momentary, and, if he was pressed to, he could say everything in one word. He could capture the moon in a dewdrop.

The aides are callow and self-absorbed, disenchanted with the work, and going through the motions. They push him too quickly in his wheelchair, set out his food too perfunctorily, and give no attention to his whispers. But John pays none of this any mind and tolerates all with a smile. Too bad, the young people have no idea they are in the presence of a holy man. What would happen if Jesus Christ returned to Earth? Well, I think He keeps on returning to Earth, and we just don't have the collective consciousness to understand and appreciate this. He is a mask of God, a representation of another kind of sublime organization within us. The young women who all hailed from another country and culture just have to confront too much blockage in ascertaining the nature of the man they are taking care of.

But over the years John has softened their hearts anyway. He has done it by resonating love and acceptance. He actively grasps the experience of dying, so that it is not a damaging resonation. He has incorporated his living with his dying and has solved the puzzle set out by consciousness in the first place, which creates an artificial split and then spends countless hours and lifetimes trying to understand it. He knows the frustration of the youngsters and does not hold it against them. As one passes by with a whoosh! he smiles and nods imperceptibly.

I only hope that there is something in me like I see in John. I look for it and I nurture it. I understand as he understands and forgive as he forgives. I value my senses and also the ineffables that we might call beyond-the-senses. Because John cannot see, he really sees. He cannot feel in his fingertips, so he really feels. As senses retreat, beyond-the-senses take over. His contemplations have led him to a spiritual life. Although he says little, he has read Buber and definitely describes his attempts at an I–thou relationship with the universe.

Lutrece began her nursing home stay with a fistfight. She hated the staff and found them insensitive and uncaring. She did not trust them, yet her only child had died and now she had to live among them for the rest of her life. After a few meetings with the staff, the negative dynamics that were so quickly set into motion stopped just as quickly. Lutrece was the staff's great-grandma. She was forceful, strong-willed, and always right. She was truly always right, and she caught the staff in a long string of empathic failures.

With me as an interlocutor, she calmed down. Bit by bit, she relented in her argumentative stance. "I know how you help people," she told me one day. "You acknowledge their right to be horrible. I have been horrible, haven't I?" She altered her modus operandi with the staff, getting to know them by name, finding out about their families, listening to their troubles, offering kindness instead of advice. "I'm 89 years old. I should know better." She showed great insight. "You were once a teacher, I can tell. I venture to say this because you remind me of me." We compared notes, and indeed we had worked with our children in much the same manner.

"I am adopting the staff," she decided. "I have never seen so many hurt and damaged people. What happened to this country after I retired?" She had gone into isolation after the mid-1960s and missed close to thirty years of cultural change. Some time after the sessions ended, she asked me to socialize with her. She became the healthy grandmother to the nursing home. Everyone came to her and knew they had her confidence and her full attention. "Some of the stories these kids tell me—I need to get some expert advice."

One aide was living in her car all winter. More than a few had borne children in the last two years and were getting no help from the absent fathers. A number had been abused so severely by their boyfriends or husbands that they had foresworn men. Some were already in gay relationships and needed to talk out their experiences. Others were on the fence. Everybody needed money, nobody was having much fun with the children, and the future looked bleak.

Lutrece just asked for strength. "I am willing to listen to these young women, but you have to be there to catch me if I fall." She never fell. She gave endlessly of her time to the hungry young women who needed a maternal feeding. She grew stronger and her influence spread to the other residents. She never yelled again, and never attacked anyone, and never reflected her frustrations. "You must understand. I feel all these things. But like you, I decide what I am going to show others." She lived for four more years in the facility. When she died, every staff member attended her wake. People got up to address the gathering, and one after another they described what Lutrece had done to make the world a better place.

Early in the treatment relationship, when Lutrece was still fuming and ready for combat, she stopped her complaining to give me a long, hard look. "You're a funny one," she remarked. "You're not what you seem to be." I asked what I seemed to be. "You seem to be easygoing and gentle. But you can rage just like I can!" She laughed with appreciation. She had found me out. In short order, she made a conceptual leap that few others can negotiate. She decided that my power was in being able to have rage without being enraged, to have love without eroticizing. She nodded a lot during that session, pondering her discovery.

She concluded that my position was the one she would have adopted in her middle age if she had had the benefit of training. She recognized that my behavior represented a resolution between what was felt and what was shown. She was able to say that I chose what to show in order to have therapeutic impact. She also speculated that as I learned to feel more over the years, I also had to develop the discipline not to show. In one deft stroke she shifted from what the psychiatrist called a paranoid position, to a therapeutic one. She decided to go all the way with her feelings and to put her emphasis on holding back and not showing. She decided to accept the sublime organization of the therapist, to not fear regression but to understand its transcendent properties.

John and Lutrece are two of the many dozens of perfectly healthy elders I have gotten to know well. This is a practice I learned at United Cerebral Palsy over a decade before. We worked with developmentally delayed infants, teaching them to sit, roll, grasp, feed themselves, walk, and play with others. It would take months, but then there would be a breakthrough. Everyone became excited and celebrated. The older staff members saw a problem of distorted perception among us and fixed it by inviting a normal infant to the program each month.

To our continuing surprise, the developmentally regular infants did all sorts of things with a speed and panache our children lacked. This doused our fires a bit, but it also served to give us a benchmark against which to compare the progress of our children. John and Lutrece demonstrate what an emotionally transcendent elder can offer, even if he is frail and ill, even if he lives in a nursing home. Through his eyes, we can see that the nursing home really is a garden, was never anything else, and that it is transcendence from within that changes everything without.

15

Contemplation

Work, love, and play: poised against each other in dynamic balance and exercised in their own right, these form the prescription for a full life. As they edge toward an integrated whole, they bring the most of Being into being that the constraints of the social contract will allow. This is the instinctual path for the acculturated human being. Eros and entropy are expressed in each of these arenas. Tensions rise and release in a way to give maximum exposure to the Being driving them.

The intrapsychic imperative to manage tension is derived from a hazarding out of what society will and will not tolerate by way of our direct expression of the impulses. Tension is the experience of impulses in the ego. Management involves the canalizings implicit in acculturation, and the advanced ego learns to accomplish this task more loosely. If its hold is too loose, instincts flee the hand like a bird set free. Then we are truly psychopath by day and schizophrenic by night. If its hold is too tight, then we strangle the animal, and there is little vent of being. In either case, it is entropic energy that is at issue. It comes out as hurt, destruction, and murder against the society, or against the self.

The strivings to exercise our tension stories freely are one with the protoplasm that we are. This is the protolanguage of the smokepot. Impulses are surging up. They are thrumming. They are wavering. They play against each other to create upward and downward movement. They rush into experience with different magnitudes. Their acceleration patterns vary, as does their intensity. At times there is an acceleration of the acceleration. They create experience as they harmonize. Eros becomes discriminable as it contrasts against an entropic background, just as it defines the action of the entropy.

The tension songs and dances settle into certain harmonics. These reflect one's personal constitution and reaction to exigency, in the search for the *just right* position. Herein lies the structure for the character. There are characteristic ways in which tension increase and discharge are going to occur, and these will later take on subjective meaning, as well as be adorned with social identity. But the protolanguage of the smokepot, if we deign to study it further and give it some attention, will take on more physical trappings.

We will be speaking of the velocity and acceleration of tension increase. This will be placed in apposition to the same dimensions of tension decrease. There will be up-and-down movement patterns. We will find psychic equivalents to the moment of force, where it is applied during various short temporal intervals. Energy will surge up, thrum, waver, and bob. To further search out what it means to *be*, we will put character at the mercy of this language. This will take the kind of introspection that is not validated at present anywhere in the society except in the arts. The dancer, the musician, the artist, and the poet surely know all about this. So do the adolescents who seek the art forms to give some credibility and shared experience to their tension songs and dances.

Therapists are in a good position to learn about this. They see what is happening to their own tension levels during the session. They come to realize that one of the goals of the treatment is to manage the tension levels in the room. They ought not get too high or too low. They learn to sense subtle changes, and this guides their talking or not talking. They sense the harmonics, the give and take of eros and entropy, and they watch what events lead to excitation and to discharge. This is a private world hidden from most people. The *ego project* has hidden tension songs and tension dances by weaving in meaning. Direct knowledge of our essential being is overwhelmed by the superflux of language.

We create an imaginary world with language that takes us away from our essence. We dance as fast as we can in order to cooperate with the greatest taboo, against knowing what we truly are. For if we stop and consider momentary experience, it is too easy to feel our tension levels waxing and waning. We become uncomfortably alert to the substructures that underlie the ego, and we feel in terrible danger of losing the ego mirage. We deconstruct toward what we conceive to be the void because in an eroticized worldview, there is either the erotic, or nothing. Entropy is not considered equal to the erotic. It is the void as death. It is as if we have not been dying all the time, from the moment we were born.

Men fetishize women's clothing in order to infuse them with their own maleness. In donning women's apparel, they can reassure themselves that the women, like them, have a penis under the dress. The awful loss of the women due to the fantastical castration is denied. All people fetishize the egoic experience in much the same fashion. If they can infuse it with enough erotic energy, they will not have to deal with the fact that it was never there to begin with. The true healing comes from noting the presence of entropy in both the sexual fetish and the ego fetish. To become a dual-drive enthusiast is to be able to relent in the ego hoax and to withdraw the erotizations that were aimed at keeping appearances up.

Psychoanalytic training does not help us to admit to an oceanic beyond the amnion. Therefore it is still easy for the analyst to consider eros and entropy as the be-all and end-all. For beyond the drives lies a truth that can be a smothering horror to those of us who have dedicated our lives to successful individuation and autonomy. We are always of Being, and our protoplasmic bubbling up is one articulation of that Being. We are as connected to everyone and everything as we could possibly imagine. We are the proverbial fish in the water, and for well-trained people who do not like surprises, this can be the most disconcerting surprise of all.

"How does the fish know that he is immersed in water?" asked the man, who was suffused in the prethought, prefeeling, the culture, the cosmos of merger, much broader than any fishbowl, lake, or ocean, not to mention being riddled through with barely felt negative ions that irritated and provoked him into asking the question in the first place. And we won't mention the embracing ether that composed the universe stretching in all directions so far that it formed a seamless torus that brought every point everywhere to bear on this man's station in space and time, since he was more ether than palpable substance, more water than scales, more water than muscle, more water than blood.

"What good would it do, for the fish I mean, if it knew about the water?" thought the man, getting the uncomfortable inkling of his own delusions of separateness and individuality. He sensed the tug of tidal forces not outside himself, but from within and through, so that the self dwindled before the wide, planar forces that grabbed equally at his mind and flesh as at the water, the sky, and the air, he being not a person so much as a slightly less-than-random collection of molecules exerting and being exerted upon, ready to give in and sway with the larger sway.

"Would the fish care to know?" mused the man, feeling himself floating, his fingers loosened from the pilings of everyday rationalizations, about *what, where,* and *who?* "Would the fish get seasick?" ventured the man, experiencing the roiling, oceanic sensation of merger-come-upon-the-self, of connection with his mother, his wife, his children, his neighbors, his fellow workers, his busdriver, his car, the waitress, priest, teller, trees, sky, wood, air, the child over there by the swings, the dog crossing the street, the grass, the cement.

"Isn't the fish going to cause a lot of trouble for itself by trying to *know* anything?" cautioned the man, who now got perfectly dizzy asking himself the ultimate questions he sought to *know* an answer to, within the arms of Being but contrarily venturing forward as protoplasm to take all that he was and all that was him to split it into two opposites and create dialogue, where none was needed, and discriminative experience, where all was continuous.

"Why can't the fish just go on with his life and do what fish do?" concluded the man, reeling in the knowledge of his connection with the fish with the water with the universe that spanned fifty billion light years that arose from a pointless point that brought past, present, and future together so it was at once a sphere of unimaginable size and dimensionless too without matter at all but vibrations within vibrations.

Being creates tension in protoplasm, and this is what we experience in our consciousness, and as our consciousness. We are not so far removed from such knowledge as we pretend. There is many a person who has managed to give himself anxiety, a headache, or confusion, or to give us startling and revealing art when such matters are explored. We are immersed in this experience, but there is little in the world that invites its more direct exploration. The ego project is so valued an exercise that this form of deconstruction seems sacrilege. It is the danger of entropy put into action that makes us hide one half of our experience, and a large part of the ego project concerns keeping the genie in the bottle.

Tension rhythms are translated into text. Love, work, and play achieve a focus only within a context. The concatenating of texts is the ego's response to the gravest of challenges. The extrapsychic world has concluded that the individual's duty is to control entropy. The entropic force is pressed into service to schematize an internal understanding resembling how the external world claims to understand itself. The dynamic of entropy is put to use to structuralize the ego and in the process a good amount of it becomes dead stuff. It creates templates that block Being but let enough through to ignite and nurture being. Relaxing this large organizing principle reveals the multiple textual skeins that exist in the world and find mirrors in the self. Protean man emerges. Neurotic man in a relaxed state surrenders his character to reveal the action of his concatenatings. This lies beyond the territory of psychoanalysis, which is committed to ego complexification and the solidification of a unitary person-

ality. It suggests a transpersonal being, closer to Being than prosaic
life generally allows.

The safest path to learning all this features contemplations
during middle age, in an environment that echoes the ego while
resonating with our deeper realities. Echo's job qualifications are
specific. She has to have solved the riddle of entropy's hiding places.
She has to know where the murder is in the room. Even the most
well-meaning religious search can still leave us praising our culture,
our race, or our credo as unique and showing contempt for the
Other. We have not learned a thing. Entropy has hidden itself within
our canalizations of images, prayers, beliefs, and is being acted out.
In fact, the need to act out entropy in order not to experience dying
is so strong that it is difficult to counter. The way to fully accommodating to connection with the universe lies with acceptance of our
two foundational drives. It takes extraordinary leadership to bring
us to this point without employing our entropic forces against us.
Because such leaderless leadership is in short supply in our culture,
it is easy to lose sight of the path.

We may miss the path for all our striving, propelling our eros
deep into transcendental landscapes and using entropy as the
cannon. It is not *what* we are looking for that will gain us answers,
but *how* we are looking. We have to see the purposeful and the
hidden, the desire to know the ineffable, and the cannon that lent
its force so we can know it. When we fall into a period of exhaustion,
we note that we are more whole. It is the experience of dying. We
find we have been on the path all the time, and our striving was the
eroticizing of experience to substantiate the ego hoax.

We may be placed firmly on the path by crisis. The most common healthful reaction to facing the abyss is to find one's character.
The protean gabbings within one's mind have been experienced as
a malaise. The protean selves have worked to cancel each other out
and to create the dumbfounded human, frozen in inaction. Crisis
clarifies. Here is crystallized a unitary character pattern that is going
to be able to make us feel most alive. Yet the path happens to lie
beyond even this healthful reaction. For we can also hover the void

and become one with it. We can decide to feel living and dying with the equal force they represent in our psychodynamics.

We may behave as if we were on the path during the last half of our life, and in the end accept this as our best gesture. If we have lived with empathy and relatedness, recognizing the value of others, enjoying others, taking gratification in our steps toward the transpersonal, we have gone farther than most. If we have been able to see ourselves in the foibles, misdemeanors, and horrific crimes of others, we have tranformed ourselves beyond all expectation. We were on the path the whole time anyway, and our experience of running parallel to it is the smallest of conceits and in no way detracts from a life experienced fully and to the enhancement of the social contract.

Can we attain this level of self-understanding without hating others who act out entropy? It is easy to avoid the zeal of the recent convert, and all the entropic enactments that suggests, if we heed the advice of Alan Watts (1972). We recognize that those people most actively pursuing individuality and autonomy, those lionizing the ego experience, or those splitting the world into good and evil and taking their roles, are to be treated with the greatest reverence. They are God playing the most frightening game of all. He has lost Himself on purpose and now is straining to find Himself again. These people are nothing less than God at His most courageous. They are us, and we can call up their organizations in us instantaneously.

THE MEANING OF METHUSELAH AND ECHO

Working with the elderly is helping me ease back onto the path. I have written and shared because this is my way of becoming more aware of the path. The elderly have given me a precious gift. They have suggested how I might go about understanding the grand issues of one's life. They have given me a way to use my fifties and sixties so that I may transcend in my seventies and eighties. They have made clear what years of schooling, training, and reading could not.

I now see that we are the universe. We are the therapy. We are everything written in this book. This book is no more than my intrapsychic processes given justification with outward examples. Spotnitz once told a gathering that every therapy book is really only about one patient. We were charged with writing a book about each new patient. I would take it a further. A book is really about one person: the author. It is about me. To the extent that my story resonates within you, it is about you, too.

Each of us is Proteus. Each of us has everybody else's story within us. Each of us has the pre-organizations and the concatenating power to reverberate with everybody else's text. Each new text that we are exposed to arouses within us a greater grasp, greater cosmological awareness, if we can perform the trick of embrace. We are each patient described in this book and the therapist who wrote the story. We are Methuselah and Echo, too. The form of therapy described here is the disquisition we engage in as part of the conscious decision to actively "treat" ourselves. We mirror Methuselah and draw him back into the garden.

We position Echo as the resonator to Methuselah's self-involvements. For the path is going to be discovered by regression. The truth that will set us free in the last half of our lives is not to be found in ego complexification. Consciousness has a developmental quality in the first half. In our old age it grows through disenvelopment. It moves backward. It is a regression in the service of transcendence. Methuselah moves toward the sublime organization of Echo, who can be aware of the experience of living and dying, who can see beyond the splittings of Being in human being, who can live in total primitive connection with all things animate and inanimate and still observe the social contract.

Methuselah-and-Echo is the middle-aged self. One part is suddenly feeling the presence of a very old man within, and the other part goes to heal that old man, to bring him into the garden rather than leave him in the corner. This act of embracing the one who is dying is the act of allowing the experience of dying into consciousness. Methuselah in the self is the entropy that culture has never allowed us to acknowledge. The invitation is the acceptance of both our drives. It is Methuselah who has been with us from the beginning of middle age. He is the new organization who is conceived in the role of patient, in order to bring out our efforts to heal eros and entropy and discover our roots in Being.

He does not have to be a bogeyman anymore, or a monster under the bed. He does not have to be a demonic presence. He is not the hateful warlord who threatens to destabilize our economy with oil or drugs. He is not the practitioner of a different religion. He is not the neighbor whose barking dog drives us to distraction. He is not Aestus of the mists. Entropy takes on the new form as our superannuated self, just one tiny lifetime—our lifetime—away from the eternal.

Accept the book as a tract, another way of seeing the world. This is not a book about old people. It is a book about the dying forces in us. We can reject its ideas and go on in the way we have become accustomed. Or we can resonate with the material and add to our contemplative inclinations. We can act as our own therapists, or we can choose a therapist to resonate with us. For we are looking for the opportunity to leave society in a way that we can function more effectively in it, to understand its enslavements, inconsistencies, hoaxes, and doublespeak and still partake of it, choosing involvement over cynicism. The bodhisattva in us is the enlightened part staying in the world to bring about the healthy growth of others.

Methuselah in the corner becomes the source of our iatrogenic intention. Left to seek out his splendid equipoise, he acts as a capacitor for entropy, discharging it in plenteous form in various acts of murder. It is his voice that plagues the work of the middle-aged therapist and his self-involvement that holds the therapist back when he ought to have a voice. His exclusion from the life of the middle-aged person prevents a healthful dialectic from ever taking hold. There is murder in the room, only the person does not know it. It is in the form of Methuselah, affecting work, love, and play.

BEING AND TRANSCENDENCE

Being is the hardest thing to talk about and the easiest thing, too. My spiritual colleagues take its presence as a matter of course and would not question it for a moment. Part of this is conceptual, but part is experiential and introspective. There was a time that man lived in an I–thou connection to the universe. The acts of seeing the sky, smelling the game, and running toes through the sand called forth a continuous *thou* experience. All were part of one. We know this is true because we remember the same experiences from our early life. There was a time we lived in the pregenital paradise, and if we work on a contemplative life, we can rearouse that time and see how we never really left it.

It is the increasingly discriminating and chatty cortex that has changed our direct connection with the universe, representing it in perceptual and intellectual constancies, and shifting us to indirect apprehensions. These are the renunciations we make to control the entropic half of our being and to find ways to live in close proximity to one another. It takes the action of unlearning to relax our defenses and to listen clearly to the oceanic once more. In this we are working against the constant training processes of modern culture that serve to obfuscate this direct experience.

Being is the great modern secret. It has been trivialized, as in "We are all brothers under the skin." The truth behind this is so shattering to modern consciousness that we can only accept the comment as a mild bromide against the guilt we feel for our prejudice. It has fallen victim to pedantic inbreeding, as in "How many angels can fit on the head of a pin?" where great minds of former centuries have turned themselves inside out intellectually rather than shift to a more inclusive and merged model of the universe.

It has been romanticized for popular consumption, "Luke. Use the force," and has resonated among millions, because the filmmakers Lucas and Spielberg know far more about the popular imagination than any of our modern spiritual leaders. They have created the texts through which modern people can more nearly experience the sense of being. Luke Skywalker feels the dark side in him but is able to use it to function within the social contract, as opposed to his rapacious father. It has been demonized by people alerted to its destructive side or willing to try to harness it, as we see in cults and in exclusive political movements.

It is the enemy of the modern ego, which is in a period of unbridled lusting for texts. How do I succeed? How do I beat out the other guy? How do I sharpen my spinmeister skills? How do I sell the jury on an alternative reality that accounts for all the data and does not arouse dissonance? How do I funnel more of the world's resources in my particular direction? How do I remain sharp enough in this mercantile universe to stay viable? These all boil down to, How do I get my hands on some superior texts? and the meaning is clear. The differentiated ego is all for itself. Eighty percent of any bureaucracy's effort is spent on maintaining itself. What is true about bureaucracy is true about its basic building block: the individual ego.

It is hard to be any other way. Forced to disavow its entropic half, being forges forward in the name of eros. All entropic enactments are considered minor flaws, lapses, or kinks in an otherwise fine machinery. We have developed a lopsided theory of humankind because we have driven half of ourselves into the darkness. It is the Enlightment against the Dark Ages, it is Life against Death, because the splits are still more profitable to the economics of today's ego than the integrations.

My scientific colleagues profess to have no idea what I am talking about. "What you are describing are beliefs, not science." But what is science? The study of emotions? They are as ineffable as the study of Being, but it does not stop researchers from writing thousands of research articles about it. We think we know emotions, but we hardly scratch their surface with our scientific approach. "I love you, I'm overwhelmed, I love you to the point of madness! Your name is in my heart like a bell shaken by constant trembling, ringing by day and night. Roxanne, Roxanne, Roxanne. Loving everything about you, I forget nothing" (Rostand 1951, p. 168). Cyrano's words to his beloved Roxanne are the most moving in our literature and came closer in capturing emotion than any scientific brief I have yet to read, but who has not smiled privately and thought, "This guy's got nothing on me. He doesn't come close to plumbing what I feel about my lover."

In our appreciation of the arts, we easily understand that our being gets only the vaguest of treatments when put into visions, movement, sound, and texts. Our dreams are more powerful, our fantasies are more breathtaking, our grasp of merger is more whole, and our ability to perfuse the other and be shot through by the other are more gripping than any play, musical, painting, or story. We hold to our descriptions of emotions as the scientific reality, over the introspectionist grasp of emotions. As long as we do this, we will never understand why a blandly kind law student could kill ten women, why the happy husband and comfortable businessman would risk everything to penetrate his 11-year-old daughter, how a nondescript and seemingly ineffective man could go on to lead his country in its "darkest hour," and how a devout rabbi could become one of America's funniest comedians.

There is a collusion here, and even the scientists go along. Entropy is central to psychopathology, but you will hardly see it or its close derivatives mentioned in the DSM. There is the passive-aggressive personality disorder, but even here the aggression is modified. Despite the action of entropy in psychopathy, neurosis, depression, schizophrenia, psychosomatics, fetishes, and addictions, there is not going to be much about it in the DSM. Where is the story about our hate for the other guy, our sadism, our control, our homicidal impulses, our suicidal acts, devastations acted out on others, self-immolations, and destruction of the body? Why is there no emphasis on breakdowns in aggression management? We are involved in a vast folly.

Our skill at murder is readily recognizable to just about every field except psychotherapy. Between 1900 and 1975, it is estimated that one hundred and twenty million people have died by violence in the world. Two world wars, police actions, coups, terrorism, atomic explosions pale in comparison to the actions of states in removing "disagreeable elements" from their borders. "This 'nation of the dead' stands as a grisly monument both to mankind's propensity for violence and our rapidly increasing technological expertise in destroying each other on a massive scale" (Allen 1983, p.13).

We are in the realm of talking about things that are hard to put into words, and things our present society has a taboo against understanding. Language itself needs to loosen to create a way to capture Being in being: the pathless path, focusless focus, whatless whatness, involved disinvolvement, disinvolved involvement, gateless gate, cork on the ocean, the ocean itself. This is stuff of the deepest understanding and internal expression, but stuff that suffers in the translation. The Jungians describe the Fisher King wound as higher consciousness (Campbell 1968). We receive the wound sometime around the age of 16 and limp around damaged for the next thirty years. The danger is revisited in our late forties, and if we have lived the contemplative life, we can learn from the wound and remain in higher consciousness. The first time around its kundalini-like transformation of our experience of being scars us. The Fisher King myth held sway for centuries, describing the very real brush with direct experience. It was a prophylactic tale for the young, and an explanatory one for the older.

I oscillate in my recognition of Being during the week, the day, the hour, the minute, the moment. I can call up my serene connection to everything and everyone as an altar boy in my church, helping the priest prepare for the transubstantiation, watching him raise his face to heaven, remembering that one time he was so moved that tears went streaming down his temples, his hands shaking slightly, chalice held high, sharing in holiness as he spoke Christ's words, "Come, partake of my body." Now here are words that speak directly to our union with one another, our most primitive act of eating connected with our most spiritual aspect in Christ. I can remember sitting with my Orthodox Jewish friends who stopped prior to lunch and prayed quietly and sweetly, filling the room with God. I cannot remember any other time as an adult that I was more moved, more in touch with the grandeur of the universe.

I remember my grandmothers. These two women, both a little

over forty years older than I, were as different as one can imagine. Thomai and Hope were products of different Greek subcultures. They spoke different dialects of their native tongue, one was cosmopolitan and one rural, one soft-spoken and one brash, one relatively cool and one demonstrative. But they were both humorous, ready to smile, fun-loving, and contentious. And they both underwent an identical transformation in shedding their corporeal form. Thomai and Hope were prepared for the body to melt away into the soil. They accepted it as natural. The more immaterial they became—which occurred about the same time—the more angelic they were able to be. As one part of them withered away, a more essential part revealed itself and burned brightly.

They both lived their last years the same way, surrounded by Greek iconography, palming worry beads, praying softly, and seeking reunion with God, spirit to spirit. The contrast between their own early differences and late likenesses was commanding as a conceptualization of the prowess of transcendence. I watched them return to the pre-egoic proximity to fuller Being. Through them I understood my ego as the diluter of my own being. It was the negative agent to the id's positive agent. It said *no* to Being, in the manner of overresponding to social interdictions. It said *when* to Being in the manner of frustration tolerance. It said *what* to being in the manner of canalizations of preferences. It said *who* to Being in the manner of character texts. It said *how* to Being in the manner of dramatic scenarios.

My grandmothers were my Echo, helping with a safe detextualization. Through them I was able to examine regression farther than before. The part of me that came from them responded immediately, and they automatically brought me forward into terrain I would not have explored on my own. Their fervor became my fervor, their easy access to the spiritual became mine. They were frankly melding with the universe and looking directly at it, thinking nothing of it. During this period I understood that secondary process does not replace primary process. It epigenetically joins it, in a way that the primary process still remains brilliant. The primitive and sophisticated live side by side. The regressed and mature live side by side. Noy (1979) described the ever-present primary process as our seeking to find *me-ness* in everything we think, feel, and do.

It was at this time I took a more reflective stance over the lionizing of character. What I had bought into so wholeheartedly my whole life I could step away from and regard from a distance. I realized that each moment in our lives is busy with mental activity. Gratifications, hurts, poignancies, all in the form of thoughts, feelings, sensations, and images, ineffable protostructures, manage to play themselves out simultaneously without erupting into cacophony. Unlike the physical universe we know, the mind oversteps and crisscrosses themes with utter disregard for the niceties of Newtonian time and space.

"It's a wonderful life and I savor each breath"/"I cannot go on and I need to retreat before I bust"/"I hate it all"/"I love"/"I don't care" have feelings, attitudes, demeanors, and autonomic conditions that prefigure them. All the pretextual reactions abound without paradox as we give our hearts and minds free expression. When someone interrupts this with, "Yes, but how do you feel about that?" there is a collapse of this rich multiverse into an identifiable response: a datum. Another ineffable, light, precipitates into either a wave or a particle state as a result of whether a wave experiment or light experiment was concocted to measure it. Light is as multifaceted a phenomenon as human consciousness and shows the slimmest side of itself in a datum. We will find that light and human consciousness have a lot more in common than their many facets. Captured in both is the busyness of the universe.

I was primed for this tranformation, for I had many Echoes. It does not take courage to change this way as much as the long-term embrace of resistances by Echo. She came in the form of my analyst, my trainers, my loving wife, and my good friend and colleague Dave Levinsky. The entropic structure of my resistance transformed under Echo's ministrations until I came to accept the experience of dying, my potential to murder, and my potential to neglect the other unto its destruction.

I sit in the backyard and watch the oak and maple leaves flutter in the sunlight and across the backdrop of the dense woods behind. The leaves lose their distinctiveness, and their fluttering takes precedence over their form. A shimmering is loosed as the perceptual constancies degrade, first to pointillistic specks that suggest the workings of my retinal cells picking up light in quanta and on to a continuity breaking, until I am there, with the trees, the rocks, the air, the grass, the sky, fused with the universe, in the experience of the oceanic, having floated through the gateless gate.

I sit with the resident who has been suffering terribly. She is staring aghast at her bandaged left leg, which is gangrenous from her diabetes and is going to have to be taken from her. Everyone has been in to see her and give her solace. But her horror has transfixed her, and not even medications can calm her because as I sit with her and I watch as she watches *I can feel I can see that it is not the loss of the leg so much as the act of sawing and she is staring at the surgeon sawing away at her flesh the thing she worked her whole life to avoid being parceled up and torn to shreds is now happening anyway a whole lifetime of guarding for nought and she just watches as the surgeon takes that leg off again and again and replays this trauma and will not let it go and can hardly breathe but cannot take her eyes off the surgeon cutting away now it is her cutting away she is the surgeon and she is cutting her own leg off like a swift and bounding marten caught in a trap way up in the woods chewing and gnawing and screaming in pain but chewing and gnawing anyway to escape the trapper because he would rather escape legless than be eaten.*

"I am going to lose my leg," she says to the leg, and then turns her eyes upward to catch me, her face frozen in panic. "I am going to lose my leg." I have been there with her and we have shared the surgeon as I have relaxed my texts to resonate with her. I ask, "What is the name of the surgeon?" In a flash that multimind, that multiverse of activity, collapses to an orientation response. "What?" she responds. I repeat, "What is the name of the surgeon?" She searches her mind. Blauenfeld, she thinks. Yes, Blauenfeld sounds like it. Well, is it Blauenfeld for sure? She doesn't know for sure, but her daughter does. Her daughter knows, and she is probably home from work now. We discuss it and she decides to call and ask.

"Honey, is it Blauenfeld who is going to do the surgery? No? Shapiro?" She hangs up the telephone. "It's Shapiro."

I explore whether she has gone over the procedure with Shapiro before. What would she like to ask him? Is she good at dealing assertively with medical people, so she gets all her questions answered? Or do they run her over like a truck and back up once or twice to make sure they left identifiable tire tracks? Perhaps we can practice some of the things she is going to ask. Here, I have some paper. I will be the secretary and write down the questions she thinks up. I leave her in a state of relaxation and repose. Her exposure to her will to cut off her own leg has been precocious. She is nowhere ready to recognize the power of her entropy. Let's put it on the surgeon and let's cut him down to size, make him someone we can subject to questions before he lays a hand on us.

The staff is worried about the new resident. She has only been in the home a month, and now her 67-year-old son has died. People imagine her keeling over in shock when they tell her the news. They ask me to go in and assess her potential for accepting this information. As far as they are concerned, it will kill her. I sit with the woman. "What are you doing here?" she wants to know. I tell her the physician asked me to drop in and see how she is doing. She is a pleasant woman, a bit abrupt, quite direct, and sad. We sit quietly and I think about her son. "Do you have any children?" she wants to know. I am curious what she perceives. "Well, I think you have children," she responds. "I would think a person in your occupation would love children."

I give none of the facts of my own life away but echo the sentiments, tempo, and affect in the room. We continue to sit. I am with her, absorbing her, and I get no sense that she is going to kill herself when she hears of the son's death. I get a very different feeling. There would have been no sadness in this life, if there had been more murder. I would not say this out loud. Who could tolerate it? She is going to be pleased to hear the news. It is the Medean act that she resisted all her life and that ruined her life. I do not have to hear her whole story. I do not have to know that when she decided to abort this son she was in total peace for the first time in her life, buoyed, serene, sober. I do not have to hear the husband tell her she'd better have this child or else. I experience her in the here and now. Her entropy burns bright and I feel it burning in me. Oh, for a good old-fashioned infanticide to set things straight!

I tell the staff she is going to be okay. In fact, she will prosper in some paradoxical way, because this will make her more spiritual. They tell her. She does not crumble. She is roused from her depression, talks freely about the son and his medical troubles, cautions others about the necessity of a good diet, and acts with a sense of completion. She gave it away in the session and allowed me to fully accept and resonate with the broadcast.

The nursing home refers a lady who has been in and out of psychiatric hospitals all her life. She is anorexic, is given to panic states, and is uncooperative in all aspects of her care. She does not mind talking to me, because I do not push her to do anything in particular. She is moody and cries frequently about her mother, who is in another nursing home. One woman is 68; the other is 87. She is guilty about having ruined her mother's life. If she could only get over this, she might be able to squeeze a drop of gratification out of her own miserable existence.

She tells me she would do something terrible to make the mother go into a panic. She cries and tells me it is so embarrassing to reveal what it was, that she is prepared to starve herself to death instead. I sit with her in session after session, as she talks about her history and tries to use it to make some sense of her present predicament. Each time she returns to some terrible words that she used to drive the mother into a panic. I relax and listen, and I let her censor what she will. She is beginning to have an effect on me, because I am skipping meals. That is not like me.

The truth is there to be uttered, but she holds back. I am with her, I am at the kitchen table, I hear them irritating each other *I hear the words back and forth I see the pained faces I sense the mother the daughter the fight the food growing cold on the plate I am with them and hearing fight after fight three fights a day three hundred and sixty-five days a year for the thirty years they lived together and suddenly, I have a very sharp pain in my throat.* What is this? When did I ever get a sharp pain in my throat?

This is physical, this feels like glass it feels like glass a piece of glass in the throat.

I ask the patient, "Does glass have to do with any of this?" She stares at me, breathless. She is transfixed. Then she bawls uncontrollably, confessing she would break glasses in the sink and tell her mother she had accidentally swallowed a piece. The secret is out, and my pain goes away. She calms down and gains weight. So do I. People ask how I knew that the subject was glass. The very question collapses a rich multiverse of activity and forces an answer. Semiotics demand a highly canalized answer. How do I describe the experience of being there/while being here/being me/being her/being the mother/feeling the glass?

I have worked with a particular resident for a few years now. He does very well with me, and he deteriorates beyond description without the support of therapy. We have met our goals twice over the past five years and have stopped the therapy, whereupon he has regressed. A continuation of the sessions revives his integrated behavior. He goes on to function even better than before. Everyone considers us a team, and as far as the physician is concerned, our work can proceed. There was a time that medicaid funding stopped for such therapy, and it took a year before we could use medicare. During that time I went to see him weekly to keep the treatment intact.

Now this man is on his deathbed. When he was still conscious he asked for me, and the staff is quick to let me know how he needs me by his side. He cannot tell I am with him, but the few hundred people who work in this building all know the story, and they need for me to be there. It is absolutely important to them that I sit with him. They come to watch us together. They are moved. The air is spiritual, not funereal. Every person in that building wants a relationship like this, where there is equal reverence, transformation, and the sharing of something special.

I sit by his side for four hours. I am in a state of splendid hovering, here and not here, at the gate, sensing everything but oblivious too, tuned in to something I do not know much about, for this is new, to sit by someone with whom I have so deeply and totally resonated, who is now resonating his all-consuming entropy. He never wakes up. His breaths come slowly. I breathe with him. He is going to die soon. The room is absolutely quiet. It is just him and me.

Then I hear the noiseless noise. I sense the immaterial material, movement where there is nothing to move. I might as well be in Grand Central Station, for all the non-commotion commotion that is going on around me. It is not his breathing, for that has all but stopped. In non-word words, I tell myself to close my eyes. Close my eyes to see. And there is the answer. The wall behind his bed has dropped away to reveal a vast plain. It is peopled by thousands of cowled figures. They are coming up to us—we are on a rise, and they are stepping right into the room. In a moment I am surrounded by figures. I am sitting on a low chair and they surround me, their garments touching my arms, brushing up against my head. The room is full.

I am one with them. There is no fear or dismay. I might as well be a 3-year-old surrounded by parishioners on Good Friday, kept safe and warm, as they sing Christos Anestes, Christ has arisen, for that is the feeling in the room. These are the man's people. Because I am at the foot of the bed, I can still see the man lying there. Three figures lean over him and place their arms under him. They pick him up, and I watch a vaguer outline of him ascend out of his dead body. The mood is prayerful, for now all the noise has stopped. They have come for him, and now they have him. He is held in their arms, and they are complete and he is complete. I am complete. They leave the room and return to the plain with him. I can still see it all. I open my eyes, and my patient has died.

How many residents have I treated who were disheveled, morose, distracted, self-involved, acting out, and not at all worried about the impression they made on others, until they became involved in the treatment relationship? The subject was eros, and it was not articulated but communicated through resonations. The tensions rose in the room through interest, on to expectation, past excitement, toward preorgasmic levels. All this was happening in the unspoken and untouched, and but for those two things, the patient was available to every aspect of lovemaking. The tumescence was immaterial but real in every other way. The erotic organization is the one easiest to access, but it also remains the most hidden, especially in this age group. These are people more likely than we to pine for someone else and not act on the feelings. I am transported by their tension dances and unbearable peakings, and I am with them, resonating. When I tell them our time is up, their usual response is something like, "It was a pleasure, doctor." Knowing in my reso-nations where we just were, I tell them, "The pleasure was mine."

When I was referred a gentleman who had not sought out psychiatric intervention even in the worst of times, I did not think there would be much success to our first meeting. In fact, he did not like talking to me at all, and at the end of the session told me he would let me know if he wanted another session. I mirrored him: I would let him know if an hour opened for him in the next few weeks. We kept meeting, and despite his gruffness and defensive-ness, he found he could tolerate me more and more. A year later we had made history together. I was with him as he faced his greatest challenges, and each time he used my help to reassert his pugilistic stance against death. He was going to make a comeback; he was going to prevail. His family needed him. He was a role model.

But the medical crises continued, he paying the price for lifelong neglect of his body. He had to leave the comfort of the nursing home and the gratifications of his social position there and go to the hospital for the fourth time. They did not understand him there, they did not answer the call bell, they let him develop bedsores, and they did not wash him. I visited and witnessed the unresponsiveness. Of the ten hospitals I have seen in the last ten years, only one would pass the rigorous standards set for nursing homes. Only one hospital would do as well as the twenty or so nursing homes I have consulted in. His hospital belonged to the other category.

Upon his return to the nursing home, the resident was seriously regressed. He moaned and cried all day, screamed at the staff, cursed vile curses, spat, struck out, and refused any of his old, pacifying stimulations and pursuits. "They broke me, doc," he sobbed. "No matter how strong I tried to be, they broke me." He was furious. I sat with him and experienced the unremitting rage, the brutishness of his youth, the sanctity of his body, the pleasure of his muscles, Conan swinging his sword against the multitudes, proud, lone, self-reliant. I hefted the huge sword, my muscles rippling, staring down the hordes, meaning to fall upon them in a moment, fearing nothing, fearing death least of all. In his worst moment, I apprehended/felt/noted/experienced/surmised/heard the pre-words for and felt as a beat in my heart and my temples that the resident held the seeds of his own redemption.

"You were an athlete, doc, just like me. You understand what I'm saying. Tell me what to do." I told him he was convinced there was only one way to win a fight. "You wage war like Sonny Liston. You plant yourself in one spot and bang away. You take your shots and you just keep banging away." He felt the connection he was looking for. "You got that absolutely right. Sonny Liston. It's the only way I know how to be." It was the only way he knew, but he had choices. Burning with his fury, possessed of his now-greatest challenge, I told him. "You can pull the aggressor onto you. You can flow with the attack. You can drop back and drop down. You can face with humility where you and your challenger will both end up. You can fight this fight as the humble warrior."

He picked up his head and stared at me. In a timeless instant we were revealed to be now, to have always been, partners of cosmic immensity, with the cosmos shining throughout us, captured by the earliest of written texts. Carnivorous dentition flashed in the sunlight even as our mouths stayed closed. Swords glistened, breath came easily, deltoids charged up, the battle for life but also the acceptance of death Gilgamesh not complete until the gods made him a counterpart, Enkidu, who he fought against and befriended and went on many an expedition with and fought side by side with until he lost him and in losing him found his own heart fellow swordsman fellow warrior kettle drums in the background dragons to slay until we find that the dragons are all in us that there was never an external threat that it was us we fought against and something in us that will kill us draw us into the humus. Humility.

Our relationship was never going to be the same again. We had shifted beyond the prosaic, and although we would use the prosaic to communicate, we would be Gilgamesh and Enkidu after that, participants in one of the first acculturating texts, where a god returns to manhood and accepts mortality out of his love for another. From that point on we communicated more in our eye contact than in our words. We found a way to access the un-relationship. "I'm going to apologize to the women. I've been awful. I heard every word you said, doc. It's all burned in my memory."

How does one understand these stories? Again, my spiritual friends will take it all as matter of fact and give a Buddhist under-standing of our complete merger within the universe. To them, such happenings are commonplace. Not all my religious friends will be so accepting. Belief in God is one thing; actual experience is some-thing different, suspect. My scientific friends will resort to coded encryptions, like "Hey, you're a lovely guy." This means, "You certainly have a vivid imagination," or "It's always good to have at least one far-out friend if you're a scientist, to prove you're open-minded."

The answer is to be in this world but not of it, to take each experience and give it equal weighting, rather than let prejudices decide what I will attend to and what I will discard. I will be neither the scientist nor the religious follower nor the spiritual person nor the artist. At the same time I will allow all of it to be me and flow through me and be aroused when I am with others. I truly enjoy my field and can think of no better way to fulfill the imperative, to work, than to practice therapy. Strong metaphors give therapy direction and structure, but they belong to a world that acts out its entropy, and this encourages me to step back and take a reflective stance.

The culture of ego is still strong and so is the idea that science reserves the best methods for understanding human growth and change. We are not ready for everything Methuselah is ready to teach us. We do not want to deal with the protean nature of the human. The closest we come to acknowledging anything of the sort exists is through the pathological dynamics of dissociation and multiple personality disorder. We ignore our own experience of reality to follow the culture's theory.

We see how Aestus not only hides in the mists, but mystifies us still. We give no credulity to the high rate of child molestation, and we maintain social structures that only increase the chance for Aestus to do his work. Methuselah is talking and telling us Aestus was an important part of his life and his troubles. The topic of countertransference is still being handled gingerly, as if what the patient feels is his pathology and we had better not be cooperating in it. Few writers are willing to describe countertransference reactions in their rich profundity, earthiness, and primitiveness, and even fewer would dare describe the therapist as the wounded healer.

In this we show that society gives advantage to the person with the superego resistance. It is better to act out entropy than it is to wholly recognize it, own it, love it, embrace it, and use it for therapeutic ends. Lest we provoke those around us with superego resistance, it is important to be in the world, even though we are not of it. But we can still privately follow our own code which is organized around our intimate understanding of the eros and entropy within us.

I have a memory from long ago that stands out in odd clarity, not only because of the incidents captured, but also because it harkens back to a time and place so different that it can never be repeated. It was the Long Island of the fifties, rural, quiet, and in some parts equally populated by animals and humans. There were dirt roads everywhere, there were horses, there was a turkey farm to the north of us, and there was scrub pine as far as the eye could see.

The town had a general store, and because there was not much to do, my brother decided he would like to buy a salt lick, to attract some of the deer that freely wandered across our property. I remember him hefting the opaque white brick with two hands; it was almost as big as he was. Thomas was about 8 years old at the time. He set the brick down in the back of the property and moved about ten yards away. He had this capacity to sit perfectly still for long periods and blend in with the nature around him. This was a patience that was not necessarily his favored style, but it was connected with a goal. This ability to sacrifice for a goal still shines in his personality today.

Thomas taught the deer to tolerate his presence by repositioning himself closer to that brick each time he brought it out. Deer must have some hunger for salt, because they would appear in a short while, tiptoeing out of the woods, and would take turns licking in small, precise movements, having given themselves to an unselfconscious posture, aware of Thomas but deciding to stay. Years later I would more correctly understand that posture as alienative rather than related or merging, enough awareness present that they could bolt should they find their lives threatened.

This continued until the brick developed a deep trough in it. By this time Thomas was able to hold his hand right above the salt. On that day I came to watch. He patted the ground next to him and we both sat cross-legged. A deer sauntered right up to Thomas, licked at the brick, and allowed my brother to lightly pet his head. It was a cool afternoon, the sun streaming through the smallish pine and burgeoning young oak, birds calling in the background, and the sandy floor strewn with dry needles and leaves. There stood this light brown animal with large wet eyes, his nose and lips quivering, leaning down to allow a little body to pet his head.

His flanks were shuddering ever so slightly, his hooves were perfect, and a white billow of fur began under his mouth and flowed over his chest. We could hear the rasp of his tongue against the brick and even hear his light breath. Never since then have I been that close to natural wildness. Thomas's measured movements prevented any startling, and the deer stayed for a few minutes, for an eternity.

As occurs with children, I reacted to this as delightful and interesting, but nothing especially outside my usual realm of experience. Children already reside in a magical and mythical place created out of their great hungers and equally great powers to invest emotionally. It was as I grew older that the significance of this incident registered. It was an external, validating incident as powerful as what a child can conjure up from inside.

I went to work in Special Education, setting out my own salt licks to attract the untamed and skittish children whose fear of educational obliteration loomed as large as the deer's fear of becoming someone's supper. Thomas went on to an English post in a high school, and after teaching himself soccer, accepted the position of coach. In 1994 the NCAA recognized him as the top high school coach in U.S. soccer.

I will not forget that sight of my younger brother, dressed in dungarees, cowboy shirt, and moccasins, thoroughly concentrating on the cup of his small hand, petting the head of that deer, having discovered his own way to transform the mundane into the miraculous, having found through contact with the deer a gateway to the oceanic.

I WILL ALWAYS REMEMBER THIS AS THE DEER AT THE SALT LICK.

Such experiences bring us closer to Being. They make clearer the trace that is found in each word, each expression, each pause, and each empty moment, too. They remind us that we were never disconnected from the universe, and if we use such experiences wisely, we can find the trace of Being. We can be at one.

16

Inviting Methuselah into the Garden

Each of the elderly people I have treated over the years has brought a necessary uniqueness to the therapeutic enterprise. Even so, there are some broad generalizations that suggest our role in engaging the person. Methuselah is not fully conscious of the meaning of his advanced age. He has experienced much over the years, but he clings to a perception of a self at the early chapters of young adulthood. It was there that he had a commanding presence, able to bring the most of Being into his love, work, and play.

The sober facts of Methuselah's life cycle are reconceived by him to be a wicked assault of disease and deterioration on a basically healthy person in his mid-twenties. He knows he raised a family, he has grandchildren and great-grandchildren, but what he knows in his conscious mind is a mere wisp of what he knows in every other part of him: In his mid-twenties he was able to escape the pain and suffering of his youth, and he is going to hold on to *that* self forever, if he can. Methuselah is Narcissus in old age and late old age.

The nursing home placement and all the facts surrounding it overwhelm his efforts to maintain his defensive posture. He regresses and most often has to employ available energies to maintain a *just right* position, an expression of his need for an emotional status quo. At the time of referral he has usually regressed further and has shifted to a relationship-destructive position. He is not engaging the great issues of his stage of life, and why would he? Where is there the chance to integrate mind, body, and soul? His medical condition may be interfering with his cognitive and memory skills, and it is certainly wreaking havoc on his body. Most often, he has not addressed his spiritual needs sufficiently and does not find comfort in any guiding cosmology.

Where is the chance for wisdom? He is not ready to review the span of his life and conclude that in fact he has been granted a precious gift. He does not demonstrate an outwardly spiritual reaction, but it is not that he is spirit-less. Working with Methuselah has taught us that spirit has developmental levels, as do emotions, cognitions, and morality. He is unknowledgeably and preliterally worshipping at the altar of his body. He perceives through the body ego and focuses on every image, sense, and proprioceptive reaction with a fervor that betrays his somatic equation. He does not consider himself in terms of a mental ego, and he will need our support in finding that he is of value in his own self and that esteem arises from his spiritual dimensions. With us he will discover that he does not have to have a whole soma in order to be whole.

Methuselah is miserable and is looking to be mirrored. He has suffered for a lack of a mirror, a lack of kind understanding, because of the special sacrifice required. To mirror him is to invite a reaction of a frightening sort, allowing entropy to find a voice. If successfully mirrored, he would relax his self-attack and more effectively release aggression upon whoever deigned to be therapeutic. Yet this is the path of maturation that was blocked when his early intimate interactions provoked self-attack in the first place.

If he is regressed enough, he is experiencing a detextualization of character, and this undoing of the fabric of his identity has him gaping in horror at the underlying abyss. He sees nothing there and is terribly frightened, for No-thing really seems to him a vacuum. Death will empty him and destroy him, and he uses these fully formed ideas, as well as a coordinated amalgam of senses, visions, and preliteral notions, to torture himself. Untrained in the proper use of his entropy, he lets it formulate to its simplest level, that of self-destructivity.

He has not learned to float over the abyss, to realize it is in fact the miasma, the bubbling smokepot of his being. He seems so out of character to himself, and it is true he has touched the place of the concatenating urge, where text does not have complete authority, and where his proteanism is laid bare to him. He believes he is light-years away from the great-grandparently vision, but he is not so far away at all. He will need us to reframe his experience of detextualization, as the inevitable path to a more sublime organization.

For if he were spiritual, he would recognize that the transcendence required of old age and late old age occurs not by working "up" toward a more complex and effective ego, but by easing "down" and bidding adieu to Ego the Hoaxer. He would not have to be religious to do this, but it would help. He would not have to be spiritual to do this, but that would also help. He has to have lived a contemplative life, but we know he did not, and so he will now contemplate along with us. If not, we will analyze the resistance to contemplating, in order to give him some access to the fourth way "to be," in addition to the love, work, and play of his lifetime.

If we are careful to preserve his self-esteem, Methuselah will allow us to reinforce aspects of goal behaviors and will even tolerate questions. He would like to put aside the whole challenge of this time of his life and be more in the here-and-now. Frequently, he gets us to reinforce the coping dimensions of his neurotic defenses. He will deny and repress better with our help and will even work with us on his behaviors. He will survey his pleasant feelings, positive ideas, hopefulness, and control over events and reinforcers in his life. At times there is a clear motivation to practice agential activity, where the patient is capable of making his own good fortune.

But he will also need to work with people who understand that suffering is fundamental, that it identifies pleasure just as pleasure defines it, that being a tiny cork bobbing on a huge ocean is also a step toward melding back with the ocean and becoming the ocean, and that the "feminine attitude" of greater and greater connectivity can sweep us past masculine autonomy, past agency, past femininity itself, and back to connection with the universe.

So we will reinforce the behavioral aspects of healthful functioning. In the more inclusive category we will reinforce the resistances in general so they can succeed in their developmental unfolding. We will help the defenses give up in their perseverings, to allow for new organizing possibilities, moving upward to greater strength and control as need be, while resonating that we are fully prepared to move downward to yielding, to connectivity, to merger, and to meeting the anaclitic needs that were missed the first time around. We get to the contemplative issues by encouraging a resonation in the patient to our own studies.

Of course Methuselah's quest must yield progress in the milieu. Our ordinary interest in matching "inside" gains with "outside" performance is intensified, even though the therapy is the patient's own. The emphasis is on results in the form that society deems desirable, and if they are not forthcoming, people will want to know why. We need to educate others about the processes of assimilation and accommodation that are a truer measure of humankind's behavior than the metaphor of a learning curve. We have to be careful, for Methuselah is more likely to punish such treatment ambition than reward it. If cognitive behavior modification does not recognize the phenomenon of treatment-destructive resistance, it can only mean one thing in Methuselah's case. When he is in treatment-destructive phase, he is simply not being dealt with. I worked for clinics serving nursing homes for six years and was regularly given situations to handle that other therapists would rather avoid. All these situations were typified by the resident, the family, or the institution itself functioning in a destructive manner.

There is an unbearable press of entropy wishing to make itself known. Methuselah has been acting out his entropy. He has not consciously availed himself of the lethal experience, or of a healthy examination of such experience. How could he? He lives in a society that has eroticized being. He has no conceptual framework for the experience of dying in the here-and-now. "I want to feel alive!" is his imperative, the text of current vogue in a semi-tumescent society that keeps itself in tantric thrall, on the edge of a petit mort, giving everything to exaggerate life in a way that will bury any perception of death.

Methuselah did not contemplate. He did not go where the Buddha went. He feels his entropy as aggression and destructivity and has otherwise denied the experience of dying. The modus thanatos is preverbal and so Methuselah is half-a-being with the entropy begging to be addressed in some way that will integrate rather than further fragment him. He has murdered in his life, murdered with stark abandon, every minute, every second. He is murdering now, with acts of mental obliteration. He has gone as far as he can toward Nirvana in this fashion, but the gate is closed to him, because his modus is flawed. He will have a chance to transcend with us, because we always know where the murder is in the room.

We can find continuity with Methuselah in a way that he decides the resulting engulfment is "what is," not "what is bad" or even "what is good," but "what is." We allow for Methuselah's fuller efflorescence of instincts and for our own, too. We come to Atman whether we like it or not, whether we perceive it or not, just by treating many elderly patients each week and by releasing ourselves from the authority of our own character text so that we become protean. This is the result of our efforts to "be" in the right way with forty, fifty, or more elderly people. We let each patient introduce us to a new side of us. Of course we stiffen up when we have to, we protect, and we libidinize the aggression in the room. We tolerate what we can tolerate. We do what we can do. But we contemplate on where this is all going and on how the patients as a group are conspiring to force a transcendence upon us, toward the collective unconscious, where the elemental quanta concatenate to build text.

This is what transforms us into the humble warrior. We accept humility—literally the degrading of our textual integration beyond salvation. But what we give up makes us more available to all our patients. We become ever more comfortable resonating with their self-organizations and their explorative regressions. Our own protean nature gives Methuselah support for his, and he accepts us as his model for transcendence.

Methuselah can be difficult. At times he is positive-suggestible, cooperative, motivated, and willing to believe in the merits of therapy and to cooperate with activities in and out of the sessions. Just as often, however, he is negative-suggestible, uncooperative, unmotivated, happy with his maladaptive patterns, and unlikely to go along with anyone else's plans for him. We work with him anyway. We work with him if he is destructive, if he is senile, if he is aphasic, and even if he does not demonstrate an awareness of our presence. We do not let third-party restrictions interfere with our ethical duties. We see Methuselah pro bono as we have to. For he needs our support, and he lives in a community that needs our support. We do not reject any resident as untreatable. The nursing home cannot reject him. They cannot turn him away. So we do not return to the staff and ask for a discontinuation of treatment because he has not gone along with our plan. We bring more of the facility into the treatment and push for transdisciplinary interventions. We enlarge the network to find the critical mass that will produce effect.

We work with everyone at his level of participation, and we work with staff to develop its élan (Liptzin 1992, Ray et al. 1993). We do not have to control all the action, we just have to remain inclusive, involve everyone in the plan, talk things up, share ideas, be taught as well as teach, and take the chance to fail like everyone else is failing. We resolve obstacles to everyone doing his part. We are shocking, we are humorous, we are thought-provoking. We tickle the unconscious of the staff by offering completely new ways to see the world.

The resident says, "I will never take a shower again, and I don't care *what* they do to me!" We respond, "You look and you smell great, just the way you are! Don't *ever* change for me!" The resident is shocked, surprised, and tickled. This "paradoxical" intervention releases him to cooperate. He becomes more amenable to staff importunings. We arouse the staff's attention to what it means to be human and to what heights humanity can reach. That unwashed gentleman was acting out the profane in the direct sense of being-in-the-world just as it appeared to him. The joining elevated him to epiphany. He "saw the light." He saw beyond the apparent and was only released by our intense, feminine connection. It was not just that he felt joined. In the joining he had a taste of connection with the universe. He had a glimpse that he was "It," and so it was easier to return to Earth and cooperate with the nurses.

We create the circumstances for everyone to experience epiphany—residents, staff, administration, families, government agencies, and politicians. I have spoken to them all. I have done it in the interest of each person learning to take better care of the elderly version of his own self.

BEHAVIORAL DIMENSIONS

The literature on psychotherapy with the elderly has dealt largely with depression. Katz and Parmelee (1994) reported on the epidemiology of depression in nursing homes. Whereas two and a half percent of the population at large is diagnosable with major depression, the number can increase by a factor of ten in nursing homes. When neurotic depression and adjustment reaction with depressed mood are added, fully forty-three percent of the nursing home population falls into the category. They found that with time these percentages increased and the staff also became more depressed.

The outcome research on psychotherapy as well as on pharmacological interventions with the elderly has been summarized by Schneider and colleagues (1994). Engel (1977) spoke of the ethical requirement to move on biological, psychological, and social fronts in providing for patients. Beitman and Klerman (1991) summarized the effects of simple and combined treatments of medication and psychotherapy. Lebowitz and Niederehe (1992) saw the need for an increased biopsychosocial perspective with the elderly. The federal mandate to limit chemical restraint in nursing homes has reduced the use of tranquilizers, antidepressives, and anxiolytics, so that psychosocial intervention has become preeminent. This happened in connection with the inclusion of psychotherapy as a medicare-reimbursable service in the early 1990s.

Cognitive behavior therapy research demonstrates efficacy with elderly patients. Scogin and McElreath (1994) and Teri and colleagues (1994) have reported on the positive results of this approach. Gallagher and Thompson (1982) specified the elements of the treatment, where the patient works with the therapist to become more sensitized to the learning principles involved in behaviors, attitudes, and affects. Events, moods, self-views, thoughts, and behaviors are discussed and explored in a way that the patient recognizes his agential powers. He learns skills such as reattributing, examining the evidence, listing pros and cons of maintaining a given idea, and evaluating the consequences of a given idea.

Continued work with the elderly has suggested to Gallagher-Thompson and colleagues (1995) that the resident be seen for shorter sessions over a longer period, that termination not be as total as with a younger patient, that the elderly patient be allowed to talk about events as he needs to, even if this does not contribute directly to the work at hand, and that audio and video aids be employed to help the patient recall and reexamine the interaction with the therapist between sessions, out of respect for compromised memory and processing skills.

The researchers are responding to the limited powers of exertion seen in the nursing home population, the need for more contact over the course of the therapy, the need for the patient to set his own agenda, and the anaclitic dimensions of the relationship where the patient is looking for something special. The approach is responsive to the data and is making the proper course changes. The researchers did not comment more on the patient's tendency to use the sessions to talk about issues of the week. I have noted this phenomenon and understand it as part of the status quo resistance, where the patient is using the therapist's stable, predictable, and dependable presence in order to introject him. The patient is "going over material," even "going over the same material" as an act of assimilation. It would be interesting to see behavioral researchers account for this particular phenomenon in the parlance of learning theory.

The behavioral dimension brings a full complement to our work with Methuselah. It adds behavioral prosthetics that give the patient greater advantage in the milieu (Pinkston and Linsk 1984). We quantify the patient's entry-level skills as well as the treatment goals. We reinforce successive approximations of the target behavior, and if the patient is cooperative, he joins us in charting, giving himself feedback, and being a more active participant. We use a contract to make clear what is expected of the patient and what he can expect from us. The contract is used to give the patient evaluative feedback on his progress.

We do a reinforcer search to identify what will help the patient move toward his goals, in an effort to "sweeten the experience" of changing toward an area he is disinclined to do on his own. If he is engaging in a maladaptive behavior in the facility, we help him with stimulus control using the proper time and place for him to display his preferred activity. If it is a behavior that the facility cannot tolerate but that he cannot stop, we work toward a decrease in the behavior rather than outright control. We study how antecedents and consequences control the patient's behavior and we alter these in session. We work with staff to alter them in the milieu. Liptzin (1992) recognized the need to empower the staff with such clinical skills.

I find that Methuselah is not the willing participant pictured in the research on cognitive behavior therapy, and I am not sure what accounts for this discrepancy. I have worked with behaviorists who have reported difficulty keeping the patient engaged because of the high level of skill required in such therapy. The patient is not so ready to do homework, to practice in the sessions, to discuss his beliefs openly, or even to engage in relaxation practices. Paradoxically, the very focus on relaxation skills makes a number of shy and withdrawn patients more anxious. Lazarus and colleagues (1992) reported on the need to identify cross-diagnostic variables that affect the viability of behavioral treatment, such as the patient's objectives, resistances, beliefs, and ideas about in-therapy and extra-therapy activities. These might be considered an effort to operationalize the psychodynamic concept of resistance.

As behavior therapy reaches out to more resistant and uncooperative patients, it is modifying its approach. Where the patient will not engage in more direct examination of ideas, the focus is on replicating elements of the milieu in the session to create role-playing situations, or the kinds of scenarios where the patient finds he is always failing, saying the wrong thing, not saying enough, being too intense, or being off the mark. This kind of work is consonant for those of us who practice analytically. The analyst will work with the patient where he is and will work with the situation as it is. Teri and Logsdon (1992) have concluded that on-site interventions with the elderly will become more commonplace in the future. If a behavioral emphasis is called for, he will focus his energies on that. This is the therapy portion of an analysis, dealing more with the immediate problem. It can also be construed as a preanalytic exercise, where the parameters are accepted in order to keep the therapy alive and the patient motivated. Creating progress with the patient is what counts. The sanctity of behavioral and psychoanalytic texts is not on the practitioner's mind.

What happens to the transference and resistance in behavioral work? The transference is there, as always. There is transference everywhere, all the time. It is in the form of resistance to transference, as is noted in the beginning of the psychoanalytic enterprise. It is worth mentioning because the therapist is picking up on the feeling state the patient is employing as part of the resistance, and it affects his personal state. The patient holds back from the effulgence of feeling, sense, and perception that there is a press to repeat, in the service of the tasks at hand. The resistance manifests as the work itself. Working on behavioral goals is a resistance to working on something else. There is no hint of pathology in this assessment, for even in the most dedicated analysis everything that is happening is acting as a resistance to something else happening. Resistance is always there.

It is important to recognize that behaviorism is a text in its own right. Like psychoanalysis, psychodynamic therapy, or any word, it is a lie. It is a metaphor for that which is really happening. It is a mask of reality. Wachtel (1973) found that behaviorists and psychoanalysts talked worlds apart but practiced much closer together. A behavioral trainer of some repute explained to us how he criticized a patient who was being resistant, by joining her negative self-description with the same asperity with which she kept repeating it. This was how he broke a treatment impasse. After the training session I asked him about this. He acknowledged it was a psychoanalytic technique. Then why was he clobbering psychoanalysis in front of his youthful audience, if he was going to turn around and use the techniques? I was given to understand that behaviorism was a reigning metaphor, no more and no less. It did not preclude an eclectic attitude.

In another training session a highly effective practitioner lambasted psychodynamic therapy and claimed to cure phobias in fourteen sessions or less. I pressed him concerning the kinds of patients we really see in the office. He did allow that he could spend nine months preparing for those eventful fourteen weeks, and he described a joining technique that helped the patient get ready. I took him to task about appropriating joining when it defied the austere categorizations of the learning principles. He winked. There is an unspoken credo here. It is natural and right that we treat people rather than apply paradigms, and that we take from each other what we need.

It is up to the individual therapist to read between the lines. Cognitive behavior therapy can surely alleviate depression in thirteen weeks. It may take forty weeks, sixty weeks, and eighty weeks. It is going to take as long as it is going to take, and it just may not work at all. To make behaviorism larger than life is playfulness. When behaviorism seems hell-bent on neutering the other therapies in its search for hegemony, that is also play, and we only need respond by offering equally attractive forms for young therapists in search of a way-to-be.

THE PSYCHODYNAMIC DIMENSION

Methuselah comes to us with the richest of psychodynamics, having been given countless opportunities to invest in others, in himself, in things, and in ideas in a way that has at once broadened him and has also refined his narcissism. He attaches subjective meanings to the events in his life with the same earnestness he always has, and he has all that history to confirm these meanings. His demeanor does not say it all, and that is why psychodynamic theory maintains its vigor with this population. It gives us the method for intuiting the private mental life that is at center.

Basch (1980) set out the basic model of how dynamics connect to behavior: "By problem-solving I mean the necessity of dealing continuously with stimulation from within and from without that must be organized in such a way as to let the individual generate appropriate responses" (p. 171). The structures of the mind have an organization and content that are amenable to re-education in therapy. Martin (1995) sees the process as one of the patient assimilating information to the point that accommodation is forced. What is being assimilated and accommodated? He believes the patient's mind is "embedding relatively lasting episodic memories from therapeutic interactions" (p. 121).

Behavior arises out of structures, and behavior change is the result of the plasticity of these underlying structures. The therapist presents himself in a way that his own structures impact on the patient's. Kohut (1971) went to Freud's formulation of how the ego wrested territory from the id. The infant felt a press for sustenance, for example, and in the absence of gratification, it hallucinated a breast. That was an act of ideation, an ego process. Kohut put the therapist at the site of this activity, for the goal of expanding the ego. By allowing minor empathic failures in an otherwise dependable emotional atmosphere, the therapist provoked the patient's ego to expand. The ego created in itself the therapist, in the dimension that the therapist would have gratified him. The patient internally met the need that was insufficiently dealt with externally. Kohut called this a transmuting internalization.

Galatzer-Levy and Cohler (1990) couched it in terms of the idealizations of the therapist fading in the face of realities. As the transference was coming under control of the reality principle, the therapist and patient were involved in the patient's own creations. "The solution to losing someone is making some of his qualities your own. If the loss is sufficiently gradual and nontraumatic, it is possible the resulting identification will be quite selective" (Galatzer-Levy and Cohler 1990, p. 98). These are concepts of long-term psychoanalysis. Elderly patients I have treated psychoanalytically function no differently than younger patients. There appears to be no disturbance to the process that is specific to age. These have been people who have been able to come to the office and keep to a weekly schedule. They are not the frail and ill elderly of the nursing homes. If there has been one distinction about age during psychoanalysis, it has been the reduction in preconscious material that can be shared, apparently due to reduced contact with the object world.

Attachment patterns as recollected by elderly residents of nursing homes correlated with healthy behavior in the milieu. Recollections were deemed important because they suggested how present internal structures were operating (Anderson and Stevens 1993). The interest is in how childhood patterns are being brought into present functioning. Strupp and Binder (1984) saw change occurring with the patient's insight that such a connection exists. He commented on the three notions concerning organizational structures that characterized psychodynamic thought: they were created by conflicts between the basic drives, by developmental arrests, or by interpersonal experiences. Strupp (1992) saw psychodynamic theory remaining vibrant: "Unconscious motivation, psychic determinism, transference, countertransference and resistance have proved remarkably durable" (p. 23). The interventions of the therapist came from his continual emotional resonation to the patient, followed by interventions about the transference patterns in the relationship. This education increased the patient's ability to move beyond the confines of the transference.

Whitbourne (1989) focused on Alzheimer's disease, paranoid disturbances, and mood disorders in the elderly. She proposed a combination of dynamic and behavioral therapy, adding family intervention where possible, based on her work with this population. Blazer (1990) encouraged a supportive therapy approach, in a way that took advantage of the environment. "Older adults do not cope with others who provide a social and emotional support without a milieu that provides a sense of connectedness and belonging" (p. 221).

Chodorkoff (1990) saw therapy as an opportunity for the elderly to resolve long-standing emotional problems, to proceed with the renunciation that marked the analytic therapies, and to do the basic work of reorganizing and reintegrating. Myers (1991) echoed Erikson's comments on the elderly person's mortal fear being related to the clock running out (p. 6). The patient might have a reluctance to commit to the work required to effect energy redistributions of a sort that could return the patient to a state of equilibrium.

Both in behavioral and psychodynamic studies, there is a clear indication that the patient benefits. My own experience is that Methuselah causes us to realign our dynamic work somewhat. He brings different energies to the sessions, his words may be fewer but carry more meaning for him, his motivational profile runs the gamut but he is also more reserved than his youthful counterpart, he does the same incremental work but also fears that time is running out for him, and yet he also reacts with a predictable amount of surprise, joy, insight, and humor to therapy. He has special issues that need to be addressed, and he arouses different kinds of countertransference, something the researchers recognized as central.

Peake and Philpot (1991) felt it was important for the therapist to have had enjoyable experiences with elders in his personal life. These authors found that countertransference arose over "biases about dying, feelings about death and mortality, anger over the patient being entrenched, pity in response to tragedies and losses, fear in response to the overwhelming nature of the patient's problems, confusion, misunderstanding and depression in response to the complexity of the problems" (p.198). Dorfman (1994) suggested that one's own emotional pain over the issues of the elderly, plus an ill-defined but pervasive ageism were enough to create a significant countertransference that needed to be dealt with educationally and through supervision.

In fact, the countertransferences are more terrifying than the researchers could have possibly alluded to. Methuselah buries his nails deep into the throat of anyone who would dare resonate with him, or even chance to get close, in order to take that other person down as the voracious Earth claims him and turns him into soil. The psychodynamic literature brings a certain gentility to what I have become convinced is a Götterdämmerung in the treatment office, where forces that seem as good and evil are in matched apposition, and where evil will win, must win, to finally have its voice in the death of the patient's soma. For clarity of purpose in the sessions, directness about the foundations of humankind, and a mask on reality that most exposes what lies beyond, I find no equal in a special variant of psychodynamic technique called modern psychoanalysis.

THE MODERN PSYCHOANALYTIC DIMENSION

Freud became enamored of the oedipal motif and thereafter chose this personality as the better candidate for treatment. The person's conflicts centered on the ages of 3 and up, his issues centered more on the erotic, and he had the capacity to put words to forgotten but accessible knowledge underlying his neurotic behavior. He experienced trust in the relationship and was able to be positive toward the analyst.

Freud did not feel optimistic about the narcissistic neuroses, as he called them. These were disorders hailing from the first two years of life. They were preverbal in nature, had strong, attendant negative reactions, included an avoidance of bonding, and were marked by lack of motivation to change. Freud (1915) recognized that hate had an eminence, that it pre-dated love in the infant's emotional life: "It derives from the narcissistic ego's primordial repudiation of the external world with its outpouring of stimuli" (p. 139).

The role of aggression achieved equal ranking to eros in "Beyond the Pleasure Principle," a paper he submitted on the heels of the Great War. He theorized that our very being was organized not only around libido, but the constancy principle as well. The former described efforts of tension increase and the latter tension decrease. Both figured in all human endeavors, indeed even in the elemental structure of the ego (Freud 1920). Side by side with this information was the image of Narcissus, who invested libido toward his own self, rather than seeking to love an object. He was someone who loved himself to the detriment of potential attachments that could bring him more healthfully into the object world.

In a brilliant act of animation, Spotnitz (1976) infused Narcissus with character, writing in the early 1960s about the myths of the ancients on this subject. He sustained the dual-drive view in interpreting the myth and looking at Narcissus's dynamics. Narcissus not only remained the subject and object of his own love, but also of his own aggression, and he died.

The therapy with Narcissus boasted some significant changes. There was transference and there was resistance, because every analytic procedure understood the presence of these two dynamics and worked with them. But the design was no longer based on confrontation, clarification, interpretation, and working through (Greenson 1967). Narcissus was not able to cooperate with such a procedure. The better alternative was to maintain a noninterpretive stance, focus more on the "inside" and "outside" together, attend to the management of resistances, and be more aware of the emotional level of what was happening in session (Margolis 1994c, p. 213).

In describing the narcissistic transference, Margolis (1994a) explained that with more primitive object relations, emotional communications became paramount, and the therapist was dealing with a lot more negative feelings. Kirman (1980) reported that insulation of the patient's ego was the priority and that the analyst must be prepared to work more with the patient's aggression. This was not Kohut's (1976) narcissistic rage, a reaction to the irritation of a poorly defended ego. It was entropy, unmanaged and un-trained, which was now channeled into destructivity, and it had to be dealt with carefully.

Margolis (1994d) explained the use of object-oriented questions as a way to direct potentially iatrogenic stimulation away from the ego. Such questions were able to better promote talk, whereas an attention to the ego could stifle movement and wound the patient. Especially in the beginning phase of treatment, it is not likely that the modern analyst would direct psychology's most famous question to the ego, "And how did you feel about that?" He would ask a factual question, a question about someone else, or even a question about himself, as a signal of his intention to preserve the ego's integrity. Self psychology made a similar observation, that the patient with selfobject transference would benefit from a contact devised specifically not to overwhelm the defenses. Muslin (1992), for example, described the importance of titrating interpretations so that shame and resultant decompensation were not aroused, when treating the elderly patient. In modern psychoanalysis, join-ing, mirroring, and reflecting became the preferred method of resolving resistances to forward movement and accomplishing the work of therapy (Margolis 1994f).

The goal of modern psychoanalysis is not to rid the patient of pathological narcissism. It is to educate this basic dimension of personality so that its healthful aspects become clarified, because it is the annealing of love and hate in the yet undiscriminating mind that has rendered Narcissus a poison to himself. It is the distinction between the drives that will mark progress, as the therapist invites a voice to each. Because we are immersed in an erotic metaphor, the primary signature of our death-denying society, it is more impor-tantly the entropy of the preverbal period that will find understand-ing, embrace, and a tongue. Meadow (1981) described the early transference states we see in therapy that place the patient in an indifferent, fearful, and hating relationship with the therapist. They are the ones to be on the lookout for and to deal with in order to keep the therapy viable. We observe and respect the patient's contact function, for it communicates to us just how he expects us to form our own comments, questions, and early relationships (Margolis 1994e).

The patient is encouraged to put words to his impulses so that he can develop more mature alternatives for expressing them. The words give at least partial gratification, and the emphasis on emotional communication brings talk to a level that it can successfully compete with id resistances such as acting out and somatizing. The therapist's role is to study what is preventing the patient from getting what he wants. This throws a whole new light on the idea of the "goal." The goal is what the patient cannot achieve on his own. It is precisely that which his character structure blocks him from accomplishing.

As Menninger and Holzman (1973) explained, the patient has every intention to seek the kind of help that would effect change. Very soon he is going to find that he is resisting giving the cooperation that is needed for change. If he is reacted to in a nondirective manner, his resistances are brought into the transference. He was hoping for magical activity to bring about the changes he wanted, and it was not forthcoming. "The analyst does not make this expected response, and there is a gradually increasing dissatisfaction and resentment in the patient that induces him to revert to less and less disguised forms of reactions characteristic of his childhood" (Menninger and Holzman 1973, p. 124).

The purpose of a psychoanalytic approach is to beckon the patient's characteristic form of interacting. The patient first resists transference feelings about the therapist. As the resistances reduce, the feelings become more available. They manifest themselves in the relationship as transference resistance. For himself, the therapist is undergoing some of the same changes. His countertransference becomes available to him, and he experiences an urge to bring them into the treatment as a resistance. The therapist will want to do something that he should not do, or he will be reluctant to do something that he should. The progress of modern analytic treatment revolves around this challenge.

The therapist searches his own feelings and uses his self-analysis to understand what it is the patient needs from him. He remains worthy of the transference obligation placed upon him and makes an emotional communication that echoes within the patient in a particular way. It is the voice of significant others from the patient's earliest years, saying what they would have said to keep him on the path of maturation. That which he searches his whole life to hear comes from the therapist who has made the empathic sacrifice to stretch beyond his own life story to immerse himself in the story of the patient and to give the right feelings (Margolis 1994b).

And what has been missed most of all during Narcissus's formative period? Some way to understand, accept, embrace, and willfully manage his entropic urges. He needed the help of those around him to bring the most of Being into being, but was left with the option of using each drive to tame the other, leaving his being in a malaise and worse. He gets another chance in the therapy to allow all of him to be acknowledged, appreciated, embraced, and loved.

What is the meaning of narcissism in the psychodynamics of the elderly person? The impact of the knowledge of death creates a clear opening to accept the foundational contributions of entropy. "I'm going to die!" is exposed directly and gives the opportunity for the patient to learn that he was dying from the moment of his conception. Every bit of his protoplasm rendered inorganic or structured was a dying that promoted living. This is the way he is built. The first irritants of his environment that registered in his system created structures of ego. The more he structuralized, the more he died. He is dying now, and he experiences it as rage, hostility, murder, or the blankness of feeling resulting from the narcissistic defense. Especially when it is hidden from view, however, does it pose the most formidable countertransference challenge.

Hayden (1983) referred to repressed rage being the most deleterious toxin in the therapy, and as the therapist was exposed to it, he could be damaged by its corrosive influence. The rage is a derivative of entropy in the ego. It is the preferred way for discharging that drive, in the absence of an emotional and philosophical education that would have allowed a more direct experience of dying.

Spotnitz (1981) saw the action of his therapy at precisely this spot. "When one employs emotional communication oriented to resolving the patient's resistance to communicating his aggression in language without action, the patient improves" (p. 134). Freud (1905) believed that people past the age of 50 had lost the elasticity to benefit from his therapy. He may have been responding to the sense of hopelessness regarding complexification of the ego in response to the instinctual demands. Fenichel (1972) offered a somewhat brighter picture: "In considering analysis at advanced age, the entire situation of the patient is decisive. If he has possibilities of libidinal and narcissistic gratification, analysis seems more hopeful than if the analysis would only bring the insight that life has been a failure without offering any opportunity to make up for it" (p. 576).

Gay (1987) gave convincing evidence that Freud was every bit the destroyer of illusions. He saw religion as offering a false hope and preventing people from working on psychodynamic issues that would more truly benefit mankind. Religion was a defense against ego development. But what has been prominent in my work with Methuselah is that his resistance against religion is one way he has worked to block his own transcendence. For hidden in Freud's formulation is the bitter axiom that anything experienced as oceanic is but a reminiscence of the fetus's time in the amnion. For our relentlessly sober Westerner, there was no Self or Atman.

Freud's therapy was not going to work well at all with older people because he had not made the connection between the experience of the artist and the experience of old age. He understood the artist's dipping into primary process as regression in the service of the ego. There was a place that psychosis was ego-adaptive. Had he opened himself up to the philosophies of the East with the same vigor that he studied ancient Western civilization, he might have fused the two ideas and discovered regression in the service of transcendence.

In the absence of a redeeming philosophy, old age seems a hell on Earth, and the therapist an unwilling Dante. "The increasing immediacy of death, the irreplaceability of the loss of objects, work and beloved persons, and the increasing dependency needs are factors that both mobilize anxiety and increase the transference and countertransference problems of the analyst" (Riess 1992, p. 22). It takes special courage and personal growth for the therapist to be with the patient and with his feelings when all these factors are complicated by severe emotional disturbance and dementia. Blumenson (1993) described the way for the therapist to be, silently mirroring and communicating at an affective level to encourage a healthful reaction in people with the most serious of challenges. Words can sometimes be used in a way to interfere with the right feelings, which in the end prove essential for therapeutic progress.

Spiegel (1993) has shown how social support increases the life span of terminal cancer patients. The therapist's presence is pivotal in arousing eros, and he has to find a way to tolerate his feelings in order to continue to supply a bonding experience. The toxic challenge of frail and ill elderly patients involves their therapist's own denial of death. If we remain purely in the psychoanalytic tradition, we are in for trouble, for to buy the illusion of our separateness and to ignore *advaita*, our non-dual nature, is to fully immerse ourselves in suffering.

The ego hoax has been a terribly exciting game, that is to say a game at once terrifying and all the more precious for its ability to keep our full attention (Watts 1972). But to give up the structures of ego and to float unmoored in the oceanic is to be able *to be* with the frail and ill elderly as they need us. "I am going to die!" is met with,

"I am going to die!"

"We were dying from the moment we were conceived."

"There is no living without dying."

The horror associated with that thought is met with our experience of dying in the moment, our sense of tension reduction, the noting of the blank spaces between the actions of living, the detextualizing of our character, our giving up our ego. The patient has transformed the experience of dying into horror. We make the emotional communication of reflecting back the whatness of the original experience, to show the patient that his foundational feeling is all he has to discover to remove the horror. His awful humiliation, a by-product of ego and its individual contours, can become the stance of the humble warrior, just by relaxing, going back, regressing, in the caressing hammock of our love and attention to eros and entropy.

The patient has never been more ready to accept dual-drive theory, not as a lecture in a university hall, but as an intimate experience of how he is in fact built. You cannot tell him. His pathological narcissism will protect him from learning in that fashion. Narcissus was notoriously resistant to learning through direct talk. You have to invite him by having the courage to know where your own loving heart and murderous heart is, while admiring his defense all the while.

What are the right feelings for an aged Narcissus who is likely to be inundated by a cosmic return to the oceanic experience? What are the right feelings for a being that is soon to yield back to the larger Being out of which it sprung, surrendering its instrumental opposites, the tools of prosaic consciousness? What are the right feelings for a being on the edge of consciousness, a reintegration with Self? They are an acceptance of where the patient has been, where he is now, and where he is going, as an expression of acceptance of where we have been, where we are now, and where we are going. It is a resonation with our foundational drives, a reverberating with how the patient has transformed them into ego derivatives that create suffering, and above all a loving embrace of the resistances that present in the therapy. It is our willingness to have all our feelings about the patient when he is most anxious and defensive, because after all, this is just God playing the most far-out game of all.

THE TRANSPERSONAL DIMENSION

In *The Book*, Alan Watts (1972) explained, "We do not 'come into' this world; we come *out* of it, as leaves from a tree. As the ocean 'waves,' the universe 'peoples'" (p. 8). He brought the philosophy of the East into the Western realm of ideas with his explanations, broaching the concept that individuality is a convention but not a reality. "As is so often the way, what we have suppressed and overlooked is something startingly obvious. The difficulty is that it is *so* obvious and basic that we can hardly find the words for it. The Germans call it *Hintergedanke*, an apprehension lying tacitly in the back of our minds which we cannot easily admit, even to ourselves" (p. 12).

Repeating sentiments held for thousands of years in the East, he described what modern physics (Haisch et al. 1994) is now calling the mirage of mass. Our solitary formation carries the energy and field of the universe, for that is what we really are. As they say, such knowledge never stopped a holy man from jumping out of the way of a charging elephant. But the elephant never stopped him from an enlightenment as to his connection to everything. Eastern ideas are proving remarkably hardy in the face of evolving theoretical physics (Capra 1985).

The *Upanishads* (1987) were written over two thousand years ago. They instruct us that there is a reality underlying life, that we have a real Self, a cosmic one, so that each of us is continuous with the power that is the universe. The ancients knew it more directly. Dossey (1989) has employed the Einsteinian concept of nonlocal events in explaining how intercessory prayer by people in one place in the United States can have a benign effect on the cardiac conditions of people far away who have not been told they are being prayed for.

But such reports have not yet captured the scientific imagination. Our present world is still gratifying the hypertonic exercise of the ego. It has lost transpersonal truths in order to deal with entropy in a different manner. Modern humankind would rather seem to wrestle with death, using greater powers of ratiocination, than fall into its arms and experience it. The entropy is availed access to structuralizations within the ego and is channeled away from direct confrontation.

Brown (1959) found death consigned to the toilet, transformed into an excremental vision. Death was equated with dirt, and that was how he analyzed Jonathan Swift's disgust as he expressed it in *Gulliver's Travels*. It was the linking of the spiritual and physical that created a special terror. Man, the angel, was made of soil. Becker

(1973) expanded on Brown's motif, "Man is literally split in two: he has an awareness of his own splendid uniqueness in that he stands out of nature with a towering majesty, and yet he goes back into the ground a few feet in order to blindly and dumbly rot and disappear forever" (p. 26).

Conrad (1983) described a young man's coming of age in *Heart of Darkness*, where the wildness of the jungle directly expressed what polite English society found ways to suppress. His assessment of Kurtz the ivory poacher reminds us of Methuselah's unhappy personal reckonings: "But the wilderness had found him out early, and had taken on him a terrible vengeance, for the fantastic invasion. I think it had whispered to him things about himself which he did not know, things of which he had no conception till he took counsel with this great solitude—and the whisper had proved irresistably fascinating. It echoed loudly with him because he was hollow at the core" (p. 133).

Gurko (1979) credits Conrad with illuminating the corrupt influences of Europe by offering up Africa in its lush profundity. Here the European sentiment could not maintain its defense, and the Western mind disintegrated before such an onslaught of generation and dissipation in pure state. Gurko marveled at the precision and color of Conrad's descriptions, because the author had adopted the English language after he was well into adulthood. My understanding is that Conrad's vision was less blunted by textual convention, by the lie that the word perpetrates. He made less of those slips, twists, and evasions that were built into the language because he took a powerful theme and rendered it more denotatively. Modern man, if caused to look directly at his foundational drives, as they are amply portrayed all around him in the natural and physical world, would die a wretch. And his last words would be, "the horror."

Rinzler and Gordon (1980) studied with Buddhists and discovered that suffering was the direct result of working against universal truths to attempt to stabilize and restabilize an "I" with its contrast in "other." Watts (1961) said this was *samsara*, the effort to save life from death, pleasure from pain, good from evil, and self from not-self. The ego had a structure and so assumed its right to permanence. *Samsara* was the vicious cycle of attempting to breathe life into such dualities, in order to keep experiencing life. Suffering was equal to that effort. McFadden (1995) identified the spiritual experience as one replacing the ordinary subject–object splits of everyday life with unity. Oneness with all is eminently available to us, but somehow we keep missing it.

These ideas would seem evident, for we coexist with cultures that can practice closer to an ideal of non-duality. Koshikawa and colleagues (1993) reported that people of Eastern backgrounds were encouraged to see themselves as an unbroken part of a dynamic whole. The attitude of therapy was to reinforce cultural givens such as *satori*, where one strived to experience unifying cosmic consciousness. This could be made concrete, in reinforcing the family ties with gratitude about everyone's contribution to the whole.

Suler (1993) reported that integration of Eastern thought into Western practice aroused discomfort in clinicians, who did not seem ready to deal with the transpersonal realm. It appears that this is one way in which present-day psychotherapy is split. It is having difficulty incorporating understandings that have been with humanity from the time it could self-reflect.

Neumann (1954) felt that man was wholly one with the universe, in a state of perfection. But as soon as man attempted to quantify experience, individual consciousness arose. His study of ancient mythologies caused him to conclude that the universe first split in the mind of man into light and dark, and it was through such action that unity continued to yield to opposites. Jung (1954) likewise saw consciousness disturbing the continuity of man-in-nature; as man withdrew the projections he had been making onto nature, it ceased to be a "thou."

Campbell (1971) saw every spiritual principle of the ancients emanating from the human physique and nervous structure. Myth was poetry designed to illuminate what man was and what he felt, to capture his being, the particular way that the Universal doctrine penetrated through the human form. Earlier, Campbell (1954) recognized the split between what the world knows and what our own field was willing to study: "And even those psychologists of our generation who do not acknowledge the spiritual betray a certain reserve when confronted with it as a problem; they stress its many meanings and point out that a spirit is scarcely a part of the individual psyche, that it is 'supraindividual,' perhaps a kind of collective supraconsciousness, to use a word both magnificent and dangerous" (p. 75).

Wilber (1990) identified the main problem. Reductionistic science sees reality through the "eye of the flesh," and its validity remains unquestioned. Yet how would it be able to convey the meaning of a poem, a play, a piece couched in its own historic time? This can better be accomplished with the "eye of reason." It is not that one is better than the other. They deal with different domains. One more level is the "eye of contemplation," which again deals with different material. The "eye of the flesh" is wrong to use for transpersonal study. Wilbur (1990) wrote, "If you attempt to translate nondual Reality into dualistic reason, then you will create two opposites where there are in fact none, and therefore each of these opposites can be rationally argued with equal plausibility—and that, to return to Kant, shows why reason only generates paradox when it tries to grasp God or the Absolute" (p. 19).

Wilber's solution was to maintain a respectful distance between contemplation and the quantifying eye of empirical scientism. The contemplative framework was complex to the point that it defied reduction. Not only that, it required study before someone could adequately move within its conceptual borders and be able to say anything intelligent about it. "When someone asks, 'Where is your empirical proof for transcendence?', we need not panic. We explain the instrumental methods of our knowledge and invite him or her to check it out personally. Should that person accept and complete the injunctive strand, then that person is capable of becoming part of the community of those whose eye is adequate to the transcendental realm" (Wilber 1990, p. 36).

Stating one of his arguments in positive terms, the student of physics must be able to carry out calculus operations. Until and unless he agrees to do so, he is not in the position to best understand what the professor has to say. To approach physics without the skills of calculus, and then conclude that physical laws are hogwash, is simply poor research. I have heard people say outlandish things about behaviorism, and they do not have the knowledge base or experience for understanding what they are criticizing. Likewise, I have regularly encountered those who misconstrue Freudian thought because of any lack of immersion in it. Their critiques generally miss the point. Even though there is much to challenge in behaviorism and psychoanalysis, these challenges best come from people who have taken the time to immerse themselves and to understand.

Whether there actually is Atman, or Self, is a question that will get short shrift from someone who is petrified of the ideas of "dying unto the self," the ego as hoax, enlightening psychotic experience, and the engulfing universe without boundaries. We can fully respect that person, who is getting a good fright by playing God's most far-out game of having lost himself completely. But we must look to others for talk, thoughts, feelings, and settings that make clear the direction to the gateless gate.

Brown (1966) felt the reality of the void, hidden by conventional words whose task was to suppress that reality. He espoused, "Not a controlled regression in the service of the ego but an active surrender of the controlling and deliberative mind" (p. 263). To have no self was to be a dead man, but not to be dead. Frankl (1984) dealt with the existential vacuum, relating it also to the great fears of the elderly. He concluded that man's work was to actualize potential meaning of one's life. May (1983) felt the goal of therapy was the radical enlargement of being. Both Frankl and May saw these are libidinal enterprises. It was up to Spotnitz (1985) to make this an entropic enterprise at the same time.

It would seem that psychology and psychotherapy have a vested interest in bowdlerizing the human drama. Bowdler was said to have gone through Elizabethan plays and stories and sanitized them for public consumption. Bowdlerizing has become a way of suppressing evidence that the *ego project* is lopsided. We know it is exceedingly difficult to find *Gulliver's Travels* in the original, or to find a story book that has the wolf raping Red Riding Hood prior to consuming her. It gives the impression that sadism, war, murder, and vengeance stand separate as a kind of psychotic expression, rather than link closely with dogmatism, racism, meanness of spirit, and destructivity in work, play, and love. It is all part of the *ego project*, to libidinize being as a life experience and steer from any telltale signs of entropy. If such details should appear, then it is just a gremlin in the machinery. It is a statistical oddity, rather than something formed out of and arising from the ground, not pure figure, but figure-out-of-ground and connected-to-ground.

Heidegger (1962) concluded one need not be at terminus to experience death, because it was available to us during each and every moment. Perhaps it is the nihilism such ideas imply that renders them unsuitable for psychology, for after all we are a field of hope. Who wants to be treated by a miserable and hopeless wretch who has no taste for life and is at death's door? (Not incidentally, the answer to that is a miserable and hopeless wretch who has no taste for life and is at death's door.) But it is one thing for the field to understand its reasons for sanitizing, and quite another to reject entropy out of hand. It is the nihilism psychology wants to avoid; let philosophy handle such troublesome topics!

But the transpersonal position is not nihilism. Washburn (1994) described regression in the service of transcendence this way: "The ego undergoes a regressus ad originem that returns the ego to, and ultimately reroots the ego in, the sources from which it originally arose" (p. 242). It is the ego whose death we are investigating, to halt the Procrustean censorship of being. Lippitt (1975) described the no-self experience as the recognition that self-images were not structures or constants. There was a freedom from them and the evaluations they carried. Fauteux (1994) used the phrase "regression in the service of transcendence," describing one's spiritual reach toward a healthy aspect of one's narcissistic base. If anything died here, it was the ego's rugged autonomy.

Grof (1990) has studied the psychological experience of the Void. Though it may be construed as nothingness, there is still a sense that all is of a unity. Even the primordial emptiness carries within it that which creates form. Otto (1950) declared our inability to more directly touch *ganz andere*, all that is beyond the reach of our basic senses. But from time to time the sacred reveals itself. In a sustained exposure, man's pedestrian personality dissolved to create the possibility of a new birth. The profane keeps its lock on our perceptions and cognitions. We believe we are one person and not many. Lifton (1993) charged us with the goal to find our protean nature. Empathy was the effort to resonate with the other person and experience him from the most intimate position. Such an effort would open our eyes to species awareness, that we are all alike, that the pieces that go to make us up are the same as they are for anyone else, that the basic building blocks are there.

We abide by the strict authority of the word, when there is no such thing. Derrida (1992) believes the word has some connection to observable reality, but its meaning is more related to what the word is not saying than to what it is saying. What each word tries to get at, and what each is not saying and cannot possibly bear full witness to, is the larger Being behind it. Fauteux (1994) saw redemption in a "dying to self," which in other terms might be described as a loosening of the authority of text, to reveal the Being it camouflaged.

Gergen (1994) saw psychotherapy as valuing autonomy, independence, solitariness, individualism, and critical thinking. We are being inadvertently guided in our work by a male-agential model. But what about a relational self, one that penetrated the male wall of indifference and connected people closely? What about an interdependent model of a healthy person? With a dissolution of the authority of text, all kinds of possibilities were created. "The self is construed as relational—as a temporary, partial and flexible emergent identity created within the social interactions among persons" (Gergen 1994, p. 19).

In the transpersonal realm are found Strupp's ineffables, the therapist characteristics that he feels are thus far immeasurable and unquantifiable, which cause healing in the relationship. They have to do with the therapist's willingness to make an empathic sacrifice for the patient. This sacrifice involves discovering all the unpleasurable thoughts and feelings we sought to repress in our own characters, questioning our most cherished beliefs about our agential qualities, giving in to the oceanic, recognizing the hoax of ego, following the patient in his ill-advised efforts to enlarge being, attracting him to less destructive ways through our own searches, and being willing to regress in the service of transcendence.

The ineffables are in fact reachable. We can experience them, talk about them, manipulate them, surrender to them, see them in cases where things go well, and find them missing in cases where we are of no help to the patient. They lie in the contemplative realm but are no less real for that. Their study is helped along if we have a guiding cosmology that places us in deep connection to one another, that admits to the co-eminence of building and destroying factors in our essence, and that has us radiating the great-grandparently wisdom that Methuselah needs to see.

For we invite the elderly patient to grow with us when we regress with him. We recognize that both are fundamental to the never-ending circle that spun us into being and will draw us back into greater Being, as surely as the great-grandparent and the unborn infant resonate with the universe and are one with it. I end with a poem by my good friend, about our ongoing search.

BECKONING

We live in a world where
Suffering (if that's the right word)
Is pretending that the pretense
Is whole, when in fact it's
The merest smidgen of a fraction
Of what's there.
We two, beyond the pier—
With lines dropped so deeply
There are no fish to catch—
Sideways glance to note

All those others who fish
For fish where fish go,
So there is hope and purpose;
And not that sense that
Something immense waits—
With dark demanding hands—
To shape and make us whole.

[David Levinsky, 1995]

References

Allen, N. (1983). *Homicides: Perspectives in Prevention*. New York: Human Sciences Press.

Anderson, L., and Stevens, N. (1993). Associations between early experiences with parents and well-being in old age. *Journal of Gerontology* 48:109–116.

Basch, M. F. (1980). *Doing Psychotherapy*. New York: Basic Books.

Becker, E. (1973). *The Denial of Death*. New York: Free Press.

Beitman, B. D., and Klerman, G. L., eds. (1991). *Integrating Pharmacotherapy and Psychotherapy*. Washington, D.C.: American Psychiatric Press.

Blazer, D. (1990). *Emotional Problems in Later Life*. New York: Springer.

Blumenson, S. (1993). The mirror of silence: a method of treating a preverbal schizophrenic patient. *Modern Psychoanalysis* 18:179–189.

Brown, N. O. (1959). *Life Against Death: The Psychoanalytic Meaning of History*. Middletown, CT: Wesleyan University Press.

——— (1966). *Love's Body*. Berkeley: University of California Press.

Butler, R. N. (1975). *Why Survive? Being Old in America*. New York: Harper & Row.

Campbell, J., ed. (1954). *Spirit and Nature*. Princeton, NJ: Princeton University Press.

——— (1968). *The Masks of God: Creative Mythology*. New York: Viking.

———— (1971). *The Hero with a Thousand Faces.* Princeton, NJ: Princeton University Press.

Capra, F. (1985). *The Tao of Physics.* Boston: Shambala.

Chodorkoff, B. (1990). Counselling and therapy for elders. *Generations* 14:27–30.

Conrad, J. (1983). *Heart of Darkness.* New York: Doubleday.

Derrida, J. (1992). Passions: an 'oblique offering.' In *Derrida: A Critical Reader*, ed. D. Wood. Cambridge, UK: Blackwell.

Dorfman, R. (1994). *Aging into the 21st Century.* New York: Brunner/Mazel.

Dossey, L. (1989). *Recovering the Soul.* New York: Bantam.

Eissler, K. R. (1971). Death drive, ambivalence and narcissism. *Psychoanalytic Study of the Child* 26:25–78. New Haven, CT: Yale University Press.

Engel, G. L. (1977). The need for a new medical model: a challenge for biomedicine. *Science* 196:129–136.

Fauteux, K. (1994). *The Recovery of the Self: Regression and Redemption in Religious Experience.* New York: Paulist Press.

Fenichel, O. (1972). *The Psychoanalytic Theory of Neurosis.* New York: W. W. Norton.

Frankl, V. E. (1984). *Man's Search for Meaning: An Introduction to Logotherapy.* New York: Simon & Schuster.

Freud, S. (1905). On psychotherapy. *Standard Edition* 7:257–268.

———— (1912). The dynamics of transference. *Standard Edition* 12:99–108.

———— (1915). Instincts and their vicissitudes. *Standard Edition* 14:109–140.

———— (1917). Introductory lectures on pycho-analysis. *Standard Edition* 16:286–301.

———— (1920). Beyond the pleasure principle. *Standard Edition* 18:7–66.

Galatzer-Levy, R. M., and Cohler, B. J. (1990). The selfobjects of the second half of life: an introduction. In *Realities of Transference: Progress in Self Psychology*, ed. A. Goldberg, pp. 93–112. Hillsdale, NJ: Analytic Press.

Gallagher, D., and Thompson, L. W. (1982). Treatment of major depressive disorder in older adult outpatients with brief psychotherapies. *Psychotherapy: Theory, Research and Practice* 19:482–490.

Gallagher-Thompson, D., Thompson, L. W., and Futterman, A. (1995). Psychotherapy with older adults in theory and practice. In *Comprehensive Textbook of Psychotherapy*, ed. B. Bongar and L. E. Beutler, pp. 359–379. New York: Oxford University Press.

Gay, P. (1987). *A Godless Jew: Freud, Atheism and the Making of Psychoanalysis.* New Haven: Yale University Press.

Gergen, M. (1994). Free will and psychoanalysis: complaints of the draught-men's daughters. *Journal of Theoretical and Philosophical Psychology* 14:13–21.

Gibran, K. (1989). *Sand and Foam: A Book of Aphorisms.* New York: Knopf.

Gordon, M. (1985). *The Iacocca Management Technique.* New York: Dodd.

Greenson, R. R. (1967). *The Technique and Practice of Psychoanalysis.* New York: International Universities Press.

Grof, S. (1990). *The Holotropic Mind.* San Francisco: Harper.

Gurko, L. (1979). *Joseph Conrad: Giant in Exile.* New York: Macmillan.

Haisch, B. A., Rueda, A., Puthoff, H. E., et al. (1994). Beyond E=mc2: A first glimpse of a postmodern physics in which mass, inertia, and gravity arise from underlying electromagnetic processes. *The Sciences,* November/December, pp. 26–31.

Hayden, S. (1983). The toxic response in modern psychoanalysis. *Modern Psychoanalysis* 8:3–16.

Heidegger, M. (1962). *Being and Time.* London: SCM Press.

Jung, C. G. (1954). Mysterium coniunctionis. In *Collected Works,* 14. New York: Bollinger Foundation, 1963.

Katz, I. R., and Parmelee, P. A. (1994). Depression in elderly patients in residential care settings. In *Diagnosis and Treatment of Depression in Late Life,* ed. L. S. Schneider, E. Frank, J. Perel, et al., pp. 437–461. Washington, D.C.: American Psychiatric Press.

Kerr, J. (1993). *A Most Dangerous Method: The Story of Freud, Tausk and Sabina Spielrein.* New York: Knopf.

Kirman, W. J. (1980). Countertransference in facilitating intimacy and communication. *Modern Psychoanalysis* 2:131–166.

Kohut, H. (1976). *The Analysis of the Self.* New York: International Universities Press.

Kolatch, A. (1984). *The Complete Dictionary of English and Hebrew First Names.* New York: Jonathan David.

Koshikawa, F., Kaneo, N., and Haruki, Y. (1993). When west meets east: contributions of eastern traditions to the future of psychotherapy. *Psychotherapy* 29:141–149.

Lazarus, A., Beutler, L., and Norcross, J. (1992). The future of technical eclecticism. *Psychotherapy* 29:11–20.

Lebowitz, B. D., and Niederehe, G. (1992). Concepts and issues in mental health and aging. In *Handbook of Mental Health and Aging,* ed. J. E. Birren, R. B. Sloane, G. D. Cohen, et al., pp. 3–27. San Diego, CA: Academic Press.

Lifton, R. J. (1993). *The Protean Self: Human Resilience in an Age of Fragmentation.* New York: Basic Books.

Lippitt, P. (1975). Self-image. In *Reflections of Mind: Western Psychology Meets Tibetan Buddhism,* ed. T. Tulku, pp. 146–159. Berkeley, CA: Dharma Publishing.

Liptzin, B. (1992). Nursing home care. In *Handbook of Mental Health and Aging,* ed. J. E. Birren, R. B. Sloane, G. D. Cohen, et al., pp. 833–852. San Diego, CA: Academic Press.

Margolis, B. (1994a). Narcissistic transference: the product of overlapping self and object fields. *Modern Psychoanalysis* 19:139–147.

––––– (1994b). Narcissistic countertransference: emotional availability and case management. *Modern Psychoanalysis* 19:161–177.

––––– (1994c). Notes on narcissistic resistance. *Modern Psychoanalysis* 19:179–186.

––––– (1994d). The object-oriented question: a contribution to treatment technique. *Modern Psychoanalysis* 19:187–198.

––––– (1994e). The contact function of the ego: its role in the therapy of the narcissistic patient. *Modern Psychoanalysis* 19:199–210.

––––– (1994f). Joining, mirroring, and psychological reflection: terminology, definitions, theoretical concepts. *Modern Psychoanalysis* 19:211–226.

Martin, J. (1995). How does psychotherapy work? A personal account of model-building. In *Research as Praxis: Lessons from Programmatic Research in Therapeutic Psychology,* ed. L. J. Hoshmand and J. Martin, pp. 104–126. New York: Teachers' College Press.

Masson, J. (1984). *Assault on Truth: Freud's Suppression of the Seduction Theory.* New York: Farrar, Straus, Giroux.

May, R. (1983). *The Discovery of Being: Writings in Existential Psychology.* New York: Norton.

McFadden, S. H. (1995). Religion and well-being in aging persons in an aging society. *Journal of Social Issues* 51:161–175.

Meadow, P. (1981). Drive theory and diagnosis. *Modern Psychoanalysis* 6:141–170.

––––– (1995). Psychoanalysis: an open system of research. *Modern Psychoanalysis* 20:7–29.

Menninger, K., and Holzman, P. (1973). *The Theory of Psychoanalytic Technique.* New York: Basic Books.

Muslin, H. L. (1992). *The Psychotherapy of the Aging Self.* New York: Brunner/Mazel.

Myers, W. A., ed. (1991). *New Techniques in the Psychotherapy of Older Patients*. Washington, DC: American Psychiatric Press.

Neumann, E. (1954). *The Origins and History of Consciousness*. Princeton, NJ: Princeton University Press.

Noy, P. (1979). The psychoanalytic theory of cognitive development. In *Psychoanalytic Study of the Child* 34:169–214. New Haven, CT: Yale University Press.

Otto, R. (1950). *The Idea of the Holy*. New York: Oxford University Press.

Peake, T. H., and Philpot, K. (1991). Psychotherapy with older adults: hopes and fears. *Clinical Supervisor* 9:185–202.

Pinkston, E., and Linsk, N. (1984). *Care of the Elderly: A Family Approach*. New York: Pergamon.

Ray, W. A., Taylor, J. A., Meador, K. G., et al. (1993). Reducing antipsychotic drug use in nursing homes: a controlled trial of provider education. *Archives of Internal Medicine* 153:713–721.

Riess, B. F. (1992). Some thoughts and material in age-related psychoanalysis of the aged. *Psychoanalysis and Psychotherapy* 10(1):17–32.

Rinzler, C., and Gordon, B. (1980). Buddhism and psychotherapy. In *Studies in Non-deterministic Psychology*, ed. G. N. Epstein, pp. 52–59. New York: Human Sciences Press.

Riter, R. (1994). Changing organizational culture within a long-term care setting. *Journal of Long-Term Care Administration*. Summer, pp. 11–30.

Roazen, P. (1969). *Brother Animal: The Story of Freud and Tausk*. New York: Knopf.

———— (1976). *Freud and His Followers*. New York: Knopf.

Rostand, E. (1951). *Cyrano de Bergerac*, trans. B. Hooker. New York: Random House.

Schneider, L. S., Reynolds, C. F., Lebowitz, B. D. and Friedhoff, A. H. (1994). *Diagnosis and Treatment of Depression in Late Life: Results of the NIH Consensus Development Conference*. Washington, D.C.: American Psychiatric Press.

Scogin, F., and McElreath, L. (1994). Efficacy of psychosocial treatments in geriatric depression: a quantitative review. *Journal of Consulting and Clinical Psychology* 62:69–74.

Siegel, M. H., and Ziegler, H. P., eds. (1976). *Psychological Research: The Inside Story*. New York: Harper & Row.

Skinner, B. F. (1976). A case history of the scientific method. In *Psychological Research: The Inside Story*, ed. M. H. Siegel and H. P. Ziegler, pp. 23–45. New York: Harper & Row.

Spiegel, D. (1993). *Living Beyond Limits*. New York: Random House.

Spotnitz, H. (1976). *Psychotherapy of Preoedipal Conditions*. New York: Grune & Stratton.

———— (1981). Aggression in the therapy of schizophrenia. *Modern Psychoanalysis* 6:131–140.

———— (1985). *Modern Psychoanalysis of the Schizophrenic Patient: Theory of the Technique*. New York: Human Sciences Press.

Spotnitz, H., and Meadow, P. (1976). *Treatment of the Narcissistic Neuroses*. New York: Manhattan Center for Advanced Psychoanalytic Studies.

Strupp, H. H. (1992). The future of psychodynamic therapy. *Psychotherapy* 29:21–27.

Strupp, H. H., and Binder, J. L. (1984). *Psychotherapy in a New Key: A Guide to Time-Limited Dynamic Psychotherapy*. New York: Basic Books.

Suler, J. R. (1993). *Contemporary Psychoanalysis and Eastern Thought*. New York: State University of New York Press.

Takeuchi, H. (1985). *The Management Challenge: Japanese Views*. Cambridge, MA: MIT Press.

Teri, L., Curtis, J., Gallagher-Thompson, D., et al. (1994). Cognitive-behavior therapy with older adults. In *Diagnosis and Treatment of Depression in Late Life*, ed. L. S. Schneider, E. Frank, J. Perel, et al., pp. 279–292. Washington, D.C.: American Psychiatric Press.

Teri, L., and Logsdon, R. G. (1992). The future of psychotherapy with older adults. *Psychotherapy* 29:81–87.

The Upanishads (1987). Trans. E. Easwaran. Tomales, CA: Nilgiri.

Vonnegut, K. (1994). *Slapstick*. New York: Dell.

Wachtel, P. L. (1973). *Psychoanalysis and Behavior Therapy: Toward an Integration*. New York: Basic Books.

Washburn, M. (1994). *Transpersonal Psychology in Psychoanalytic Perspective*. New York: State University of New York Press.

Watts, A. (1961). *Psychotherapy East and West*. New York: Pantheon.

———— (1972). *The Book: On the Taboo of Knowing Who You Are*. New York: Vintage.

Whitbourne, S. K. (1989). Treating the older adult: a diverse population. *Journal of Integrative and Eclectic Psychotherapy* 8(2):161–173.

Wilbur, K. (1990). *Eye to Eye: The Quest for a New Paradigm*. Boston: Shambala.

Wolinsky, S. (1993). *Quantum Consciousness*. Norfolk, CT: Bramble.

Index